MAKING

LIFELONG

LEARNING

MAKING LIFELONG LEARNING WORK:

Learning Cities *for a* Learning Century

Norman Longworth

KOGAN PAGE

First published in 1999

Kogan Page Limited
120 Pentonville Road
London
N1 9JN
UK

Stylus Publishing Inc
22883 Quicksilver Drive
Sterling
VA 20166-2012
USA

© Norman Longworth, 1999

British Library Cataloguing in Publication Data

A CIP record for this book is available from the British Library.

ISBN 0 7494 2727 2

Typeset by Kogan Page Limited
Printed and bound by Biddles Ltd, Guildford and King's Lynn

Table of Contents

CONTENTS

Foreword by Markku Markkula, Member of the Finnish Parliament

I am delighted to be asked to write the foreword to this book. In the first place, Professor Longworth and I have both been instrumental in helping to set up the European Lifelong Learning Initiative over the past six years, and in the second he has, over the years, been one of the most passionate and knowledgeable contributors to the cause of European lifelong learning. 'Passion to learn' is one of the key phrases in the Finnish lifelong learning strategy, which I believe to be one of the most forward-thinking documents to appear in this century as a preparation for the next. We in Finland take lifelong learning seriously. For us it is, in Professor Longworth's words, one of the most important paradigm shifts in educational history, and will affect both what we do and the way we do it right across Finnish society for many years to come. We note that we are not alone in this opinion, since governments around the world are now formulating policies based on similar principles.

In his first book *Lifelong Learning*, written with Keith Davies, Professor Longworth demonstrated an impressive knowledge of the basics of his subject, which will remain valid for many years. It received superb reviews and has informed the thinking of governments, education institutions and industry in the past two years. I believe that this new book will be similarly received, describing, as it does, one of the most significant developments in lifelong learning at the level of the 'Learning Community'. I and my colleagues fully support Professor Longworth's contention that cities, towns and regions will be the lifelong learning laboratories of our nations, the places where the innovative advances into the learning society will take place. In Finland and elsewhere, the growth of interest at municipal level over the past two years has been phenomenal. This book will contribute many insights into the what, the why, the where and the how of learning cities in the minds of civic leaders, professionals in local government, university and school-teachers, and the many citizens who take an intelligent interest in the development of their own communities. No city should be without copies in all its major departments and institutions. That, in my view, is a measure of the importance of the subject. As I contemplate the excitement and the opportunities ahead in what Professor Longworth calls 'the Learning Century', I am reminded of the title we used when putting together the Finnish national strategy. It is 'the Joy of Learning'. This book supports that view.

Markku Markkula

UK Foreword by Bob Hogg, Executive Director of Education, Southampton City Council

It gives me great pleasure to write a foreword for this much-needed book. Southampton, as a major port with a long history of co-operation with other countries and cultures, has an openness of spirit and outlook that gives it a natural advantage for the development of lifelong learning. The learning relationships we are building with many parts of the world affect all age groups and all sectors of the city. This is why we are putting lifelong learning at the forefront of our educational policy, and why we have already started the process towards developing Southampton as a 'City of Learning'. As Professor Longworth emphasizes in this book, we recognize that this is a long-term project, an outward-looking, co-operative venture involving every educational organization in partnership with business and industry, local government and the rapidly-growing voluntary sector.

We recognize too the value of encouraging contribution by our citizens in order to give them ownership of their own city's development. Such individual and collective commitment gives a focus to learning outside of that for their own needs, and enriches immeasurably the common pool of talent and skill available to the city's growth as a learning city. The highly successful European Conference on learning cities, which Southampton hosted in 1998, is one example of our commitment to continuous improvement, and I can demonstrate many others in the city's institutions. It was here that the Charter for Learning Cities, described in Appendix 1, was first proposed. Professor Longworth has an unusual breadth of experience, having worked in schools, in industry and in universities, including periods as a research fellow and as a staff member at the University of Southampton. He has lived and worked nationally and internationally to develop understanding of lifelong learning as a practical concept applicable to all, and has contributed much to the development of governmental and organizational policies and strategies through his work with the European Lifelong Learning Initiative, of which he was President for a time. He, like me, recognizes that lifelong learning goes well beyond education into every aspect of community life, affecting values and attitudes as well as knowledge and skills. He has brought all this experience and insight together in this excellent book. It will be a source of great interest and counsel to every city, town and community which wishes to orient its policies towards coping with the great changes inevitably affecting their future.

Bob Hogg

Dedication

This book is dedicated to my wife Margaret whose patience, forbearance and long-suffering understanding has made her into the lifelong learner to end all lifelong learners, to David, Jeannette and Mandy, from whom we both learn much without knowing it and to Charlotte Megan, who will reach my age in the year 2060 and experience learning delight throughout most of the Learning Century.

Introduction

Like most of us, I am frequently asked by friends and people I meet in business situations or round the dinner table what I do to earn my crust. It's not an easy question to answer. 'Well, I'm President of the European Lifelong Learning Organization and a lifelong learning consultant working with organizations such as universities, cities and international non-governmental organizations. Oh, and I'm setting up a Centre for the Learning City at a UK University' is not only long-winded, but also more than a little pompous and self-important. Even with the most sympathetic of people I can see the glazed eye, the panic reaction, the unexpressed wish to be somewhere, anywhere, else long before the sentence is completed.

So another strategy like 'Well, I work for a small European organization for promoting lifelong learning' might work then. Don't believe it. The word 'promoting' has immediately identified one as a salesman – which is of course what I am in one sense. So what do I sell? – er lifelong learning? Immediately the unreal panic sets in again, and a situation of high conversational promise based on the ignorance of one person about another becomes a determination to avoid future congress at all costs. Lifelong learning? – what in the name of heaven is that? Is it a religion? – if so it sounds like a dangerous sect. Is it a healthy living drug for prolonging life? – one look at me would confirm that isn't so. Or is it just another fancy name for education and training? – in which case why doesn't he just say he's a teacher or a lecturer?

Occasionally, through politeness or persistence – or even sometimes, interest – the conversation continues. Lifelong learning huh – what's that? Now it's my turn to panic! How on earth can one convey the richness and diversity of a whole philosophy of education, the urgency of the whole world's need to embrace a new approach to learning and the fundamental psychological approach to the development of one's human potential in one short sentence? And the question is often asked in such a way that a short answer is exactly the requirement. One feels like an

1

untrained Jehovah's Witness who has suddenly, against all expectation, found his foot successful in stopping the door from being closed.

One could try the ELLI definition: 'Lifelong learning is the development of human potential through a continuously supportive process which stimulates and empowers individuals to acquire all the knowledge, skills, values and understanding they will need throughout their lifetimes, and to apply them with confidence, creativity and enjoyment in all roles, circumstances and environments.' Hardly short! and definitely not terribly illuminating at first hearing! – and certainly not a reply calculated to prolong a dinner party communication.

Of course, there isn't an answer to that problem. There is no short answer and even many people who purport to be promoting (there's that word again!) lifelong learning differ from each other. To some it is adult leisure education – rows of eager wannabe cooks understanding the basics of Chinese cookery or macho dog-owners learning rottweiler-handling techniques or throwing pots, or languages for holidays in Spain. To others it is University-Industry partnerships and Continuing Education for employment and employability. To yet others it is the practical application of Open and Distance Education and Training with a sophisticated feedback system to stimulate discussion and follow-up.

For me, it is certainly all of those things, but much, much more. In the first place it has to be 'lifelong' – from cradle to grave, from maternity to eternity, from hatch to dispatch, 0–90 (and why stop there?). Secondly, it has to be 'learning' – not teaching, not course provision, not training, but out and out focus on the needs and demands of the learner, however strange they may be. Thirdly, it has to marry all of this into a seamless infrastructure which makes available all the resources of the community, including the human resources, for the development of the full potential of all the human beings (and why not other species?) in that community.

So I got to thinking – if this is what it is, what else distinguishes the bright new product of lifelong learning from plain old boring Education and Training? And so this is the second of the books in answer to that simple question. If the first *Lifelong Learning – new vision, new implications, new roles* explained the why and the what of the subject, this one is meant to describe the how. How can lifelong learning be turned from an often diffuse and vague concept into a living and working model for today and tomorrow? Where are the examples of good practice to guide us in our search for a perhaps illusory, educational nirvana? How can the excitement of 21st century learning be transmitted to the sceptical, the cynical, the unimaginative, the fearful, the disinterested, the overworked and the genuinely worried? And there are many of those.

The following question and answer paper has appeared in several magazines and journals over the past two years. At least five people have commented to me how it helped clarify their thinking, so at least five people have read it. On reading it again, it acts as a perfect Executive Summary for this book.

INTRODUCTION

Lifelong learning is suddenly big news. Why?

One reason is that several European countries have published White and Green discussion papers on the subject, and the debate is also hot in North America. Britain's government has even appointed a Minister for Lifelong Learning as a demonstration of its commitment to developing a new approach to Education and Training, the economy and society. It was the European Year of Lifelong Learning in 1996 and that was so designated to explain to everybody what lifelong learning means and how it will affect them not just in 1996 but for generations ahead into the 21st century.

Yet another reason is because just about all the major world organizations – from UNESCO to International Corporations, OECD, National Governments – are developing plans to introduce lifelong learning within their spheres of influence. And it isn't just at international level – local organizations, local government, schools, small companies are beginning to take an interest.

This thing is big – it's going to influence every one of us and our children's children over the next century. And we are just at the beginning of the process. It's an exciting time.

So lifelong learning is something new then?

Not at all. Plato used the phrase 'Dia Viou Paedeia' 2000 years before Christ – for him it meant the obligation of every citizen to develop his or her own potential and participate in the activities of the city. The Chinese philosopher, Kuan Tzu, in the 3rd century BC said, 'When planning for a year – sow corn, when planning for a decade – plant trees, when planning for a lifetime – train and educate men.' While that may seem to be sexist, I think that he meant humankind. More recently Comenius, in the 16th century drew up a picture of the whole world as a school for mankind and said that learning is the most basic human instinct.

Arthur C Clarke, the famous science fiction writer defined the minimum survival level of the human race as 'everyone being educated to the level of semi-literacy of the average university graduate by the year 2000'. Science fiction writers are allowed to be apocalyptic. HG Wells defined the whole of human history as 'a constant race between education and catastrophe' – he thought the latter was winning – and as we look around us at some of the more horrific activities of some of our fellow creatures, who can say he got it wrong?

So what's different about lifelong learning today?

In the late 20th century, there are many differences. As a race we are slowly but surely coming to terms with the fact that this planet is finite – that we cannot continue to exploit its mineral wealth, its food resources in land and sea, and change its natural life-sustaining ecosystems without threatening our very existence. And with an expected 5 billion new members of the human race in the next 50 years, learning to adapt has got to play a large part in the future for all of us.

In what we call the developed world we have moved into an entirely different sort of employment situation. In the middle of this century we have come to expect to be employed in one job for a lifetime – that is no longer true for the vast majority of us and is becoming even less true for future generations. The workers of tomorrow will have several different jobs, several different careers – they will have to be adaptable and flexible and versatile, mentally as well as geographically – they will constantly need to be trained and retrained to a much higher level than today, dipping in and out of education as necessary to renew their store of knowledge, skills and understandings.

These are just two of the many reasons why I am calling the next century, the 'Learning Century' – because, unless it becomes just that, the alternative is more and more unhappiness, social disorder, deprivation, poverty and a breakdown of civilized and democratic structures.

How do you persuade people to respond in this way? Education isn't the most popular word in many people's vocabularies.

That's true and that's why this is going to take time. We need 20–20 vision. Lifelong learning has profound implications for all parts of the system – not just the education systems in the schools, colleges and universities, but also the social, political, economic and cultural systems we have built up in our societies. I believe that the age of education and training is dead and that the future focus has to be converted into a new era of learning in which education has to be brought to all people in the way in which they want to receive it. Integral to it, not separated from it. Learning has to become fun, enjoyable, a pleasurable thing to do – whether it is for work, for leisure or for life it has to become a part of our lives in much the same way as shopping or banking or playing games.

But in order for that to happen, the education providers at all levels have to start focusing on the needs of people as learners – finding out why, when, what and how people prefer to learn, discovering new learning methods, identifying the basic skills which people need in order to learn better – learning to learn, developing our potential, handling information, developing thinking skills individually, in groups and in families – and using modern education delivery technologies and tools to provide new learning for people wherever they want to receive it.

Are the Education Providers ready for this?

There are pockets of good practice around – there are one or two schools for example which are developing continuous education and personal skills updating

4

programmes for their teachers so that they can respond better to their own learning needs and those of children. Some universities are widening their intakes and modifying their courses to become responsive to the needs of a much more polyaccessible educational world from industry and the community around.

But, perhaps surprisingly, the greatest breakthroughs have come in industry education departments, and we can all learn from this. Here there is a much greater take-up of the tools and techniques of the new technologies and a much greater democratization of the learning process. This is because modern companies have realized that their strength and their future lies in the performance of their people and that the development of individual skills and values is the most important thing they can do to survive in a very competitive world. Most major car manufacturers, for example, have taken a deliberate step to 'empower' their workforce, to put decision making in the hands of those who do the work. This creates a whole new set of skills needs among adults which lead right back into schoolroom practice.

However, it has to be said too, that for the majority of education providers there is still a long way to go. They are providing an industrial-age education for a post-industrial environment. The emphasis is still on information and memorization rather than knowledge, high-order skills, understanding and values – teaching what to think and commit to memory, rather than how to think and how to discriminate between good, bad and indifferent. In an age in which information doubles every five years and then feeds upon itself to produce new knowledge, this is a nonsense.

But isn't it the Government which tells education organizations, particularly the schools, what to do?

The Government has financial levers and uses them to get its own way. That's why there is a need for mindset change (if the first part of the word can be located) in all parts of the system. The Government has an important part to play in understanding and creating the conditions for a true lifelong learning society so that both the nation and the people prosper economically and mentally.

There is a very strong correlation between the economic health of a nation and the learning health of its citizens. But it must base its actions on research and understanding of the true needs of everyone, rather than ill-considered political dogma or reactionary prejudices nurtured in an elitist past. If, for example, we use a failure-oriented examination system, that is one which creates failure in some in order to celebrate success in others, we can expect to take the consequences of coping with those who fail.

Separating academic sheep from non-academic goats is one model. There are other, less divisive models – for example, a target-based system which takes the development of human potential as its basis might use examinations as learning opportunities to give feedback guiding the learner to eventual success. Sure, successful learning must be celebrated and rewarded, but let's make it possible for everybody, or as many as possible, to participate in the fun of success. Nor is there any advantage to be gained from starving teachers and schools of the mental and physical resources and values they need to succeed, and then claiming that they are failing the children.

You keep mentioning values. Is this deliberate?

Oh yes. Lifelong learning values and attitudes are as important as lifelong learning skills and knowledge. Ask anyone over 30 what they remember about their schooldays. Very few will mention subjects and classrooms. Most will remember the extra-curricular events, the games, the plays, the choirs, the camping holidays, the playground activities where values and attitudes were created. A love of music, consideration for others, a talent for acting – these are acquired from participation in activities rather than taught by teachers.

But values go further than people. There are organizational values – a company develops a set of values about the worth of its people and invests in their development accordingly; a school, college or university develops a set of values which may, or may not, go beyond its statutory responsibility to provide a basic knowledge of the standard curriculum. Each is an investment in a lifelong learning future for both the individual and the organization. A well-governed nation promotes certain values as an investment in social cohesion and economic progress. This too is an exercise in survival in a competitive world. A Learning Community, whether it is a city, a town or a region tries to inculcate into its citizens the values of co-operation and harmonious living.

A Learning Community?

Yes – that is a model for the future. It is a community in which business and industry, schools, colleges, universities, professional organizations and local government co-operate closely into making it a physically, economically, culturally and mentally pleasant place to live:

- from which no-one is excluded from learning and in which learning is an enjoyable and rewarding thing to do;
- which makes all its resources, especially its human resources, talents, skills and knowledge, available to all;
- which looks outwards to the rest of the world and encourages its citizens to do likewise;
- which uses modern communications technology to link people internally and externally;

- which encourages its citizens to develop personal learning plans and to use guides and mentors to develop their knowledge and skills;
- which mobilizes special interest groups – birdwatchers, botanists, scouts, guides, church groups and the many informal organizations in which people congregate – in the monitoring and preservation of a sustainable environment;
- which celebrates learning frequently and encourages whole families to participate.

This may be a learning utopia – an impossible dream. But already some cities – Liverpool, Sheffield, Southampton – are taking the first steps towards the dream and declaring themselves to be Cities of Learning. There are others in the world setting up similar initiatives and it is not impossible to imagine, soon into the new millennium, a new world of linked Communities of Learning in which knowledge and expertise and talent are shared with each other through electronic links between third-age citizens, schoolchildren in their studies, universities in their research activities, companies for trade, hospitals for medical assistance and knowledge.

Has this anything to do with the Stakeholder Society we hear so much about?

I think that the concept of the Learning Community goes further than the Stakeholder Society. Certainly there are similarities and many of the features of one are also features of the other. Empowerment of the workforce of a company for example, and the idea that citizens should play a large part in the development of their own community. The stakeholder society, quite rightly, gives rights and decision-making powers to individuals. But a Learning Community is also a model for genuine co-operation and partnership between dissimilar organizations for their mutual benefit. It recognizes that rights entail responsibilities – the responsibility of making efforts to understand the problems of others and to help to solve them.

For example, in the Woodberry Down School/IBM Basinghall Street schools–industry twinning scheme in the late 1970s (both locations exist no longer) the close co-operation programme between the two organizations led to the skills, knowledge and talents of more than 500 highly qualified professionals being theoretically made available to enhance the education of staff and children at the school. Since this was a two-way co-operation the educational skills and knowledge and the facilities of the school were made available to the company. Both organizations gained immeasurably from the 30 joint projects and the interaction between two dissimilar organizations. Energy flowed creatively.

I am sure that this could also happen in a stakeholder society, but it might not be an essential feature of it. What both need though is leadership by example from the Government, and a large programme for creating leadership skills in all sections of the community.

So lifelong learning is about developing learning communities?

Not just that – that is a means to an end. Lifelong learning is principally about people and the way in which they can develop their own human potential. In some cases people have been so scarred by their learning experiences that they have been put off it for life. It was Einstein who proposed that none of us, not even himself, ever use more than one-third of the capacity of our brains. Experimentation with brain-damaged people has shown how the deficit can be partially made up by other non-damaged parts of the brain. We are all capable of learning and we are all capable of enjoying learning. But many people put limitations on themselves. Good lifelong learning practice takes away those limitations and provides the new tools, techniques and motivations to learn.

Quite apart from the new economic necessity for everyone to learn throughout life in order to survive at something above a basic level, lifelong learning aims to create, or recreate, the habit and the joy of learning. The Ford Company, for example, makes available a sum of money for each employee every year to take a course in something – as long as it has nothing to do with the job or the company. Now the Ford Company isn't daft or even altruistic. It is in fact now a successful company as a result of these apparently strange practices of giving money away. It recognizes that, by creating the habit of learning in all its employees it is building the foundation of its success in the marketplace. The new working practice of empowering workers means that they have to make decisions right down the line – and they have to make the right decisions. That's where the value of learning comes in.

Sounds like a lot of empowering everywhere. How are you going to satisfy all these new learners?

That's where the new technologies come in. They're not very well-developed at present and resistance is high in schools, universities and elsewhere. But there is a promising future and they are becoming ever more sophisticated in what they can do to help learning. I have already mentioned the vision of a new world of linked Communities of Learning using communications technologies which are available now, like the Internet.

But there are other tools and techniques in the Open Learning firmament using a mixture of sound, text, vision, graphics and motion picture to stimulate a learning response. Technology is therefore one of the keys to lifelong learning and the Internet provides one of the media. The trick is to develop ever-more creative use of these links both within and between communities.

For example, the Lifelong Learning University of the future will use modern, Open and Distance Learning technologies to provide services for Continuing Education in Industry and Government Offices, support for teachers in schools, extension courses for adults wherever they may be – in the shopping centres, the pubs, the home. They will use all the media at their disposal – television, local radio, satellite, cable, ISDN networks and the Internet – to make learning the number one activity in each community. They will interact internationally to open up both learning opportunities and minds, and make research more applicable to those on whose behalf it is carried out.

For example, schools will make an extensive use of networks.

- Teachers will develop and teach collaboratively common curricula between schools in the community and internationally. Children will learn collaboratively with children from other cultures, regions, countries.
- Children will access databases and stimulating people to enliven and enhance their learning.
- In environmental studies, for example, children and teachers will participate in joint project work with community organizations and industry.
- Schools will build up their own geographical, historical and biological databases and share them with others.
- Language teaching will be given a new dimension through interpersonal contacts.

And they will use sophisticated open learning software to give them the skills, concepts and knowledge which allows them to cope with the more complex society they will inhabit. These are not threats to teachers – they are the tools of their future trade.

Business and industry will profit from such networks, developing their own wealth, creating contacts between communities for the community and receiving from the community aware, committed and open-minded employees with an in-built habit of learning.

The possibilities to use learning technologies creatively are endless, the opportunities to liberate minds and mindsets abundant in all parts of education and training. And all of this will contribute at last to the development of the potential in every one of us. This is what I mean by lifelong learning. We have the means to make it happen. Do we have the will, the vision or the bottle to make the 21st century really 'The Learning Century'?

So lifelong learning is here to stay?

You can say that again, and again, and again. The alternative doesn't bear thinking about.

Lifelong Learning Today

That article does no more than give a flavour of the content of this book. Its intention is different. Because lifelong learning is such a fast-developing concept, it brings the reader up to date with changing perceptions and changing practice. Lifelong learning is no longer a philosophy, remote from the mass of people who will benefit from it. It is a growing, vital and dynamic basis for the future educational practice in many countries of the world. But let us not be fooled into thinking that it will be easy to implement. This journey into the learning future will take many decades to complete. Reluctant and opinionated politicians and administrators will have to be convinced, over-burdened teachers will need to be both won over and re-trained to understand learning, a sceptical public will need to be reassured that this is not another exercise in social engineering, and above all mindsets will have to change.

But the process is already happening in a big way. In my research for this book, I have been almost overwhelmed by the sheer number of worthy projects carried out in every country and every community. They have been implemented by every sector of the city – business and industry, universities, schools, adult education organizations, professional associations, local government offices – often in partnership with each other. Such has been the quantity, and in many cases the quality, that I have had to make a decision on which sector of activity to focus upon. In the event, because the learning community in its geographical sense comprises every social sector, I have presented a mixture of examples from each.

Most of the project descriptions and case studies illustrate and support the various fundamental principles of the way in which a community can become a Learning Community, a nation a Learning Nation, an organization a Learning Organization, and an individual a Learning Individual. In the end it comes back to the latter. One of my favourite exercises in lifelong learning workshops is to ask people how they will know when we have a Learning Society. One of my answers, as a proud old Boltonian, is that we will know we have succeeded when the half-time topic of conversation at the Reebok (soccer) Stadium is how much was learned last week and how that will lead to more learning next week. And that isn't going to happen next month, next year or within the decade. Or is it not?

I finish this introduction with a series of statements, which I call Learning Beatitudes. They are not intended to replace the original set, but they have inspired some people to think more positively and more deeply about learning. They have caused others, mostly of the academic persuasion, to turn a bright shade of puce. But then, that's life in the melting pot of learning.

INTRODUCTION

LIFELONG	LEARNING
1. LEARNING LIBERATES	IT FREES THE MIND TO EXPLORE THE UNIVERSE OF KNOWLEDGE
2. LEARNING EMPOWERS	IT MAKES POSSIBLE THE REALIZATION OF OUR DREAMS
3. LEARNING AWAKENS	IT AROUSES HUMANITY'S NATURAL CREATIVITY AND IMAGINATION
4. LEARNING RELEASES	IT ENABLES US TO DEVELOP THE LATENT POTENTIAL WITHIN US ALL
5. LEARNING NOURISHES	IT GIVES VITALITY TO OUR HUNGER TO KNOW AND TO WONDER
6. LEARNING INSPIRES	IT ENERGIZES THE SPIRIT OF DISCOVERY WITHIN US
7. LEARNING NURTURES	IT SUSTAINS GROWTH AND UNDERSTANDING IN THE MATURING INTELLECT
8. LEARNING GROWS	A LIFELONG LEARNER HAS NEVER HAD SUFFICIENT LEARNING

Part 1

New insights into lifelong learning

Chapter 1

Into the learning century

_____

Living with uncertainty

The reasonable man adapts to his environment and adjusts to the circumstances in which he finds himself

The unreasonable man questions the environment and circumstances in which he finds himself and tries to change them

Therefore, all progress depends upon unreasonable men

(Old parable)

Every new civilization takes ideas from the past and fashions them into the reality of the present. In this respect the times in which we live are little different from times in history. There are those for whom the notion of progress is firmly linked with a burning desire to change outlooks and ideas. They will espouse new causes, new knowledge and new concepts sometimes for their own sake, adapting comfortably to a life of uncertainty. Others, probably the vast majority, seek stasis, a more ordered and prescribed existence in which change takes place more slowly, and where tomorrow will not be too different from today or yesterday. For these, the state of uncertainty is a state of fear, and to be resisted. Similarly there are those whose vision encompasses the recognition that they are living through one of history's more violent paradigm shifts, and those whose perceptions are more mundane and practical, preferring familiar standards, values and lifestyles. Delors, in *The Treasure Within*, the report of the Commission on Education for the 21st Century, speaks of 'the major danger of a gulf opening up between a minority of people who are capable of finding their way successfully about this new world that is coming into being, and the majority who feel that they are at the mercy of events and have no say in the future of society, with the consequent danger of a setback to democracy and widespread revolt'.

Such binary generalizations, dividing people into one or other type, have a superficially observable truth. But often they tend to ignore the complexities across the spectrum of human behaviour, and the schizophrenic thought processes from which individuals often extrapolate their world-view. The enhanced empowerment available to many people, mainly through the applications of modern technology and the changing patterns of the workplace, is changing perceptions rapidly. There *is* an awareness, albeit inchoate and inarticulate, that world events are affecting lifestyles, leisure styles and work styles in all parts of the global community – a sense of the planet in transition. The question is whether these new perceptions are reaching a sufficient number of people and quickly enough to avoid massive social unrest and disillusionment. In the late 1970s, the journalist Alvin Toffler, expressed it thus. 'A new civilization is emerging in our lives,' he said. 'And blind men are trying to suppress it. This new civilization brings with it new family styles, changed ways of working, loving and living, a new economy, new political conflict; and beyond all this an altered consciousness as well. Pieces of this new civilization exist today. Millions are already attuning their lives to the rhythm of tomorrow.'

More recently Charles Handy, management guru and author of highly regarded books for the business world, has written in *Managing the Dream*: 'When the future was an extension of the present, it was reasonable to assume that what worked today would also work next year. That assumption,' he says, 'must now be tossed out. The world is not in a stable state. We are seeing change that not only accelerates ever faster but is also discontinuous. Such change lacks continuity and follows no logical sequence.'

Handy and Toffler are not alone. Just about every thinking writer looking at the years ahead uses words in the same vein. Change is endemic in the modern world. Globalization changes the nature of work and our perceptions of nationality. Television, which presents us nightly with often violent images of nations, regions, organizations and people in the process of change, de-sensitizes our brains and re-sensitizes our emotions. New governments, new company leaders, new authors present new ideas, new visions and new goals. While Europe becomes more cohesive and cooperative in response to the global challenge, other national groupings, like Rwanda–Burundi and Yugoslavia, become more fragmented, tearing themselves, and often their people, apart in the name of ethnic unity. The fundamental direction of our societies changes. After 20 years of increasing individualization and less intrusive government culminating in the fall of communism and Margaret Thatcher's announcement of the death of society in the 1980s, there is now an increasingly strident movement to revive the sense of community and the 'stakeholder society'. In *Lifelong Learning*, Longworth and Davies drew attention to Naisbitt's words 'the triumph of the individual'. In the past three years, the scene has changed again. The age-old concept of lifelong learning, so well developed in Damascus, Athens and Alexandria thousands of years ago, has again become an icon for educational development into the early 21st century. And so the harmonies and the discords, the cadences and the rhythms of the symphony of our times is conducted once again by a more participative, more contributory philosophy under the banner of lifelong learning.

Change, history and the sense of community

Why is this phenomenon variously called lifelong learning or lifetime learning arousing the interest of governments, organizations and people, not only in the so-called developed nations, but also of those in the developing world? The answer might be encapsulated in one word – change. Change, rapid, all-pervasive and confusing for many, is the basic driving force of the last years of the 20th century, and the progenitor of the need for lifelong learning. It is not an ephemeral trend. New developments in technology will cause it to accelerate over the coming years and affect the lives of more and more people, whether or not they like it. Only a major human catastrophe can slow it down. Educational structures cannot resist its progress, they will have to accommodate it and prepare individuals for it, by themselves embracing and welcoming the new contents, methodologies and approaches.

For many there is a sense of déjà vu about lifelong learning. Historians will argue, and with some justification, that there is nothing new in education. Plato dispensed some very pertinent thoughts on lifelong learning and 'Dia Viou Paedeia' – the responsibility of every citizen to educate himself – some 1500 years before Christ. Damascus and Alexandria were true Cities of Learning long before the crusades. In the 16th century, Jan Comenius suggested that 'Every age is destined for learning, nor is a person given other goals in learning than in life itself.'

More recently, in the 1970s and 1980s, OECD, UNESCO and the Club of Rome were signposting the path to the learning society through reports and actions which were considerably ahead of their time. Original work by Paul Lengrand in a 1970 UNESCO report, *An introduction to lifelong learning*, was followed up by the Fauré Commission Report of 1972. This was considered by many to be one of the most important educational reform documents of the second half of the 20th century. Among many other things it proposed:

- the development of human skills and abilities as the primary objective of education at all levels;
- support for situation-specific learning in the context of everyday life and work so that individuals could understand, and be given the competency, creativity and confidence to cope with, the urgent tasks and changes arising throughout a lifetime;

- the creation of the sort of learning society in which independent learning is supported and provides an essential part of the continuum of learning as people move into, and out of, education during their lives;
- the involvement of the community in the learning process and the wider social role of education in understanding conflict, violence, peace, the environment and how to reconcile differences.

Certainly present-day lifelong learning advocates would recognize most of those words. OECD was not far behind. Its landmark report *Recurrent Education: A Strategy for Lifelong Learning. A Clarifying Report*, produced in 1973, was equally forward-looking. Unlike UNESCO, which tended to use the concepts of 'Éducation Permanente' and lifelong learning interchangeably, it drew a clear distinction between lifelong learning and lifelong education. The latter, it said, is systematically organized, specific teaching-learning activities usually isolated from other activities and the pressures of life, while the former is the process of learning through life experience.

The standard was raised again by the seminal Club of Rome report of 1979, *No Limits to Learning*. 'Innovative Learning' was the new focus and the new context, requiring individuals to be able to analyse and transform new knowledge and information into creative problem-solving, through which they could develop responsible values and attitudes. A broad-based mobilization of the creative talent inherent in every human being was considered to be the only way to allow him/her to understand, adapt to, and make progress in, an increasingly complex world. Thus more research into human learning processes would need to be carried out as a prelude to the great leap forward in human capability and international understanding.

However, political, social and economic trends during the 1980s and early 1990s changed attitudes considerably. The unfettered visionary idealism of a global, learning-based society became more unfashionable, while the gradual rolling back of the state and the firmer placing of responsibility for personal development onto the individual induced a more utilitarian view. Until the mid-1990s, vision and idealism took a back seat to practical method and 'back to basics'. But lifelong learning refused to die. Papers were written, rationales rationalized, justifications justified and reasons reasoned. The two philosophies are even now in combat for the hearts and minds of a generation raised on the purely functional and the economically advantageous.

Education and training are dead

The recent renaissance was again led by UNESCO and OECD, though the European Commission and the Council of Europe will also, justifiably, want to claim some credit. The Delors report on Education for the 21st Century was published only months after the 1996 OECD ministerial conference on lifelong learning and its subsequent book *Lifelong Learning for All*. Meanwhile the European Commission was declaring the same year as the 'European Year of Lifelong Learning' and preparing a White Paper on the subject, closely pursued by the European Round Table of Industrialists which collaborated with the Council of University Rectors to produce a booklet on the learning society. Longworth and Davies also published their book *Lifelong Learning*, spelling out its implications for schools, universities, business and industry, teacher training and the community at large.

All agree that, as the old century dies, the difference is one of the *urgency* with which these ideas need to be implemented. Governments, business organizations, professional associations are finally catching on and catching up and, at the same time, developing a new set of requirements for the millennium. They are now aspiring 'learning organizations'. Indeed, in keeping with earlier comments on the speed of change, the momentum of lifelong learning is rapidly accelerating at an astonishing rate. Scarcely an educational, commercial or governmental conference goes by without a mention of lifelong learning as the key to future progress. It is the core of the European Education and Research Programmes for the next five years. Most major organizations and governments are incorporating its concepts into business plans, national strategies and recommended activities.

So where are we now? Change has almost become a paradigm of itself. Small wonder then that uncertainty and confusion reign supreme, and that a proper response to these challenges is unclear. Both Toffler and Handy put the onus on improved education. 'The responsibility for change,' says Toffler, 'lies with us. We must begin with ourselves, teaching ourselves not to close our minds prematurely to the novel, the surprising, the seemingly radical. This means fighting off the idea-assassins who rush forward to kill any new suggestion on the grounds of its impracticality, while defining what now exists as practical, no matter how absurd, oppressive or unworkable it may be.'

At some levels Education and Training perceptions are fast changing into practical learning precepts. Kent – Region of Learning's strategy suggests that 'Learning is not synonymous with education and training. It includes the products of education and training, the processes of both formal and informal learning and the various types of learning – skills, knowledge, understanding, values, experience, attitudes.' And it is evolving strategies to change all of those in the people who inhabit that county.

Lifelong Learning somewhat provocatively and optimistically – and perhaps even arrogantly – announced the demise of the education and training age. 'It has served us well in the past half-century,' it said, 'and it deserves a decent burial, but the time has now come to address a much wider, much more numerous and much more demanding audience. In its place will be the first dawn of an era of Learning, when the focus will be on the needs of all learners and these will take precedence over the power of teachers and trainers. Ownership of, and personal participation in, learning will be the prime motivator. The use of Education Technology and

Open and Distance Learning methods will give the necessary forward impetus to such a movement.'

That was written in the heady days of the European Year of Lifelong Learning, when nations, organizations and people struggled to understand and to come to terms with the new educational ideas which lifelong learning plants in the national and corporate mind. And indeed the European Year caught the mood of the changing educational times. More than 800 projects took place and, since that time the European Commission Socrates, Leonardo and Adapt programmes have funded more than 2000 new and larger projects, the Organization for Economic Cooperation and Development (OECD) has initiated vast monitoring and measuring programmes world-wide in response to the demands of its nation members for action, and UNESCO and the World Bank have alerted developing nations to the value of new educational structures. In addition, national governments have published Green and White Papers for implementing lifelong learning in their countries. Finland, the Netherlands and the UK are among the first to do so and others are following quickly behind. The USA policy document makes its appearance in 1999.

Putting it together

In 1995 The Action Agenda for Lifelong Learning suggested the following:

> It would not be an exaggeration to suggest that the survival of organizations and societies in an advanced technological world depends on the development of lifelong learning skills and values as an essential part of their culture. The smarter company, the shrewder university, the better school, the more enlightened government, the more perceptive association – they are already exploring the challenges, implications and opportunities of creating and sustaining lifelong learning organizations for their own long term durability and self-respect.

But it is not only in an advanced technological world that lifelong learning is important. As we have seen, it is equally relevant to the developing world, and to communities and nations as well as to organizations and societies. If this were not so, countries so diverse as South Africa, Venezuela and China would not be spending time and money developing sophisticated lifelong learning strategies. In some ways lifelong learning is quite new – in others, it is as old as humanity itself. In the view of most educationists, the engine of lifelong learning change is the development of human potential at all levels and the focus of education is the satisfaction of the needs of every learner.

In lifelong learning we know very well what lifelong means. But we are not at all good at knowing what learning means – what learning styles are, how to use the new technologies wisely and interactively to provoke a meaningful response, how to switch people, many of whom have learning difficulties, on to learning on a mass scale. In some languages the concept of learning is not well expressed, but putting the focus on the learner is the first step to understanding the rules of today's game. Learning surely does not mean not training, nor is it teaching and, in many senses it is not even education any more. In its purest meaning, learning focuses on giving learners the tools by which they can learn according to their own learning styles and needs. But if it is to mean anything at all it must be for everyone – excluding no-one and proactively creating the conditions in which learning develops creativity, confidence and enjoyment at each stage of life.

Since the flurry of publishing activity in 1996 the drip of information, knowledge and action in the subject has become a deluge. Ideas feed upon ideas and produce new insights, understandings and approaches. Part 1 of this book, therefore, brings the current state of our knowledge of lifelong learning up to date and highlights the more important differences between the new lifelong learning paradigm related to the needs of the 21st century and the old paradigm, rooted in the education and training traditions of the 20th. This will be done under five headings, each an important and distinct facet of lifelong learning, and each promoting a set of actions to which governments, educational organizations and people have to respond.

Chapter 2

The land of learning

The first set of lifelong learning insights deals with the effects of the change towards learning as the major focus for educational, and indeed many other, activities. Government, educational organizations and learning communities will need to understand that this is a significant 180-degree shift from existing perceptions of the way education and training has been carried out in the past, and how this can be used as a motivating factor. Thus the premise is as follows:

The lifelong learning focus is on *learning* and the needs and requirements of *learners*. This means:

1. It makes greater demands on the educational expertise of the learning provider

It was a conference in Bratislava, a typical academic event in which, for 3 hours, many worthy experts with 10-minute slots had spoken for anything from 15 to 20 minutes about many worthy things from the platform. The audience, from schools, universities and government, was now visibly restless and hungry. The chairperson looked at his watch and reminded the last speaker of the morning that lunch would be in 5 minutes and could not be delayed because of staff difficulties. The speaker blanched, the audience breathed a huge inward sigh of relief.

As the speaker reached the platform, he looked at the audience, and then at the chairperson and very visibly tore up his notes. 'Thank you Mr Chair,' he said. 'I was going to talk about what my organization has been doing to promote lifelong learning in Europe. Instead I now only have time to say what I really think. So since food is imminent, I want to present the first course – that is food for thought.'

He waved the morning newspaper. 'This,' he said, 'represents today's news,' and he listed the national and international doom and gloom of wars, burglaries, murders, crime, divorces and poverty in that edition. 'This is not the sort of world I want to live in. This is a world created by present structures, including the educational ones, which you are helping to maintain. What I do not want is more of the same. We do not even need better than the same. What we want, and can create between us, is more and better of something different.

So, what is this something different? Let me try to change our mindsets from the way we see things as a progression from what we have. I therefore recommend a three-point plan.' The audience, now hanging on every word, relaxed. Only three points. That we can cope with.

'Number one,' he said. 'Close down the Ministry of Education!' One third of the audience paled and others gave a nervous laugh. There was even a cheer or two. 'But,' he continued, 'only for one week.' Another sigh of relief. 'And then it should be re-opened under an entirely new name.' Puzzlement in the audience. 'I suggest,' he said, 'the Ministry for the Development of Human Potential.' Further puzzlement and a few pennies dropping, as they thought about the meaning of what was being said.

'In the week it is closed,' he continued, 'there should be brain-stormings, creative development sessions, team meetings, new job descriptions for everyone, written and re-written by the employees themselves, and all of this activity focusing on exactly how the human potential of Slovakia's young people will be developed and allowed to flourish.' The audience considered this – OK what next?

'Number two,' he said. 'Close down the Schools!' Another third of the audience stopped smiling, while two-thirds relaxed. This was not their problem. 'That's everybody's problem,' said the speaker, contradicting thoughts, 'because during the week they are closed down, they should have the same brain-stormings, creative development sessions and new curriculum development programmes. And they should bring in parents, children and members of the community into all those sessions, ready to re-open as "Institutions for the development of Human Potential", focusing on the best ways the youngsters can be persuaded to do that.'

The audience briefly considered this. Mindsets softened and insights flashed. 'Lastly,' said the speaker, 'you know what is going to be closed down next.' The University section of the audience nodded. 'And I don't have to tell you what happens – simply that Universities now become "Institutions for the further development of Human Potential". And while we are at it, companies in industry, business and commerce might become organizations for the application of human potential.' The few businessmen in the audience clapped.

'Lastly,' said the speaker, now in his last minute, 'I know you won't do any of this. But at least regard it as a metaphor for what might need to be done to create a lifelong learning society in Bratislava and in Slovakia as a whole. From now on your learners are your customers. Thank you and enjoy your meal.' It was a noisy lunchtime.

Educational organizations are not generally accustomed to the idea of learners as customers. But when the focus is on the needs and demands of the learner in order to promote a more personal commitment, this is what they become. They are accountable to the learner as customer. In order to facilitate better learning, learning providers must take into account the learning styles and preferences of each individual and tailor courses to them. It must also use a wider variety of learning approaches and be much more acutely aware of how learning takes place in each individual. This is a radical shift both in mission and expertise.

Learning providers are hampered by the sparseness of research into the ways in which people learn and prefer to learn. Howard Gardner's studies into multiple abilities offers new insights and tends to be the most frequently quoted example of modern learning research, but other researchers are now taking up the gauntlet. Richardson, in *Bringing Learning to Life* points out that the acquisition of language by the age of three or four years, is probably the greatest intellectual achievement any human being will ever make – and 99 per cent of children do so. But, he goes on to say, none of this is as a result of formal training. He extrapolates from this, and uses evidence from the psychologists Vygotski, Brown and Butterworth, that the most effective 'teaching' is the acquisition of knowledge-in-context, allied to an internalization process on the part of the individual based upon reconstruction and creative diversity. The most effective learning, he says, takes place by personal participation. He rejects as irrelevant and self-fulfilling the Darwinian notion that each learner has a limited potential for learning.

Such a view is borne out by Gardner himself. He observed the advanced mathematical skills demonstrated by ten-year-old Californian, Texan and Pennsylvanian children, who had been three years behind. They were learning from a system where the teachers hardly ever provided answers but were specially trained to ask questions. From this, Bradshaw concludes that 'serving teachers need help to rid themselves of out-of-date over-reliance on rule-of-thumb procedures and they need thorough acquaintance with the new approach to understanding and its applications.'

Learning through experience is one strategy much in vogue over the past 20 years. The exhortation 'to do and to understand' has resurfaced frequently throughout history from the time of the Ming dynasty. Both common sense and the personal experience of every learner confirm its power to motivate, notwithstanding its current reputation in some countries as a 'progressive' idea and therefore a failure in practice. Such backwoods' attitudes suggest both that professional teachers should not keep up to date with trends in creative learning practice, lest they become 'trendy teachers', a term of abuse in some countries. They also believe that the past 30 years has seen a vast increase in active learning. Both are demonstrably untrue.

The sector which has seen the most quantitative and qualitative increase both in active learning and in the number of people participating in it, can be found in business and industry, as a strategic thrust into the development of employees' capacity to learn. In many ways it has been highly successful there. Many industry education departments, led by cost-efficiency considerations, demonstrate a strong interest in the psychology of learning and its translation into new educational methods, and they devise ways of putting these into practice. Such foresight and willingness to experiment with new perceptions of learning can hardly be said of many of the formal education sectors, outside of the funded research departments of a few universities. There are of course good non-educational reasons for this, particularly in the schools, where no parent would like to see the child as a guinea pig in a great educational laboratory. Bayliss acknowledges this, but it does not take away her concern. In her 1998 address to the British Royal Society of Arts, she asks the question 'should we continue simply to tinker with what remains essentially a 19th-century philosophy and structure of schooling, if we want the system to meet the needs of the 21st?'."Our schools,' she says, 'are at real risk of being left behind by external change.' Her discussion paper, *Redefining Schooling*, laments the sheer lack of understanding that education needs to take major changes in the environment seriously, rather than continue to evolve inside a mindset which is demonstrably and even dangerously out of date.

But not all schools are learning deserts. Some of them attempt to take good practice from other sectors and reflect the coming focus on learning by alternative presentational approaches. The Schools Council Industry Project (SCIP), a schools/industry-based organization in Britain, identifies and recommends 15 examples of active and experiential learning methodology as follows.

Group Discussion	Role-playing	Visits
Problem-solving Activities	Investigations	Simulations (inc computer)
Data-handling Activities	Games	Visitors into the Classroom
Case Studies	Active Writing and Reading	Presentations
Memo-driven activities	Work-based assignments	Work Experience

These are certainly methods used widely in industry as ways of improving understanding, as opposed to giving information. They are also used widely in Adult Education Colleges where educational practice is less constrained by external considerations and methods of teaching are more open and attractive.

In industry lesser-known, but nonetheless successful, approaches are used, based upon new revelations of how people learn more easily when they are relaxed and when they are self-aware. They include methods based on Tai' Chi, meditation, transactional analysis, structural analysis, relaxation therapy, visualization, brain-storming, creativity stimulation through music, right brain exercises, imagineering, virtual reality – and to a further extreme, hypnopaedia and subliminal suggestion. Recent research also makes a strong connection between music and intellectual stimulation. Naisbitt tells us that the Singer Company takes this seriously enough to recommend periods of musical day-dreaming with portable walkmans to relieve stress and improve creative productivity. In other learning experiments, Dr Bevan Morris, President of the Maharishi Universities of Management, claims to have discovered new information about how the brain works through Vedic knowledge, and to have applied it with great success in the schools under its control.

While many new breakthroughs in our understanding of how learning best occurs in individuals are relatively untested and regarded with suspicion by many people, if not dangerously occult by some, the education departments of industry which have espoused them also have some positive tales to tell. Certainly more emphasis needs to be given to research into the way people learn and learn better, but this has been true for many years. Paradoxically, resistance to educational change based on new knowledge tends to be at its highest in the educational sector which is responsible for producing this new knowledge.

But these new approaches are not all. We are told by the media that learning-enhancement drugs have been in circulation for several years, that their use will increase vastly in the future, and that even the implantation of skills microchips in the brain are in store for us by the year 2020. To many, this is the ultimate in easy learning, to others it is a horror story demonstrating the depths to which advocates of the use of technology will sink.

All of this is not to suggest that every new fashion in learning should be adopted by schools and universities. It does however confirm that new tools, techniques, methods and approaches are available, and that teachers should, if they are to remain updated in a professional manner, be aware of them and their implications.

2. The learner will have a greater involvement with the content and methodology of his/her own learning and a more developed sense of ownership of it

The concept of ownership has been in constant discussion since the early computer-assisted instruction experiments of the 1960s. How to apply it in practice is more problematical. But strategies do exist. The schools outside of the mainstream, Rudolph Steiner, Montessori and others, have evolved methods to develop a love of learning in students through the involvement of students in the education they receive. OECD, in *Lifelong Learning for All*, talks of individual pathways to learning, suggesting open-ended and interconnected learning targets within a system of personal learning plans and individualized assessment methods. This would allow learning to take place in a variety of environments – at home, in school, in specially designed centres. While such structures are some time away, it is probably the way in which education at all levels can escape from the straitjacket of institutionalized provision.

Such thinking passes the schools by. In the state system, few schools make the attempt to put the curriculum into context to those who are on the receiving end of it. Real learner-centred education is still in its infancy, though the Nordic countries of Europe particularly are addressing the method with vigour. In the Finnish national lifelong learning strategy, reference is made to the individual child's learning ability as the first, and most crucial, pillar of lifelong learning. Markkula and Suurla put it thus: 'It is in very childhood that learning principles and attitudes are adopted…If a person learns to learn in early childhood the capacity for learning will be tremendously enhanced…Earlier, no-one could picture a 3-year-old child capable of using a computer to acquire new knowledge in the way children do today.'

The Finnish strategy recommends that a child's natural inquisitiveness and willingness to learn new things should be developed into a 'passion to learn' and an openness and receptiveness to everything. The Mankaa school, for example, in the city of Espoo, devotes every tenth day to a 'virtual working day' in which all children are given the freedom to develop their own learning, studying whatever they want to study and wherever they want to study it. Computer technology plays a large part in the co-ordination of this. Moreover, it is successful. In a personal conversation, teachers told me that more real learning takes place on that day than on most of the other days. And they also said that the idea had improved the attitude of the students so much that other aspects of their work had been considerably enhanced. And from Markkula and Suurla again, for learners of all ages: 'It is the purpose of lifelong learning to make people independent, to encourage them to develop personally and to tap into more resources in working life. This succeeds only if people are made to discover possibilities available to them, if they are given support and freedom to develop themselves along with more responsibility for planning and accomplishing their tasks. We must learn to see a person as an entity, capable of far more demanding accomplishments than the conventional work machine.'

However, in some countries, the thought of handing control of learning to the learner has received a bad press. In England, for example, the same 'trendy teachers' who advocate learning by doing are reviled by government ministers, newspaper proprietors and Chief Inspectors alike. Perhaps as a result, very few teachers are urged to give a rationally acceptable explanation of the syllabus for each subject to their students, nor are they required to transmit a sense of anticipation and excitement in the knowledge and skills the learner will acquire. Sometimes, indeed, there isn't one. Most teachers try to make learning interesting, of course. It is after all their professional function. But they are often fighting against both a cultural apathy, which sets little store by learning, and administrative hostility, which sees learning as a means to demonstrate results rather than a desirable end in itself.

Setting aside the arguments about whether schools ever did move toward participative learning, most educators agree that a strong motivation to learn, wherever and however it originates, plays a crucial part in successful learning.

Given this, some attempt to put the learning people do into its wider human context would help the process of motivation at all levels. Dr James Botkin, principal author of the Club of Rome *No Limits to Learning*, confessed that he was disappointed with progress in innovative learning in the state systems ten years later. In Dee Dickinson's book *Creating the Future* he confesses that only in Austria, Finland and Japan does he see progress, and expresses surprise that leadership has come from the most unexpected source, ie the international business community. The twin forces of inertia and reaction, it seems, have successfully held back development in most other developed countries.

Ownership of learning has not yet reached most universities, even though students are over 18 and adults in their own right. In many, students are often given a detailed syllabus, with reading lists and recommended additional courses, but in very few are the rationale and expected benefits explained in any detail. Indeed the joy of learning becomes, to many students, and not a few lecturers, the chore of learning. And yet, the somewhat long and convoluted fifth article of the Hamburg declaration, produced at Confintea V in 1997 offers another vision. It states 'the objectives of youth and adult education, viewed as a lifelong process, are to develop the autonomy and the sense of responsibility of people and communities, to reinforce the capacity to deal with the transformations taking place in the economy, in culture and in society as a whole, and to promote co-existence, tolerance, and the informed and creative participation of citizens in their communities, in short to enable people and communities to take control of their own destiny…' That might have something also to say to other parts of the education system.

As Botkin says, it is to the private sector that one turns for further inspiration in this field. The need to insert principles of total quality management has led in many companies to an entirely new empowerment of the workforce. They have smashed, for example, the long-held view that somehow there are limits to learning based on intelligence quotients or whatever. For example, Mercedes-Benz opened a huge new factory in Alabama, the poorest state in the USA. Logan tells us that, within a few years, it transformed agricultural labourers and people who had never worked at all into world-class car workers. In a Learning Organization like this, individuals and teams are given the responsibility and the privilege of working out their own solutions to new processes, new procedures and the acquisition of new knowledge and skills. Such a transformation from the imposed to the acquired is encapsulated in Figure 5.2 and also in Figure 6.2.

In an environment requiring personal development, personal responsibility and driven by the needs of customers, the ownership of the tasks and the sense that learning is a continuous activity is the minimum needed to ensure a school's, a university's, a company's success. Appendix 2 of the Finnish National Strategy neatly encapsulates the new role. 'The Information society is going to change teaching methods by replacing the excessively passive relationship between teacher and student with a new interactive relationship. The teacher will increasingly become an advisor and a coach. The 'guide at the side' of learners will tend to replace 'the sage on the stage' of older education systems.

However, if anything will galvanize educational organizations to hand over control to the learner, it is the use of the new technologies for learning. The increased availability of options offered by sensitively developed new learning tools and techniques can help promote the learner-centred approach which links people with their goals and their dreams. This is a topic for exploration in later sections.

3a. In being more responsive to individual learning needs teachers will develop a more versatile range of skills and competencies

Teachers would become 'learning counsellors', with a knowledge of all aspects of educational approaches including the use of learning technologies, the development of leadership skills and a knowledge of the tools and techniques of lifelong learning.

3b. The learning counsellor would also develop the proficiency to empower others to learn – a much more sophisticated and complex set of abilities

A vital part of the curriculum of the developing and practising teacher must be not how to teach teachers how to teach, but to teach them how to stimulate learning and confident self-development in people of all ages.

The notion of a 'learning counsellor' (the label varies) as a versatile 'teacher' who would be at home anywhere within the educational system has been raised at several European conferences. The idea has been received with a great deal of interest and not a little scepticism, since the profile of such a 'teacher of tomorrow', as the European Lifelong Learning Initiative calls it, is far more sophisticated than anything we have at the present time. And yet almost every book or report on lifelong learning – the OECD report on Learning for All, the UK and Finnish Government's Green Paper, The Fryer Report, the USA National Strategy for Learning – forecasts great changes in the role of the teacher. All of them describe a very different world of learning – new approaches, new curricula, new knowledge, new technology. All of them require a much wider range of skills, knowledge and competencies than presently exists in schools, universities, colleges and industry. Indeed this is not just in the world of teaching. It is so in every other professional walk of life and teachers should not be exempt from it.

The Finnish National Strategy for Lifelong Learning recognizes that the role of the teacher in the school will have to change. It is highlighted as the second of four pillars of lifelong learning. Markkula and Suurla put it thus: 'The teacher's new role is the second pillar of lifelong learning. It involves a total change and reform in the role of people working in teaching jobs.' They go on to expand the definition of a teacher as a person who is a helper and a support – also in the learning equation are managers, experts, parents, grandparents, supervisors, coaches and mentors. They are all part of the physical, mental, emotional and intellectual nurturing and support process. The trained teacher in this scenario becomes the expert co-ordinator, the motivator and the enabler of the learner and of the learning.

Again such a view is supported by the European Study Group on Education and Training. 'Teachers play a primordial role,' they say, 'because they are the only people in our societies providing a service of such multidimensional character. Contemporary trends are that their role is becoming ever more multi-faceted, because it increasingly incorporates social, behavioural, civic, economic and tech-nological dimensions.'

What is true in schools is also true in industry. The European Round Table of Industrialists recommends in its publication on *Lifelong Learning in Industry* that 'large companies should have their own lifelong learning counsellors, who can ini-tiate co-operation and collaboration with universities and advise employees about Continuing Education.' And again they considered that universities too should follow this lead – 'Every University should have a lifelong learning office to work with companies, and a study counsellor to advise adults working in SMEs, the bulk of Europe's workforce.'

These views are expressed from both a school and an industry lifelong learning viewpoint. But if they are relevant in one part of the educational system, why not in others? The answer is of course that a true Learning Counsellor would be equally at home in any environment, education and non-educational. He/she would be competent in schools, in industry, in universities, in the community, in adult edu-cation, since the required skills are similar in all those places. The new skills are many and various. Figure 2.1 below shows how the teacher of tomorrow will need to adapt to a poly-educational world.

Learning Counsellors – Teachers of Tomorrow

√   Create the habit of learning in people through a thorough knowledge of how people learn and their individual learning styles

√   Optimize the use of open and distance learning technologies to make the best use of their power to create interactive feedback between the learner and the learning programme(s)

√   Understand how to develop and administer targeted evaluation techniques and personal progress modules

√   Network learners with other learners on a local, national and international basis and develop all the ways of using communications technology to stimulate innovative learning

√   Support learning by developing and using partnerships between industry, schools, higher and further education, local government and the informal education system

√   Empower each learner by helping to set and monitoring personal goals through personal learning plans, mentors techniques and individualized learning modules

√   List all the learning needs of people in a database by carrying out learning audits in companies, the community and wherever people congregate

√   Link these needs to learning opportunities locally, nationally and internationally and make use of all funding sources

√   Organize information programmes and schemes to mobilize the skills and talents of the whole community for education and learning

√   Research new learning techniques and incorporate them into courses

√   Stimulate learning into an enjoyable and creative experience through a thorough knowledge of the psychology of learning motivation and how to overcome barriers to learning confidence.

Equally at home in industry, schools, adult education, universities and all parts of education and social systems

Figure 2.1 Learning Counsellors – teachers of tomorrow

4. A wider range of the skills, talents and knowledge available from the community at large will need to be mobilized in the service of learners

Within every community there exists an enormous untapped resource, that is the talents, skills, knowledge and wisdom of people from every walk of life. Some schools already make use of them in a formal way. Policemen regularly talk to schoolchildren about road safety or aspects of crime; nurses and doctors are invited in to talk about aspects of health. But there it generally stops. The skills of the engineer, the experiences of the single mother, the wisdom of the philosopher or minister, the expertise of the practising biologist, the knowledge of the professional musician, the enthusiasm of the amateur bird-watcher – all are kept firmly outside the walls. Chapman and Aspin deplore this: 'It is unfortunate that many school doors have been firmly closed against the entry of the community. It is difficult for schools, that in the past have seen themselves as closed organizations, to change their attitudes towards becoming open institutions...'

At the Southampton Conference on Learning Cities in June 1998, Longworth described the problem and the opportunity thus:

> I live in a particularly beautiful area of Southern France. My village of some 300 souls is one of those villages perchés and one of the 100 most beautiful villages in France. The view from my office opens out across the valley onto the Canigou, a 9000 foot mountain, snow-capped for ten months of the year. In the foreground are peach, apricot, almond, cherry and nectarine trees which, during blossom time, form a rich carpet of pink, white and green on which, it seems, one could float into El Dorado. Prades, the nearest town, comprises about 7000 inhabitants. Its secondary school and college are fed by the families of the town and the many villages around. On its curriculum at all levels are languages, including English and German, Biology, Music, Geography, Mathematics, as well as a host of other subjects.
>
> I am not the only British resident of this paradise. Among our small community of 100 people are a much-travelled world-class biologist who was secretary to the Prince of Wales Environmental Trust, a former teacher-trainer in geography, a mathematics teacher who has taken early retirement, three English as a foreign language teachers, two former opera singers also trained in music teaching, a former dietician and a former professor of German. These are just the skills I know about.
>
> The application of logic seems to point to the marriage of these talents with the schoolchildren who might benefit from them, enriching their learning world with the stories, adventures and experiences of those who have personal immersion in the subject, and from time to time giving the teachers a rest from the stress of the schoolday. And if asked, all of those people would be happy to devote a few hours a week, a month or a year to making their knowledge and assistance available. But of

managing time constraints between school education, multimedia entertainment, physical entertainment and household chores.' The messages invading the senses come from every quarter and constitute a richness, a diversity and an overabundance for which learning strategies must be devised, both for adults and young people. They can only become more urgent and demanding.

Most teachers are unaware of this richness, and in some countries, would be unable to use it if they obtained it, either because deviation from government-prescribed, content-heavy curricula does not permit it, or because they do not have the time to evaluate or participate in it. The curricula of our education providers, mainly schools and universities, have not been updated to provide the information-handling skills that harness the power of the information at our disposal.

6. The creative use of networks in collaborative learning strategies between people of different cultures, creeds and colours to enhance both international understanding and learning outlook and performance

The simplistic world seems to be divided into binary segments. Developed and developing nations; authoritarian and liberal democratic governments; multi-ethnic and homogeneous societies; over-populated and under-populated territories; ageing and youthful populations; religious and secular societies; societies in which women are free and those in which they are not. The real world is more complex and rich, but the fault-lines between one philosophy and another are real enough. What constitutes lifelong learning for the peasant boy in Pakistan is not the same thing as that for the research scientist in the USA. What comprises learning for women in Afghanistan is different from that for women in Australia or Europe. What the Brazilian street-boy can aspire to differs in content and kind from what is available to the Vietnamese immigrant in Canada. Opportunities, information, peer pressures, parental influence, religious customs, household budgets – they all conspire to create diversity and fashion opportunity.

This is where the power of the technology to open up hearts and minds to new learning really comes into its own. What happens if we put the peasant boy in touch with the research scientist, the South African ghetto girl with the Chelsea pensioner, the unemployed Scottish labourer with the Japanese banker through the Internet. Perhaps nothing, perhaps a whole range of surprises. While these may be extreme examples to stimulate creative thinking, there are other examples where such links can, when used properly, so energize the motivation to learn that many of our prejudices about its limits are set aside. The PLUTO example and others are given in Chapter 13. But the possibilities of using networks to learn, about each other, about the world as others see it, about the knowledge we can obtain from experts and non-experts alike are only constrained by the limits of human creativity.

Certainly it would, and should, have a great effect on the curricula of schools, universities and other parts of the educational system. It will put an increasing emphasis on the acquisition of skills, particularly information-handling skills, and values, particularly the virtues of flexible and adaptable thinking. Such creative learning is discussed in Chapters 14 and 19, with examples of how it has increased the motivation of children and adults alike.

Chapter 3

The common constituency of learning

The second group of new insights into lifelong learning covers the cross-departmental, cross-sectoral, interdependent nature of the concept. In a learning city for example, several departments of local government and several sectoral organizations might be responsible for devising and implementing lifelong learning plans and strategies, often in partnership with each other. The premise, then, is:

Lifelong learning is more holistic. It is an economic, social and cultural, as well as an educational, concept. This means:

1. Exploiting the potential relationship between high levels of education, economic success and low social costs

The 1995 OECD Jobs Study establishes a link between the economic and the social value of lifelong learning. 'Long-term unemployment lowers self-esteem, and has the potential to impact adversely on health, interpersonal relationships and social and community structures, leading at its most extreme to such individually and socially dysfunctional phenomena as crime and substance abuse.' Not all governments are willing to make such an explicit link between social conditions and social problems. Yet almost every social study made into the effects of education on material and mental well-being agree that a greater potential to earn and a richer lifestyle is available to those who take advantage of their educational opportunities, no matter how flawed the system may be. Highly educated people are less likely to need welfare benefits, vandalize park benches, spray graffiti or get involved in drunken brawls. In financial terms alone, the savings to be made in addressing problems of social exclusion and dysfunction and moving to a more attractive and successful learner-centred education system has a high value.

And yet in many systems there are still in-built inequities. In study after study, children from poorer families are less likely to achieve higher education, though the problem is often more one of low expectation, lack of aspiration and a negative sub-culture than of lack of acceptance. Financial constraints exacerbate the problem. Those countries which formerly subsidized students are now demonstrating less willingness to do so. Many governments are trying to address this situation. The British Government's Green Paper, *The Learning Age*, describes some of these. The 'New Deal' programmes expect employers to share the cost of education with those students on their temporary payroll, so that they too are investing in skills development in their own longer-term interests. Career development loans help to pay for vocational education or training. In a state version of the Rover scheme, described by Longworth and Davies in *Lifelong Learning*, one million 'Individual Learning Accounts' of £150 are available to start people on the way to a learning future. Smart cards will provide a record of what, how, when and where learning has taken place. The 'New Start' programme will try to re-motivate young people from the age of 14 who are disenchanted with learning by offering alternative pathways, as recommended in OECD's *Lifelong Learning for All*. Childcare support is planned for women wishing to return to work after pregnancy. In the USA 'Headstart' programmes for disadvantaged youngsters have been made available for more than 20 years. The European Commission's 'Youth for Europe' scheme tries to raise horizons for young people by providing work experience in other countries and offering grants for disadvantaged youngsters to start up their own organization, be it a business or an association. Governments and local government in all parts of the developed world recognize the problem, and implement hundreds of programmes to ameliorate it.

However, the predominant need in most countries is for a break in the cycle of deprivation. Low-income families expect their offspring to contribute to the household budget as soon as they are legally able, and often before. Books are a luxury, newspapers an occasional purchase, and what they read there does not encourage a change of culture. Low functional literacy in adults – OECD put this as high as 25 per cent in some developed countries – breeds low aspirations in children, and an ignorance of how to break out through learning. It is a condition that has existed through the centuries. It is a situation which a new lifelong learning approach should seriously aim to solve in the 21st century.

2. Re-assessing and re-designing financial programmes – social, economic, educational, fiscal, cultural

'If learning were a valued resource like clean air and fresh water, neither individuals nor society as a whole would hesitate to provide the necessary funding.' So says the Kent – Region of Learning book, and, as Chapter 25 indicates, Kent is in the process of examining the integration of budgets. Traditionally, Government and Community departments have jealously guarded their autonomy and their budgets. Education has diligently pursued its path of providing for primary, secondary and tertiary education within the establishments created for the purpose. Social Services departments have picked up the pieces of failure and cater for those who have not fitted into the norms of society, while others have dealt with the physical and mental deficiencies of those who have succumbed to illness and upheaval. Yet other departments have devoted themselves to the detection and punishment of crime and wrong-doing. Outside of the governmental systems, company education departments are increasingly remedying the damage done to individuals who left the education system as failures. Longworth and Davies recount the award-winning success story of Youth Training Scheme students who left IBM for other jobs, and retrained with a new set of personal skills, values and attitudes after personal development skills had been put at the forefront of their skill profile. Many other projects relate success stories of this kind.

It is only recently that authority has come to realize the interdependent, interlocking and interactive nature of all these social systems, and started to initiate programmes to deal with the problems at source. The example of Japan in requiring different functions of the state and the community to formulate lifelong learning plans (see page 41) is already one beacon to follow at governmental and local level, while many developing countries often have no other option than to combine their social, educational and police budgets. UNESCO's *Mumbai Statement* also recognizes the issue: 'The imperatives of education throughout life are driven by the diverse demands of the global economy and those of equitable and sustainable societies. For the majority to benefit we recognize the interrelatedness of the economic, the social, the political and the ecological.'

Somehow, however, one feels that real life is not so simple. Power structures built up over many years do not yield territory easily. Convincing research evidence needs to be shown before the premise that lifelong learning, carried out as a holistic exercise in co-operation between departments, social sectors and organizations, will redistribute resources by reducing levels of crime, increasing good health and combating exclusion. Many governments are uncomfortable establishing a link between poverty and crime for example, preferring to believe that a lack of individual responsibility is the cause. And so it is, but where does the sense of individual responsibility originate and how can it be fostered but through learning?

The NIACE study on 'Adults' Learning' describes a study carried out in Wales highlighting the importance of co-operation, innovation and expanded vision. The manifesto it produced recommends greater co-ordination, the collective mobilization of resources and a greater investment in lifelong learning to ensure social and cultural vitality as well as economic success. From studies of this kind, which establish the direction of the vision, and often the ground rules for action, can come a mould-breaking advance. But to have the consent of the people, it must also involve the people. And to involve the people it has to catch the imagination. A co-ordinated effort, as recommended for Wales, to present lifelong learning as a practical project to improve both the standard and the quality of life in the next century would do much to help light the candle of learning progress. Presented only as another educational initiative it will not have the same effect.

Even within the education services there is a much greater scope for the greater sharing of resources and the development of a common cradle to grave policy. The UK green papers on lifelong learning, higher education and adult education are both visionary and open. They begin to chart a new 'third way' to a lifelong learning future. But the Schools' White paper might have been written on a different planet. While the need for lifelong learning is referenced, the schools' paper appears to be so obsessed by Victorian classroom teaching methodologies, didactic curriculum content, and failure-oriented assessment strategies under the guise of 'standards', as to be indistinguishable from the new approach recommended in the others. Both Whackford Squeers and B F Skinner would have been proud. Of course reading, writing and arithmetic, the basics, are important, but, as Naisbitt says, 'to stop there is to equip children only with the skills of their grandparents. It is like giving them a wrench to fix a computer. There is nothing wrong with a wrench, but it won't fix a computer.' The cradle to grave holism of lifelong learning demands a more seamless and intergrated policy, horizontally and vertically interdependent with each other, rather than isolating the schools as an entirely different phenomenon.

To be fair it mentions the importance of computers in the teaching process. But in tone and vision it contrasts strongly with the all-encompassing Finnish lifelong learning strategy paper, quoted frequently in this book, emphasizing the contribution of schools as an equal partner in the creation of a lifelong learning society, and the importance of drastic changes in teacher training, both in-service and pre-service. Consequently the British strategy is skewed heavily to lifelong learning as a concept for adults, and especially for adults in or seeking employment. This was not the intention of the more visionary Fryer report, which preceded it, and which recognized the importance of what happens in school to the development of lifelong learning values and attitudes in individuals. Nor was it the message of OECD which devotes considerable space in *Lifelong Learning for All* to recommending action in the early years of school. To be fair, Britain is not the only country with a problem in recognizing the lifelong aspect of lifelong learning. France, Italy, Germany and Spain, to mention just a few, have great difficulty in presenting a completely comprehensive cradle to grave framework for lifelong learning. All of them make strong reference to the importance of the early years, but few are able to translate this into a holistic vision in practice.

3. Developing lifelong learning schemes and programmes across and within sectoral and departmental boundaries

In Japan, where, in general terms, crime levels are low and health care is good, lifelong learning is not seen as the preserve of the education ministry or education department. The comparative study carried out by the National Institute for Education Research in conjunction with UNESCO Institute for Education describes how each separate ministry devises its own plans.

The Ministry of International Trade and Industry (MITI), which helped to enact the Law for the Promotion of Lifelong Learning, has also established a Division of Lifelong Learning Policy within the Ministry, and is currently conducting professional educational activities through the medium of the Chambers of Commerce and Industry. It has created a budget for the implementation of lifelong learning programmes.

The Ministry of Labour has produced a plan to develop lifelong learning by establishing centres for workers, and in particular, working youth and working women. Furthermore, this Ministry is developing lifelong learning professional skills, and is creating centres for the advancement of lifelong education within companies to develop a system for the advancement of the professional skills of people in industry.

Industrial development and town improvement for lifelong learning is part of the responsibility of the Ministry of Agriculture, Forestry and Fisheries, mainly to improve rural mountain and fishing villages, and for the preparation and deployment of village resources. Many examples of the construction of facilities connected to lifelong learning can be seen in every community. The Ministry of Construction is pursuing lifelong learning in relation to a policy of residential housing. In order to plan for the enhancement of the community and to support the policy of town improvement, a lifelong learning community structure is being developed by the Ministry. Furthermore, this involves the National Land Agency, which is considering the practical use of community centres.

Meanwhile, the Ministry of Health and Welfare is concerned with lifelong learning from the point of view of national health care. There are public health centres, welfare centres, municipal health centres, senior citizens' homes, each with a mandate to use lifelong learning as an aid to health improvement and to speed up the participation of elderly people in social activities. The Economic Planning Agency promotes lifelong learning activities directed towards leisure activities within national life. Even the Prime Minister's Office is involved in lifelong learning. Its interest is to strengthen measures for both the fostering of sound body and mind among children and the encouragement of international exchange among youth. Each ministry has its own independent objectives and roles to perform in the promotion of lifelong learning policies. For Japan, lifelong learning encompasses all the qualities of human nature and life, from learning related to individual objectives such as personal hobbies and health management, to learning that covers many social objectives such as town improvement and interpersonal development on a systematic basis. All these are set in motion through the support of the various ministries. Governments in the rest of the world can learn from this. It demonstrates a keen awareness of the multidimensional character of lifelong learning that is the responsibility of everyone. Learning Cities too have much to learn here. More cross-departmental projects leading to a breakdown of existing autonomous structures, would also lead to the rebuilding of new co-operative lifelong learning frameworks in local government. Here again the imperative of lifelong learning is fighting against inertia and the vested interests of existing power structures. This is why, to succeed, it needs a strong and highly influential personality at its head.

4. Special fiscal measures to encourage and reward learning

The 5th recommendation of the high-level policy committee to the EU proposed the following: 'Governments should use their financial resources to encourage industry–university collaboration for adult education. Lifelong learning should be treated like a social investment. All costs to the individual and the employer should be tax deductible. When companies give work-time for education, they should receive tax benefits in return.'

Tax breaks are just one of the many instruments within the power of Government, and, as a fiscal measure, it is a very powerful one. The UK Kennedy Report on Adult Education, 'Learning Works', made just such a plea. 'The Government should ensure that education up to level 3 is free for all young people and for adults without basic skills or who are socially or economically deprived; tax relief should be extended to all learning programmes up to this level, which are funded by individuals.' And again, 'The Government should extend tax incentives to encourage private sector employers to establish employee development programmes.' This latter may be influenced by the moderately successful and often creatively interpreted French system of 'taxe d'apprentissage', in which all companies are expected by law to devote a proportion of their profit to educational activities, though the paymaster in this case is not government.

In fact, tax relief does exist in England and Wales on study, examination and registration fees, accreditation of prior learning assessments and payment for an award or certificate. Much more can be done. It doesn't yet cover equipment or textbooks, essential course materials (eg photocopied course notes) provided by a trainer and not generally available commercially; living or travelling expenses in connection with the training, the provision of which is a real barrier to learning for the poorer student.

Another recommendation in the same document suggested a 'Learning Nation fund'. 'The Government should create a learning nation fund,' it said, 'from the national lottery funds released after the millennium to achieve the quantum leap in participation in post-16 learning needed to tackle the backlog of underachievement.' This was to be allied to a 'Learning Regeneration fund' to provide incentives and reward for local strategic partnerships. The British Government, in its reply, has promised to look into the idea. Many other sectors of the community could also benefit from the same fund and so the problem would be one of targeting those areas where real progress might be made.

Other stratagems might include the funding of local learning festivals, as is also done in Japan, or by financing one person in each educational establishment, such as a school, to exploit all the resources of the community around it. Although it would include income generation, he/she would not be simply a fund-raiser, more a resource generator, taking a wide view of the nature of resources. Alumni funding in United States universities is a good example of creative fund-raising, and a number of British public (ie private) schools have adopted a similar idea. A good brainstorming session would uncover many more such initiatives producing a large return on the investment of relatively little. But commitment is needed. Once convinced of the need to foster and develop lifelong learning as both a wealth-creating and a social development strategy, the mental leap towards fiscal support measures by both government and the community is made vastly easier. The problem perhaps is to persuade others of the need, and this leads to:

5. A proactive approach to the value of lifelong learning

OECD, in *Lifelong Learning for All*, has provided many statistics on the cost-benefit accruing to nations, organizations and individuals from the move to a learning society. 'The evidence,' it says, 'supports the assumption of lifelong learning as an investment that more than pays for itself.'

But there is another, non-financial, aspect to the business of presenting learning in a positive context. In *Lifelong Learning* the practice in the Rover Company of displaying the seven principles of its learning business function can act as a model for education organizations. 'Learning is the most important human characteristic' is the first of the seven, and that can equally be applied to the university laboratory or the school classroom. Although only a slogan, it has the effect of constantly reminding people that they have learning potential and that that is one of the reasons why they are there. While this is a common practice in industry, it is rare that one can walk into a school classroom or university workshop and see the benefit of being there, writ large, for all to mentally ingest. Because of this the European Life-long Learning Initiative is applying for funding to develop two series of posters aimed at both practitioners and students, to be available from 2000. The first series will deal with general characteristics of lifelong learning for display in staff-rooms, common rooms, learning centres and offices. The other will aim to switch people on to learning through short messages for exhibition in classrooms, public places and community centres. An example, without the graphic support, is shown in figure 3.1 below. It takes no great stretch of the imagination to build upon this idea as a focus for competitions, displays and learning events without waiting for the ELLI posters.

IT'S YOUR LIFE

LEARN

TO TAKE CONTROL OF IT

Figure 3.1 A Slogan

6. Learning audits, carried out regionally, of the present and future learning requirements of all citizens. The resultant database to be updated and maintained on an annual basis

Neither nations nor cities can satisfy the learning needs of its citizens without know-ing what they are. Only when the community knows the extent of the need, and in a learning community it will be a rapidly growing need, can it provide the infrastruc-tures to satisfy its citizens. The number of unexpressed, and therefore unsatisfied, needs is probably as much as five times the range of satisfied needs. The learning audit carried out by the European Lifelong Learning Initiative in 1995 bears out this thesis. Fifty per cent of the people interviewed had never before been asked what their learn-ing needs are. In many cases it was believed that they had none. In the event the very asking produced an explosion of unsuspected, unfulfilled learning dreams.

The learning audit was developed with a grant from the Force Programme of the European Commission. It was carried out in small companies of between 50 and 100 people and took into account a wide range of learning needs from the point of view of the individuals working there, rather than from the narrower point of view of the company's training needs. All employees were involved. A report on learning needs was generated for management. Naturally, the company is not expected to satisfy all these requirements, but the responsible company with a commitment to the maintenance of learning habits in its workforce may wish to discuss them with a range of providers in the locality.

Although this was carried out in small companies, a creative brainstorming session carried out in a city can produce some interesting ideas on where and how to collect this data – in the shopping centre, the pub and the restaurant, on the train, the plane and the ferry-boat. As to who and how, there are many suggestions. The unemployed – to give them a glimpse of the need for education, trainee teachers – to give them an insight into learning needs in a whole community. Schoolchildren could be used to help collect and analyse the results and realize that an adult's world is a learning world. Irrespective of who and how, the learning audit is best carried out under the supervision of a university or another type of education provider. They have the expertise and the equipment to interpret the results. If it is to be carried out in industry, a sympathetic person should carry out the interview – in that way employees have more confidence in the confidentiality of their responses. This is important because a good learning requirements' questionnaire will solicit data about past, present and future learning experiences and needs, and opinions as well as facts. In other words, it will try to involve the individual in a detailed personal discussion about the world as he or she sees it, and the place of learning in it.

Thus there will be questions about personal learning styles and preferences, observations on the company and its performance in satisfying their needs, the answers to which an open learning organization will be happy to receive. There will be enquiries about their own view of themselves, and discussions on dreams for their children. It is a complete document, opening up the mind of interviewee and interviewer alike, and supplying more information about the individual than most surveys of this type. In the original survey, an analysis package was developed including data-entry sheets into a commonly used spreadsheet programme and an interrogation program which produced the graphs, charts and tables for management action.

Learning audits may not yet be in common use, but the company and the city of the future will make increasing use of them both as a motivator of learning, and as a means of obtaining a full picture of learning needs. Certainly, the results obtained in Europe were interesting. The major difference in perception occurred between northern and southern Europe. The concept of lifelong learning as a whole-of-life activity, in which life at work and life outside of work are part of the same continuum is more resisted in southern Europe, where the lines of demarcation between one and the other seem to be more rigidly applied by both individuals and companies. It is perhaps a perception of the difference between living to work and working to live. Similarly the burden of deciding who takes education, and when, is more a matter for the individual in northern Europe than in the south.

These seem to affect workforce perceptions in those questions where an opinion was required on the likelihood of education and training being made available easily and freely to individuals. In all parts of the survey, even where the company provided schemes and cash for the individual employee to enjoy learning, there was some scepticism about this, reflecting on the one hand a failure in the company information and communication system and on the other hand a lack of insight into the true nature of lifelong learning. There is a long way to go before the concept of developing one's own human potential through learning, or even realizing that one has a greater potential, is well accepted. Formal education systems seem to have done a good job of hiding it from the vast majority of people. And yet, raising consciousness of its existence is important for the future of business and industry, education and society in general.

7. The encouragement of towns, cities and regions to declare themselves as 'communities of learning' and to develop and implement strategies which develop their human potential

Cities around the world seem to require little encouragement to do this. The increase in the number of cities designating themselves as Cities of Learning over the last two years makes it one of the growth industries of the decade. Governments and non-governmental organizations can pontificate and set targets, but cities and towns know that most of the real development will take place at local and regional level, where organizations are situated and where people live. Organizations to link and service their needs are also proliferating. Eurocities, Educating Cities, ELLIcities, the North American Association of Learning Cities, and national bodies for learning cities have all been created in the 1990s, most of them recently, and offering varying support programmes. The ELLIcities initiative, for example 'intends to be the major forum for the development of European Cities, Towns and Regions as vibrant, innovative and exciting places whose citizens accept Learning as a part of Life.' Its prospectus states that it:

- Provides public and private electronic forums for productive discussion between administrators, teachers, councillors, counsellors, city workers and all who contribute to the development of a learning city, town or region;
- Runs courses, conferences, seminars and workshops in member cities for people in all walks of city life;
- Initiates action research through programmes funded by the European Commission, the cities themselves and other funding bodies;

- Develops case studies of good practice in learning city development and action for member cities;
- Keeps member cities up to date with the latest developments through newsletters and journals.

But of course any city can decide to designate itself as a 'city of learning' without changing one item of its policy. It remains no more than a label until it implements new projects to become a true centre for lifelong learning. This is why Part 2 of this book is devoted to the topic of the learning city, the place where lifelong learning will be made to work. It is also why Sheffield Hallam University in the UK has opened one of the first 'Centres for the Learning City' in the world, and has applied for European funding to establish a full network of such centres.

8. Schemes to share resources within communities and to develop partnerships which entail transfer of resources, including human resources, between sectors

Vast sums of money will not be made available by Governments to create a lifelong learning society. In the first place they cannot afford it, and in the second place, as we have seen, their vision of lifelong learning is linked to a more cohesive and holistic society in which resources are shared, where voluntary activities increase and economic returns outweigh the costs. Theirs is a long-term view.

The OECD, in *Lifelong Learning for All*, is quite categorical on the subject. 'Historic costs are of limited use as indicators of future cost,' they say. 'The key to progress in making lifelong learning affordable is to ensure that there exist the framework conditions that a) encourage innovation in the provision of learning opportunities; b) overcome the problems arising from externalities, and the delay when the costs of lifelong learning are incurred and when the benefits are realized.' Externalities in OECD-speak are the productivity and personal gains made by people and organizations who are successful in the tertiary system and which are not ploughed back into the education system. As a result, OECD foresees:

- The greater use of education technology tools and techniques and an understanding of how they can be used interactively as learning stimulators as well as content presenters;
- Curricula in all parts of the formal education system emphasizing the acquisition of skills, values, and turning knowledge into understanding, rather than information content and memorization.

But while OECD explains that new money for lifelong learning will be a scarce commodity, it does not identify the source of new resources to be made available for its development. For this we must look at the merging of resources from existing programmes and the innovative exploitation of the unused talents and skills of people and organizations in every community, and seek the best use of resources through sharing, as discussed in Chapter 2. Chapman and Aspin recognize this. 'It is difficult for schools, that in the past have seen themselves as closed organizations, to change their attitudes towards becoming open institutions that can provide many sources of information and possible avenues of expansion to cater for the needs of people who have different learning needs from those of children.' They continue by describing how schools, which have responsibility to the community, should make greater efforts to make their resources available to that community: 'We need to see the school as a resource centre which is open and available, where facilities are made available to those who have learning needs of any kind.'

The concept of public bodies giving and sharing as well as taking is also relevant for other organizations. Universities, industry training centres, churches and church halls, theatres and those offices in every organization with unused computers during the evening, for example. Resource-sharing is basic to the development of lifelong learning, as are the partnerships which may stimulate, or result from, it. Now recognizing lifelong learning as a holistic concept, we can combine its economic, political, cultural, social, environmental and educational wealth and needs to create a more open and contributory learning society.

Chapter 4

A fiefdom without failure

The third group of lifelong learning insights examines the issues around assessment, evaluation and accreditation. The premise is:

In a lifelong learning world, examination and assessment methods are used to confirm progress and encourage further learning for everyone rather than to highlight success/failure in the few. This means:

1. National and regional systems of target-based assessment structures

Assessment is a sensitive and delicate issue. Opinions range from the élite and laissez-faire 'cream rises to the top' argument, in which human beings are the subjects of a great IQ determination experiment in an infallible examination system, to the anarchic position that all examinations are divisive and should be abolished. In view of the overwhelming evidence that success in school-level written examinations does not guarantee similar success at university level, and the new research into such aspects as emotional intelligence (Goleman – see Chapter 2) and multiple intelligences (Gardner – see Chapter 2), there is little room for belief that the current system of SAT scores, Bacs, GCSEs, Abiturs, IBs etc does any more than test a good memory and the ability to use certain parts of the left hemisphere of the brain. Further, failure is writ large into the whole system, success for an increasing few being dependent on failure for a decreasing, but still, many.

Chapman and Aspin suggest that 'People's capacity to and willingness to learn throughout their lives depends to a considerable extent on whether they draw positive experiences from their period of initial education.' Self-evident perhaps, but many students might be forgiven for believing that the only purpose of initial education is to sort out successful sheep from unsuccessful goats so that organizations can reduce the interviewing lists for jobs. Often, no other message – the intrinsic value of learning, the fascination of knowledge, the acquisition of a valuable skill, the development of their mental potential – is given to them than the demands of the final examination, the skills of second-guessing the examiner and the requirement of a good memory. In many educational establishments, the threat of examination failure is used as a means of keeping discipline. When this reaches down to young children in the infant schools, the combined pressure of parents and teachers to succeed in a single subject at a single time in a single test, can not but have a deleterious effect on subsequent attitudes to learning.

This is no basis for a lifelong learning world, as the European Round Table of Industrialists confirms in its 3rd definition of a Learning Society. 'Examinations should confirm progress rather than brand failure,' they say, and coming from an organization which co-operated with the Council of European Rectors to produce this document, something must be stirring in the groves of academe too. Again Longworth, in the *Journal of Higher Education in Europe*, states 'Present assessment models are not based on concepts of lifelong learning – rather the opposite, they tend to be based on division and the celebration of success for the few at the expense of failure for the many.' Similarly, a UNEVOC study on Technical and Vocational Education acknowledges that 'the effects of bad practice (in assessment) are more potent than for any aspect of teaching.' The authors, McDonald *et al*, say 'Students can, with difficulty, escape from the effects of poor teaching; they cannot escape the effects of poor assessment. Assessment acts as a mechanism to control students that has more effect on students than most teachers or administrators are prepared to acknowledge.'

And yet the answer is not to abolish examinations, as happened for a short period in some Danish institutions. People have a need to understand and measure their own progress, to have a standards target, by which they can measure themselves against an independent norm. In most people it is a natural human requirement. But no-one is interested in being a failure. And so there is, perhaps, a need to devise a failure-free system in which each individual knows at what stage he/she is in a personal learning path, perhaps in several subjects and skills, and what is needed to reach the next stage of maturity or knowledge. Such a system was first mooted by Longworth and Davies in *Lifelong Learning* and is further discussed later in this chapter. A similar view is also supported by OECD. It advocates a system of value-added learning which 'presupposes individualised instruction and personal growth targets in learning achievement'. Smethurst's words in his 1995 RSA lecture, 'In order to succeed in life, you need not just academic skills but personality, independence of mind and autonomy of spirit', are universally true and self-evident, but, because such attributes are difficult to measure, they tend to remain the stuff of academic comment rather than assessment action.

As yet the assessment industry is not keeping up to date with new requirements. Universities in particular are often obsessed by a rigid maintenance of high measurable standards, believing that the status of the institution depends upon the preservation of high quality research and teaching. And so it does, but the (generally low) level of teaching and (usually higher) level of research in many universities is rarely related to the assessment issue for students, potential and real. Better to concentrate on those things which improve the performance of lecturers, students and researchers than the content and examination issues in which university committees spend so much time getting themselves bogged down.

A new assessment vision would predicate a national system of education which recognizes late development, interpersonal competencies and different approaches to learning, and which values equally practical/vocational and academic achievement. It would focus on the improvement of personal performance rather than efforts to prove it inadequate. It would use examinations as part of a continuous learning situation rather than a terminal point in a period of learning, and an opportunity for educators to say 'gotcha'.

2. Assessment of prior experience programmes giving credit for non-standard experiential learning

Assessment of Prior Experiential Learning might be simply described as giving credit for learning gained from work and life experiences. The average age of students wanting to take post-secondary courses in colleges and universities has been steadily increasing in all parts of the world. This is partly because adult learners are becoming more aware of the need to be competitive in the job market, particularly in cases where technological changes affect employability. For a variety of reasons, many of these students do not have the qualifications to enter the courses, but they have acquired knowledge and skills gained from years of working and living. A system such as APEL looks at ways of formally recognizing such learning. It takes away more than one of the barriers to learning frequently quoted in polls and surveys, by potentially making it less expensive, providing initial encouragement and self-worth and by ensuring a better use of public funds.

APEL is a topic of great interest in North America and Europe. The Finnish National Strategy states the following:

> There should be an extensive programme to develop the capacity of educational institutions to assess skills. Once sufficiently standardized and high-quality facilities have been put in place, a system should be developed from the network of educational institutions or parts of it to provide private citizens with generally acknowledged certificates or diplomas on their skills in relation to the certification system. It is a public recognition of previously acquired knowledge which forms a

necessary part of the programme for raising the knowledge and skills level of adults with the weakest educational background.

It goes on to describe the need for a skills passport, in which can be entered the skills individuals have demonstrated in the course of their working and non-working experience. It would include whole or part completion of certificates or diplomas and comprise a portfolio of personal skills developed at work, pursuits outside work and in studies not forming part of the examination system. It could be used as a basis for developing a personal learning plan (see Chapter 11).

Finland is not the only country examining prior experiential learning. Many government departments are looking at APEL as a means of encouraging people to become learners again. But in practice it is a much more complex activity than would initially seem to be the case. It strikes at the heart of education's current pre-occupation with assessment as a means of preventing people from taking education, and this is supported by some sections of the press as a process of 'dumbing down' educational achievement.

Much work has been done in this area in all Canadian provinces. And the following description of one college's processes to recognize APEL is typical. 'The assessment of an applicant's non-credit experience,' it says, 'generally involves a variety of evaluation tools, including written examinations, interviews, essays, performance evaluation, simulation, and mini portfolios. Documentation is an essential part of the assessment. For example, all conferences, workshops, seminars, and job experiences must be fully documented. Students are asked to give a written chronological record of any activities or experiences which they then "challenge for credit".'

This is hardly the stuff of lifelong learning, however good its intentions. Let us look at a hypothetical case. The applicant might be a 35 year-old mother of two with an outgoing personality who has minimal qualifications, since her school dissuaded her from taking them in case she brought down the percentage pass rate in the league tables (this system exists in the United Kingdom, though not everywhere). As a result she considered herself to be an academic failure and did not take any post-secondary training. She became a waitress in a restaurant for two years, followed by a spell as a children's nanny before becoming an unmarried mother and living off state benefits. However, she also got herself involved with community work and helped out in an old people's home, where she gained new self-esteem through helping people in a worse situation than herself. Now her children are relatively self-sufficient, and in order to make herself an earning useful member of society, she now wants to train as a community help worker, preferably in a hospital or a residential home. She hasn't really written much in the past 20 years, though she has maintained an intelligent interest in current affairs through television and the media.

She is now asked to run the gauntlet of written examinations, interviews, essays, performance evaluation, simulations, and mini portfolios. She is asked to provide documented evidence of attendance at conferences, workshops, seminars and her job experiences, and to provide a 'written chronological record of any activities or experiences so that she can "challenge for credit".' What are her chances of success? Indeed what are her chances of ever walking through the door of the college?

Such protectionist attitudes are so common in education that an educationist would possibly not recognise the irony or the problem. It is not surprising therefore that OECD states, in *Lifelong Learning for All*, 'Recognizing and certifying prerequisite and acquired knowledge and competencies is one of the major problems for tertiary education institutions confronting lifelong learning.' It is this mind-set which will be most 'challenged for credibility' in a poly-accessible lifelong learning world. Students do learn a great deal outside of the formal education system, but the thing 99 per cent of them don't do is attend conferences, workshops and seminars, some of them have not had a job for many years and nor have they kept a record of achievement. It is precisely to remedy that that many of them choose to return to education. But in the meantime they have picked up useful skills and knowledge which makes them more mature and more knowledgeable – and they hope that that can be used to a welcome mat at the door of the educational institutions. The initial response they receive is crucial to their educational self-esteem. The European Commission Socrates Programme has a large project investigating APEL and is due to report in 1999. Hopefully it will take the side of the learner rather than defend to the death the honour of the educational institutions.

3. Schemes and strategies to enhance the non-threatening nature of learning and bring educational dropouts back into the system

Those who fail to complete secondary education are at serious risk of economic and social exclusion, not just in their teenage years but throughout their adult lives. A scrutiny of OECD figures on the relationship between qualifications and unemployment rates confirms that those who dropped out of the system, or did not take full advantage of it, are less likely to be employed, more likely to turn to a life of crime and highly likely to be low in self-esteem. Alexander reports 'Opportunities for training later in life depend heavily on the qualifications with which one enters the labour force, and learning opportunities open to the unemployed, employees of small firms and the disadvantaged groups in our society are far fewer.'

Those countries where a secondary school certificate is considered a minimum requirement for entry into most jobs, seem to suffer most. The reverse is not always true. In France and Spain for example graduate unemployment is high in spite of a high educational level.

OECD figures show that more than 12 per cent of 16 to 19 year-olds in OECD countries are in neither work nor education/training. They also show that young women are more severely affected than young men. Two to three per cent of young Danish, Dutch and German men in neither education nor work contrasts with a figure of over 15 per cent for young women in Greece, Italy, Portugal and Spain.

The European Commission White Paper on Teaching and Learning expresses concern about exclusion of this kind. Indeed, the fight against exclusion is one of its five major action points, recognizing that, however many projects there are to skill, up-skill and provide new learning opportunities for those who are already in the workforce, the presence of a sizeable minority of non-learners excluded from the employment market will cause instability, social unrest and increased crime. 'Access to knowledge is crucial to fitting into society and finding employment,' says the European White Paper, while on the other hand it recognizes that family and social circumstances prevent many from gaining the self-confidence and sense of self-worth to know how to fit into society. Its solutions are two-fold.

They are providing youngsters with the best training and support arrangements in 'second chance schools'; and European voluntary service initiatives to give young people a chance to engage in an activity serving the common good in their own, or a developing, country.

For the former it recommends that the best teachers are employed and paid a higher salary. Learning would be customized, the pace of teaching and innovative methods would be tailored to each student. It should be a meeting place for the community, offering education outside of school hours as well as during the day-time. Reference is made to the success story of 'accelerated schools' in the USA, where under-achievers work at an accelerated pace by setting ambitious targets and taking away the possibility of failure. Pupils, parents and teachers are involved in order to present the school as a responsible community in which each member has a part to play. Their procedures echo the words of the Kent Region of Learning booklet: 'Existing systems and structures produce existing results – to achieve something different the system must change also.'

In Britain, several programmes under the heading of 'Welfare to Work' and 'New Deal' provide similar second-chance activities. The Welfare to Work Programme is based upon a similar programme operated in the United States for several years previously. In this, long-term unemployed people are offered train-ing opportunities with companies to make them employable for the future. In the new deal for over 25 year-olds who have been unemployed for two years or more, support services and training is provided to up-skill or to reskill with an employer. Costs are met principally by government and participating companies and between them they put together a personalized training programme for each learner. The new deal for 18–24 year-olds has five options. Youngsters who have been unem-ployed for six months can choose to study full-time, study part time and train with an employer, join an environmental task force or the voluntary sector, or train to become self-employed. They are subsidized by government grants during this period. The 'no skills, no job' message of lifelong learning is explicit in all of these programmes.

Britain is of course not alone in putting together creative schemes to keep people out of unemployment and into work through skills development. Many governments now recognize what was evident since the recessions of the early 1980s – that national prosperity depends on a high skills base, that the content of the national skillbase is changing rapidly and that the money spent on paying people to remain unemployed might as well be spent on giving them these new skills to create national prosperity. The argument is circular and self-generating. There is, and always has been, an alternative.

4. More partnership programmes between industry and education

Industry–Education links have existed for many years, more in the Anglo-Saxon part of the developed world than in other parts. As a result of the building of Europe, the urging of inter-governmental organizations such as World Bank and OECD, and the globalization of industry, such links have proliferated at all levels in many more countries. At higher education level, for example, the close collaboration between the Society of European Rectors (CRE) and the European Round Table of Industrialists (ERT) has resulted in an excellent series of European booklets on aspects of lifelong learning, the use of technology and industry–education links. At an entirely different level, there is hardly a secondary school in the United Kingdom or USA which has not established mutually beneficial links with one or more companies in their own localities.

The principle is now well-established. Such links break down stereotypes, provide work experience, share research, provide new resources and insights and can furnish good learning experiences. Only the more dogmatic of people on both sides find a reason to refuse to co-operate. Companies provide educational resources on the Internet, help with curriculum development, and make extra resources available to educational organizations.

Jim Botkin estimates from figures in a 1993 National Alliance of Business Study, that there are more than 200 000 Schools–Business alliances in the USA. These include University schools and 90 per cent of the money goes to research. Most of the schools-level projects involve such initiatives as loan-a-teacher, and adopt-a-school, which would be difficult to establish in some countries where business is kept away from the process of teaching. But there are some interesting initiatives aimed at ameliorating long-standing educational problems. For example the Walt Disney corporation operates a challenge programme in Florida, in which high school students at risk of drop-out are offered a way to stay at school, and merit awards are offered to innovative teachers. The Georgia Pacific lumber company funds teachers to teach computer modelling and simulation as a new way of thinking developed at MIT. Sara Lee supports arts programmes on the grounds that creativity in the arts can lead to creativity in the development of new products. Apple and IBM have donated thousands of computers to schools and paid for research into computer-based learning techniques.

Partnerships – Engines of Organizational Change
1. Partnerships should provide benefits for all partners. A one-way flow of information or service will lead to a loss of motivation
2. Partnerships should involve as many people as possible in the respective organizations in its activities
3. All people in the organizations should be informed about the partnership's objectives and progress
4. People in the organizations should be free to suggest improvements to the partnership and its activities
5. Each partnership should have clear objectives and goals, with time-scales and benchmarks for achieving them
6. At least one high-level person from each organization should be responsible for ensuring the success of the partnership
7. Regular meetings of the partnership should be held, at least once per term
8. The partnership should have a manager with secretarial support and ownership of making it happen
9. Partnership management should be pro-active, encouraging people to contribute and participate
10. The partnership should be celebrated as frequently as appropriate to maintain interest and commitment

Figure 4.1 Partnerships – engines of organizational change

Not all such alliances are based on philanthropy and altruism. In many cases, there is a large element of self-interest, but where the objectives of the company coincide with those of the school, and control of the project is properly established, it can become a win-win situation for both. But these alliances need to go further than mere public relations exercises. Many companies are now using the expertise of third, non-profit oriented parties such as the American Council on Education to evaluate and advise on useful projects and alliances. Business has much to teach the schools about teamwork, learning, management, evaluation, the use of equipment, motivation, the world of work and many other subjects. Properly organized and controlled, and given a genuine two-way interaction of real benefit for the students, there is a wealth of opportunity to make schools–industry relationships into dynamic and productive learning experiences. It is yet another resource management exercise for both.

Fruitful partnership examples occur in many places and many fields of interest. Others involving schools, universities, business and industry and the voluntary sector are described at other points of this book. But perhaps it would be useful to describe some key points for a successful partnership, taken from the European Lifelong Learning Initiative's 'Eurotoolls' development programme under the Socrates programme of the European Commission. Figure 4.1 describes ten essentials for successful partnerships.

5. A new look at the purpose of examinations and the development of credit-based, linked modular education systems into which everyone can be accommodated wherever, whenever and however they wish to study

The traditional learning paradigm at school, university and college level concerns itself with the content of individual courses and how to measure several levels of success or failure after its completion. Quantity is often more important than quality, memorization more rewarded than understanding and teacher contact hours more regarded than student working hours. Organizations are measured on their outputs and their facilities – the number of student hours taught, the faculty contact time, books in the library, classrooms with desks and pupil–teacher ratios. Learning activity is the percentage success rate as measured by the number of good passes in the final examination. The learning process is the teacher giving knowledge or information to the passive, receiving student. Learning is a competitive activity with built-in failure in order to satisfy the requirements of the statisticians. As for the students, their preoccupations are concerned with grades, hours spent in the classroom, second-guessing examination questions and how it helps them in their career.

This is not a paradigm for a learning century. Somehow real learning, the sort that sticks, is enjoyable and becomes a part of the student's behaviour, becomes lost in the morass of procedures, protocols and traditions. It is neither the product nor the process it should be. This is why OECD states in *Lifelong Learning for All* that ' there is a real economic and professional need for new types of certification that link them to work experience.' That need, together with the rise of education and training in the non-formal sectors, will create pressure for change.

Finland, in its national strategy, suggests that skills are the missing link. Following Longworth and Davies's ideas on the skills-based curriculum in *Lifelong Learning*, the strategy recommends a 'skills pass'. 'The manner of defining certificates and diplomas should be developed in such a way that certificate or diploma requirements describe the skills needed and thus support skills assessment,' it says, and proposes that individuals collect entries for their 'skills pass' from the skills they have demonstrated during their studies.

The future may be even more radical. In a learning century context, learning may be enabled by an institution, but it need not take place there. The curriculum is decided in a consultation between teacher and taught, and meets the needs of the student in terms of time spent, relevance of the subject, the method used and the level of the reward. Textbooks and lectures are not the only information sources, and personal deviation from the syllabus is equally important, since it reflects the student's desire to learn more than the minimum requirement. Students learn from and with teachers, from and with each other, and from and with the community. Learning is a contribution to everyone involved in the process. The staff themselves are continuous learners, updating themselves on new materials and methodologies and learning how others learn. While the results of learning are measurable and achievement-focused, failure is taken out of the system. Student performance is outcome-based. The purpose of measurement is to encourage continuous improvement rather than to find defects.

Chapter 2 suggested renaming schools, universities and industries as respectively 'organizations for the development of human potential, organizations for the further development of human potential and organizations for the development and application of human potential'. This, they thought, might change the perception of educators from a subject-centred, pour-it-in-and-hope-some-of-it-sticks model, to a student centred, co-operative, how can I give this student the learning tools? approach. This tongue-in-cheek proposition serves to make a lifelong learning point that the focus of operations has shifted from teaching to learning and the focus of all systems, including examinations, is to assist in the development of human potential.

While the need is for a much more flexible system of personal target-based assessment, as described in the first section to this chapter, such a system has its drawbacks, particularly where national and international comparisons and equivalences need to be made. As many more people are travelling to other countries to work, and, until the learning society is a global condition, there is a need to demonstrate an achieved standard. OECD again in *Lifelong Learning for All* recommends 'Certificates ought to become transferable or portable from one work situation to another, from an academic to a professional position, and vice versa, and new elements can be added to existing evaluation schemes to reflect advancement over time, learning performed in different places and the individualisation of learning geared to employment and a career development.'

The simplest adaptation to the present system at university level would be a credit accumulation system which clearly defines the content of each module, the skills it has intended to develop and the level of knowledge achieved by the learner. The basis of such systems has been in operation in the United States for many years and many European universities are adopting the principle, if not always the spirit, of co-operation in this. Competition and mistrust still misrule.

But greater flexibility still can be found. New delivery technologies, smart-cards and learning passports take away the time and space constraints in present systems. In this new flexi-world, no-one should be excluded from demonstrating that he or she can achieve a credit standard, no specific time of the year, like 'we take our examinations in the summer' should be set aside for that demonstration, and the organization where the accreditation takes place can be any of several around the world to take into account the mobility of people. A potential student should be able to define the content and methodology of a course of study with a personal tutor and agree the credit rating for it. This is then posted into a database such that a variety of tutors can advise, teach and accredit. In practice most students will stay with the same tutor, but there should be the option to change on grounds of mobility or incompatibility. The student who believes that he or she has studied enough to achieve the standard and wishes to prove it should then be allowed to do so within a period of time – one week being normal – at any of the organizations accrediting him/her. Obviously some rules will have to be put in place to avoid abuse, but these should be as few as necessary to avoid abuse and to support learning.

This is a foretaste of the flexible learning world of the 21st century, where students will vote with their feet. Certainly, if traditional universities are not able to satisfy this new requirement, many others will. The likely proliferation of universities making courses available on the Internet will force others to take into account flexibility of assessment methods, as they are doing themselves. The University of Phoenix for example, has grown in the last few years to more than 48 000 students undertaking vocational degrees in areas such as business, IT and teacher training, mostly via distance learning. It gives working adults access to learning wherever they happen to be. Another example is the California Virtual University, offering 700 courses from 81 public and private institutions throughout the United States. This is a real learning revolution and a threat, or an opportunity, depending upon the point of view, to traditional universities.

More than that, the vast increase in Corporate Universities based on multinational companies – British Aerospace, Motorola and the Disney Corporation to mention just a few – offers the prospect of much greater competition in the years ahead, to which the universities will need to respond. The jokes about Mickey Mouse degrees and so on will certainly engage some of the smaller academic minds, but the joke could equally be on them. Standards at many of these are high, and degree courses are normally taught jointly by university and company lecturers, and accredited accordingly. Disney managers for example receive courses via satellite from places like Carnegie Mellon University, Babson and the highly regarded Wharton School of Business.

In the United Kingdom too, similar things are beginning to happen. British Aerospace now offers four Masters degrees in subjects within its own sphere of activity. The Body Shop has devised two Masters degrees with the Universities of Bath and Lancaster as a part of its 'Academy of Business' and, because of the language similarities, most universities are anticipating, with fear and dread, the invasion from across the Atlantic. While some universities are responding early through industry–education course development pacts, it requires a sage of Nostradamian proportions to predict the world of higher education in the year 2010.

Chapter 5

The territory of eternal learning

The fourth category of lifelong learning characteristics examines positive actions to be taken by nations and communities in order to develop learning cultures. The premise is:

Lifelong learning proactively encourages the development of the habit of learning in everyone in the community rather than re-actively responds to specific needs at specific times. This means:

1. Investigating how national and local education systems can improve positive encouragement and feedback to all learners

Past sections have emphasized the virtues of active learning based on the needs of individuals as a means of motivating students to learn. This is of course more relevant where the motivation does not exist in the first place. Some students in schools were an example in mind. But not all students are unmotivated and not all learning is by doing. A more sophisticated approach would combine a wide variety of learning tools and techniques. It would recognize that much of learning can indeed be hard (though rewarding) work, and that there is subject matter to be retained as well as skills to be acquired. Memorization is a valuable human skill and should not be discounted simply because it is taken to excess in the traditional examination systems. But before we can tell learners that they have achieved the competency of learning, we need to know something about learning itself. How do we recognize the competency of learning?

Early research into learning competencies was carried out by Sylvia Downs and her colleagues for the British Department of Education. She discovered that there are a large number of ways to learn and that most people use very few of them. The DSL (Developing Skilled Learners) approach derived from that research.

How will we know when we have reached the point where learners are regarded as skilled? Barry Nyhan has developed the following to help with this:

- Skilled learners take responsibility for their learning and generally adopt an active role.
- Skilled learners can distinguish between things they have to memorize and things they need to understand, and things that are best learned by doing.
- Skilled learners use more ways of learning and choose between them according to the material to be learnt.
- Skilled learners do not fall back on trying to memorize things they should be trying to understand.
- Skilled learners make conscious decisions on how they will learn something.
- Skilled learners make sure they learn despite poor teaching.
- Skilled learners ask more questions and ask particular kinds of questions to ensure that they learn properly.
- Skilled learners seek feedback on their own performance.
- Skilled learners realize that difficulties in learning are not always a lack in their own capacity to learn but frequently lie in inadequacies in the delivery of learning/training.
- Finally, skilled learners are confident to take on new learning opportunities.

But having now defined some of what we are looking for, how can it be made to happen in the majority of learners? As has been emphasized several times, the initial training of teachers and their continuous professional development is one answer. The Finnish National Strategy recognizes this in its national strategy. 'The in-service training of teachers and other instructors required for the realization of lifelong learning should be taken up as one of the focal points of the policies to promote learning over the next few years,' it says, with impeccable logic. There can be little doubt that a teacher who encourages, persuades and gives positive feedback has a more cathartic effect on learning than one who criticizes and carps, or gives no feedback at all. In my teaching days some colleagues and I used to take some of the most difficult children in the school camping and hill-walking during the school holidays. Those were the children with whom other teachers had endless battles to persuade them to work, but we had very few of those problems back in the classroom because of the positive personal relationship we had built up with them. Indeed, many of them progressed in leaps and bounds after such trips.

Another stratagem, though, lies in the reward systems put into place to recognize that learning has taken place and that it is appreciated. Multinational industries have long recognized the value of rewards. Appreciative gestures for employees include restaurant tickets for the family (to recognize that they too have played a part, and presumably to persuade them that there is more to come), seminars and workshops in exotic places to combine work and pleasure, straight monetary gifts (which sometimes fall foul of income tax officers), theatre tickets and other creative prizes. Most of them pay a high proportion, if not all, of the fees on successful completion, while others, such as Ford, Rover and most of the major motor manufacturers make available sums of money to all employees to take courses of any kind in order to get them into the habit of learning. Some companies organize a celebration event similar to a graduation ceremony for all employees who have successfully completed an external course during the year.

What is done in industry might be difficult in the world of the community. It takes some imagination to guess the reaction of members of the local community to the prospect of free family dinners in a good restaurant for graduates on the local taxes. This might be a matter of culture. In Japan it would be acceptable since the bestowing of honours for learning achievement is a part of the culture. In many Japanese families, for example, every member who has a birthday at 20, 30, 40 etc is expected to recount what he/she has learned in the past ten years to make him/her a more knowledgeable and skilful person. In some families it is done every year. Learning is taken seriously there, and highly valued, as it is in Korea, Malaysia, Singapore, Taiwan and many countries on the Pacific Rim. But there is also an economic return to both the family and the community from learning, though it is not always one which can easily be given a monetary value. In that sense, reward schemes on the rates are perhaps not such a bad idea. They help the community to increase its wealth.

Nor do rewards necessarily come from the community purse. In some USA adopt-a-school programmes for example, industry itself provides the learning rewards in the schools, and there are perhaps many other types of non-monetary gift to be uncovered by creative application of the human mind. But the source of the reward is not as important as the fact that there is a gesture of appreciation. It is this that will help to create the new culture of lifelong learning.

2. Promoting and advertising the value and attractiveness of learning nationally and locally

Modern marketing techniques are sophisticated and well-researched to aim at persuading people to desire a product or a service in order to sell it to them. This happens whether or not there is an intrinsic need or reason. If this can be done to generate profit for companies, then similar techniques can be used to generate long-term profit for a nation through the marketing of learning. Educational purists may shudder, but this is the way the real world works. People will buy into education only of they are convinced of its benefit or if they can be convinced that it is a worthwhile use of their time. A continuous information and promotion campaign presenting the benefits of learning to the nation, to organizations and to individuals is the responsibility of both national and local governments, which they may choose to pass on to other organizations.

The UK Campaign for Learning exists to promote learning through a series of workshops and seminars designed to sensitize people to the value of learning. Supported financially by several of the country's major companies, it seeks innovative ways of passing the message on to the places where it will be of use. It organizes three 'Learning Days' per year – a 'Family Learning Day' (see Chapter 22), a 'Learning at Work Day', and a 'New Year Resolution Learning Day'. It has helped to place an 8-page insert on lifelong learning into a mass-circulation tabloid newspaper. It works in partnership with its sponsors and with other organizations in the field of learning, and produces quarterly a visually attractive newsletter on good practice in lifelong learning. It is an interesting example of an organization with a learning mission and none of the self-interested academic baggage which might affect an educational organization trying to do the same thing, nor the accusations of political pressurizing which might affect government's ability to deliver the message.

At the European Level, the European Lifelong Learning Initiative performs the dual role of publicizing lifelong learning where it can and providing a professional organization for lifelong learning organizations across the board in Europe. To the former end it has developed a series of information leaflets and briefings for organizations in different sectors and is building up strong European Lifelong Learning action networks which it calls ELLIversities, ELLIndustry, ELLIschools, ELLIteachers and ELLIvoc, etc between cities and regions. The ELLIcities initiative cuts across these, providing links and partnerships. The ELLInets are the national arms of the organization, providing governments with a pool of qualified and knowledgeable people to help develop lifelong learning strategies and activities. This is again another interesting example of an ideas-and action-generating membership organization with national, international, sectoral and cross-sectoral projects, events and activities. Appendix 3 gives more background.

Media campaigns are expensive but they are effective. Government and local government both have the responsibility to promote the value of lifelong learning by whatever means will be most effective. They need to be supported by the learning providers who could do so much more to make the product attractive and seductive to the doubtful candidate. Again industry has provided a lead in its poster campaign to switch employees on to learning as described earlier in Part 1. If we want people to believe that learning can be fun, perhaps we should say so out loud. Figure 5.1 suggests a simple slogan, and no doubt more capable spin-doctors could improve on this. It is hardly an academic message, but then the majority of learners are not academic. Again the idea of loyalty cards so much used by supermarkets today could be useful in passing the message of learning to customers. An advertising campaign to emphasize how much the supermarket is a learning organization and how its staff will learn from its customers, could do much to fix both the image of the company and the value of learning in the customer's mind. Equally one of the rewards for shopping could, by arrangement with a local education provider, be a learning voucher to be cashed as a course at the local college.

Lastly, we can learn much from the techniques of the Internet. Most educational organizations now have a home page, and many are highly creative in their presentation. New techniques using sound, animation, text and graphics allow great sophistication in the delivery of a message. Most have the facility to be interactive, if not immediately then with e-mail facilities so that questions can be asked and answered, either by e-mail or through the post. While most of the target audience is not in touch with the Internet, the techniques of simple message delivery there can be replicated in other ways.

LEARNING CAN BE FUN

BUT ONLY YOU CAN MAKE IT SO!

Figure 5.1 Another slogan

3. Political recognition that learning is important to national and local prosperity in a globalized world

Countless reports, and not just those by educationists, have made the link between learning and national prosperity. It is an argument already won. In the past twenty years, industries have expanded rapidly into new areas of the world. The combination of political change caused by the fall of communism, and technological capability, exemplified by the rise of education technology, has accelerated this process during this decade. Greater accessibility to consumers, the need to develop new marketplaces, the availability of cheaper labour, high wage costs in the developing countries, proximity to raw materials and higher growth are attractive to companies building new factories and facilities in countries they would have left severely alone in the earlier part of the century. In 1984 the massive UK chemicals conglomerate ICI, Imperial Chemical Industries, did 80 per cent of its business and employed 90 per cent of its workers in the United Kingdom. Now, in the short space of 15 years, it does less than 10 per cent of its business there and employs workers in 84 countries of the world.

Finland, recognizing the international nature of the marketplace, is setting itself up as a European laboratory for the information society. 'Globalization and internationalization are pre-requisites for the success of the knowledge society,' say Markkula and Suurla. 'Companies, institutions of learning, political parties, civic organizations, labour-market organizations and other interest groups must all contribute to the development of their international aspects.' Already more than 80 per cent of Finns are equipped with mobile telephones, many of them also have sophisticated portable offices, while the ownership of computers per capita is one of the highest in the world. This is what underpins its new lifelong learning strategy since it realizes, with ERT, that an information society can only happen with an accompanying learning society. Accordingly, great changes are being made to curricula and methods in Finnish schools, adult education colleges and universities to sensitize the Finnish people to the ramifications of this and its effect on their own future prosperity.

Countries in the former developing world, particularly those on the Pacific Rim, recognized the power of learning some twenty years ago. They invested heavily in an education-led dash for growth, with those in Latin America following close behind. Although more recent events have pricked the bubble of perpetual rapid growth, it is highly unlikely that any of these countries will ever revert to their former developing nation status. They have tasted the fruit of prosperity and, for them, it is good. This puts great pressure on the countries of the developed world to improve their own educational performance in order to remain competitive. Labour-intensive manufacturing industry which provided the bulk of employment for workers in these regions is fast migrating abroad to lower-cost suppliers and new, knowledge-based professions, requiring a much higher level of understanding and competency, are replacing them. The new knowledge worker is international, polyglot, mobile, highly-educated and infinitely adaptable. Education and Training models based on the limited mass schooling needs of an industrial society are in no sense able to cope with the new demands.

An excellent example of this was given in the film 'Primary Colours'. A scandal-rocked President seeking re-election is speaking to an angry assembly of dock workers who have recently lost their jobs. He knows that he is behind in the opinion polls and decides to take a chance. In a percipient speech about the realities of the modern world he takes on his audience by delivering a few home truths about what politicians can and cannot do. In essence he gives seven reasons why things can never be the same again.

1. A globalized world has no borders – millions of dollars can be transferred easily from one country to another. The secret of operating in such a world is to understand it and work with it.

2. Manufacturing jobs will go where labour is cheap. Countries in an advanced technical world have to find alternative jobs – those which use brains and knowledge rather than hands and muscle.
3. People who want to work will have to go back to school and learn and relearn new trades, techniques and skills, throughout life.
4. That makes education the number one important industry in any advanced country.
5. Coming to terms with this is not easy. But no-one can do it for anyone else – the motivation has to come from the individual.

The film uses more colourful and accessible language, but the message is plain and incontrovertible. What is true for America, as in this film, is true for every nation which aspires to maintain high employment, ensure economic survival and avoid social instability.

In this is encapsulated the dilemma of the developed nation. Toffler's 'third wave' is becoming a tsunami, a tidal wave, and engulfing the more vulnerable members of developed world societies. The more perceptive countries are developing lifelong learning strategies to take their citizens 'back to school', to raise performance levels in education. They are aiming to develop a 'Learning Society' in which learning is the central tenet of the culture and internationalism is the vision which enables citizens to take their place in a global community. Not all politicians, or even educationists, understand the vast implications of this, or are prepared to risk losing the sympathy of the clients who give them power, but there can be little doubt that the voyage to lifelong learning is now underway in many countries, and is necessary.

Further afield, the background paper of the 1998 Arab Regional Conference leading up to the UNESCO Higher Education Symposium, states: 'It is now globally recognized that a country's workforce, with higher education providing its core leadership, is the most effective resource for determining its economic future, and its ability to deliver competitive goods and services to world markets.' The Arab Universities have learned a great deal about the new role of the university from western experience in the past two years, and indeed appear to have given it a position of leadership in the community.

There are now signs that governments are taking lifelong learning seriously. As was seen in Chapter 1, 1996 was a key year. The European Year of Lifelong Learning did much to educate politicians and civil servants, while OECD devoted its major inter-governmental conference to educating Ministers on the subject. UNESCO pledged its medium-term strategy to peace and lifelong learning. Since that time both the content and tone of educational policy documents have changed dramatically. Britain, USA, Finland and the Netherlands have all produced Green Papers on lifelong learning in 1998 and others are following suit rapidly. Each of these demonstrates a willingness to embrace change as a preparation for a very different 21st century. In many ways change itself is setting the agenda and the papers are an acknowledgement that this is so.

But slogans and protestations of support for learning are one thing. It is the political willingness to provide the leadership for making the necessary extensive policy changes which counts. Democracy may be, as Churchill said, the best we have, but it is an imperfect instrument for transforming society quickly. Good politicians have an eye for understanding how far they can oppose popular culture and embedded traditions. And herein lies a dilemma. The argument for change is comprehensively described in these pages and in innumerable research and conference reports, but these reach only a few academics, administrators and politicians. It has neither the understanding nor the consent of the people who, in a democracy, make the ultimate decision. Making lifelong learning work is a long process of persuasion, marketing, information and cascade-model projects carried out where people are – in cities, towns and regions around the planet. It is a partnership process encouraging contribution and joint action between electors and elected. Without a massive effort to change cultures, allied to a real understanding of what Lifelong Learning is and a willingness to come to terms with it, few of the words will ever come to fruition.

4. An emphasis, in schools particularly, on teaching methods which can compete with the sophistication of the media, which do not turn children off learning and which give them the habit and skills to learn for life

The arguments for active learning have been well rehearsed in this book as well as in many others. This requires investment in materials and equipment, which should be up to date and professionally prepared and presented. The same is true of the new approaches to learning. They too are competing with the sophisticated, people-manipulating and interestingly-presented programmes normally seen on television, in computer games and virtual reality experiences to which people, including children, have regular access. Given a choice of learning method between computer graphics and a blackboard, the former is likely to win hands down. It is a difficult dilemma. While some very rich schools may have access to multimedia equipment and the staff to make the most of them, the majority are as far from sophisticated studio equipment with the resources to handle them as they are from the moon.

And so the trick might be to enlist the support of the sophisticated people. 'Edutainment' games can be developed which powerfully present educational concepts in a way which entails real intellectual effort on the part of learners, without the pain and boredom of rote. The copyright laws for television materials such as documentaries and educational programmes need to be amended so that they can be used in educational environments. The English and Scottish National Grids for Learning are setting an example by developing a database of films, videos, graphics material etc suitable for use by schools and other educational organizations. These too can collaborate with the media in the making of programmes, the putting together of the newspaper, as in the excellent 'Making the News' competition between children which used to be run by News International in the early 1990s. Students themselves can work in creating their own video presentation of a topic to be learned at school or university.

In addition, there are many possibilities of the Internet to enhance learning and the acquisition of knowledge and understanding. A vast library of downloadable materials highly relevant to many curricula, including video clips, graphics, text, sound, motion picture, is now available there, much of it free of charge. Want to know about Kangaroos? Look up the Kanga company's Web site for educational materials suitable for geography, history, natural history and home economics. Want information and materials on oil and petroleum? Look at any of the oil companies' Web sites for graphics, learning materials, clips and sample lessons for teachers. This new richness of resource, while industry-based, is not always an advertising gimmick and much of it is professionally prepared by active educators.

The European theme conference on lifelong learning recognized the need and the opportunities for increasing the excitement in learning. In its booklet, the *Joy of Learning*, published by IACEE, it commented, 'The comprehensive schools and secondary-level educational institutions should encourage their students to acquire a wide range of learning experiences and also organize such opportunities themselves. The experiences and the lessons they provide should then be discussed in class. Educational Institutions should approve the knowledge and skills acquired by their students in other learning environments as part of the study package.'

The drive for more open and transparent learning methods has also reached the universities. The Council of European Rectors reports in its submission to the UNESCO Higher Education conference:

> Universities no longer have a monopoly on knowledge. Companies are also realizing the potential of information technologies and the education market. Universities will find themselves either collaborating with public and private educational corporations, enterprises designing educational delivery systems, computer firms, and telecommunications companies, or they will find these groups becoming competitors. HE institutions need to create real strategic alliance outside the university. However not all universities have clearly identified either their competitors in the field, or the best partners for co-operation. Nevertheless, the pressure for change cannot be ignored. Universities should seize the opportunity to influence the production of educational multimedia, as an aid to better teaching.

Children particularly are influenced by the media. The opinions of their role-model heroes and heroines and the exploits of cartoon characters are as important in their minds as the opinions of teachers and the subject matter of lessons. Schools are in many senses in competition with the outside world, the real world of peer groups, crime, divorce, and media exploitation. The more the school is divorced from this world, the more it becomes an ivory tower, the more children will switch off from it as an irrelevance. It is not, as some say, a haven of reason in a mad world. Children do not compartmentalize their lives in this way. So the more the teacher can enlist the support of the media and sporting personalities, the more their presentation methods can compete with the sophistication children see when they get home, the more the children themselves are engaged actively in their own learning, and the better the chances of building the foundations of a lifetime of learning.

The newspapers too are an aspect of the media deserving closer scrutiny. A UK Schools Council project describes how one school in particular learned to understand the media a little better. The students from years 4, 5 and 6 developed a special supplement to a local weekly paper, the objectives of the project being to research and write the articles, supply photographs, find people to advertise, and design the advertisements. The focal point of the supplement was the study of the local river. This built upon work already being undertaken in the school by the three year groups. The project gave a focus and a real audience for their work. It covered planning, drafting, revising, proof-reading and presenting their own work. They met with the sub-editor who explained guidelines and analysed newspapers for examples of layout, content style and the use of pictures. Local companies linked to the river were contacted and interviewed. A reporter visited the school to explain the job and how to interview. As an example of active cross-disciplinary teaching methods involving geography, biology, English and ecology linked to an awareness of the world of work and the development of skills of written and oral communication, teamwork, design and technology and interviewing, this was invaluable – and learning was fun again.

It also encouraged children to look outside of themselves, which leads to:

5. More outward-looking educational techniques which encourage learners to look outside of themselves and to understand the way they can fit into a democratic society

Many governments and communities are seriously worried about the level of ignorance of basic democratic structures among young people. Direct teaching of 'citizenship' has again become yet another requirement for an already over-crowded curriculum. The European Parliament, for example, believes the purpose of education to be, 'To develop each individual's personality, to teach values of private, social and public life as solidarity, tolerance and understanding of cultural diversity, to promote the ability of various cultural groups to communicate and to promote the involvement of all the citizens of Europe in democratic decision making.'

The *Mumbai Statement* expresses similar views: 'The notion of citizenship is important in terms of connecting individuals and groups to the structures of social, political and economic activity in local and global contexts. Democratic citizenship highlights the importance of women and men as agents of history in all aspects of their lives. The act of learning, lying as it does at the heart of all educational activity, changes human beings from objects at the mercy of events to subjects who create their own history.' This idea of people creating their own history is also connected with the development of self-esteem and self-worth, topics which have been discussed in Chapter 4. People confident in their own ability to contribute will participate more willingly and less fearfully in democratic decision-making. In so doing they can reach outside of themselves to see the world as others see it. This is a process which can start in the schools, and which the CL4K project, described in Chapter 14, addresses.

But the answer is not to endlessly develop and deliver classroom materials on 'civics' or 'citizenship', as many local communities and European projects are doing. These have their place in the scheme of things, but it would be far better to teach citizenship in practice by sending children in schools to old people's homes; or inviting adults to participate in a neighbourhood or environmental 'watch' scheme; or building bridges between university and community; or visits to the council debating chamber in session; or any one of the hundreds of projects already taking place in hundreds of communities around the world. This is civics in practice, learning by observation and action. The classroom is then the place to discuss what happened, why it happened and how it could be improved.

The Japanese National Institute for Education Research reports that among the curriculum guidelines for teaching young children issued by the Japanese Ministry of Education (Monbusho) to schools are the following:

- encourage good manners, self-control and attitudes to observe social rules;
- help find out about oneself and seek one's 'way of living';
- encourage participation in the learning experience;
- increase comprehension of subjects and why they are learnt;
- clarify subject matter through innovative teaching;
- develop well-rounded personalities;
- encourage broad and strong-minded young people in every facet of educational activity including subject teaching;
- nurture children's capabilities to cope positively with social change;
- foster children's creativity;
- stimulate children's spontaneity to learn.

It finishes by extolling 'the significance of helping children to find solutions to problems on their own through analysing the situation, thinking independently, making positive decisions and fully expressing themselves rather than providing them with only conventional knowledge and skills'. Notwithstanding that it is also reported that many older Japanese teachers have difficulty in following such visionary guidelines, the incorporation of personal development, community involvement and creative learning into the modern curriculum in Japan provides something of a contrast to those distributed by other countries supposedly with a longer record of innovative teaching.

Today's learners need to be able to process complex information, solve problems, make decisions against the background of uncertainty and relate their knowledge and skills to novel and ever changing situations. Learning therefore should be active, constructive, goal-oriented and systematic. The use of the information and communication technologies is one tool which will offer everybody the opportunity to become a constructive and creative learner. Other, more sophisticated techniques such as simulations and community contribution take learners outside of the self and prepare them for life in the community.

6. A greater use of partnerships and work experience programmes to improve collaboration and understanding outside of the classroom

At one level there are national and international measures to deal with national educational and social problems and to improve standards within the compelling concept of learning as a lifetime activity. Down at the grass roots things are rather different. Grand ideas of an educational renaissance tend to be met at the chalk-face rather more suspiciously, and exhortations to change are treated with much greater resistance and scepticism. Here, after all, is where the resources shortfall is most keenly felt and where the magnitude of the professional updating task is most acutely perceived – that is, where it is acknowledged that there is a need to update in the first place. The concept of continuing professional development for teachers is sometimes lost in the continuous pressure on budgets.

As any manufacturing company will testify, installing a new system requires not only a change in skills but a widening of perceptions and a new mind set. How to persuade the 140 or so teachers and administrators of a 1000 pupil school to embrace concepts of lifelong learning, often in the face of parental and community hostility, is a task of the first magnitude. Indeed, at these levels, the pressure on Education and Training *not* to change is strong. It is often seen as the one immutable, invariable rock in the sea of uninvited turmoil which is the changing world. Parents, whose attitudes to school are often rooted in the values of their own parents, do not like to think of their own children as the subjects of a great educational experiment. They themselves, though not their children, are sometimes uncomfortable with technology, not having had the benefit of computers during their own schooldays. The modern trend to impose targets, testing and core curricula can be at odds with the life skills of flexibility, adaptability, versatility and personal decision-making needed by children to cope with the world they will inherit. Journalists, even those in the more liberal papers, and administrators right from the top, delight in dismissing those teachers who are prepared to inspire their pupils and prepare them for life as 'progressive', and therefore beyond the pale.

Thus the portents are not propitious for a rapid leap into a future in which people become learners for life in a caring and contributing Learning Society. And yet, even within the schools, there are some islands of good practice and a willingness to take on board new, personally fulfilling, ideas. Outside the educational walls, there are even more. Business and industry, perceiving the constant need to train, retrain and empower workers with the skills which enable them to operate independently and in teams, and yet keep a permanent eye on costs, have made great strides in learner-focused education. The field of Adult Education has spawned many projects at both national and international level. Some universities, like the University of Sunderland, described in Chapter 14, are going out into the field, initiating innovative programmes to meet learners wherever they may be found, in shopping centres, in the street. In the fullness of time these will percolate down into the schools and teacher-training establishments. But this will be a process taking many years, perhaps two generations, and provoking much reaction from the more conservative elements of the profession.

A much more effective and more interesting way is to combine the best educational activities of the private and public sectors into a common pool of skill, knowledge and talent, creating partnerships in which good practice and new vision is shared between them. At the same time this will give ownership of the need to change to those who have to make the changes.

It is at the community level that this will be enabled, and already many cities and towns encourage at least one week's work experience, and preferably more, for students in the last year at school. The pressure is on local industries to provide meaningful work placements for such short periods of time. In the United Kingdom, it is now commonplace to see students in industry, in shops, in hairdressing salons to fulfil their obligation to a week in the world of work. Not all of it is effective or useful. After all, in a hairdressing salon (where I met a student last week), it is not wise to let a work experience trainee loose on the customer's coiffure, and the alternative is a lot of waiting around and chatting.

This is why the Schools Council Industry Project issued guidelines to the organizers of work experience placements. 'Ideally,' it says, 'preparation should have started at primary school with their first introduction to the world of work.' Experience can be further developed through workplace visits and meeting experts invited into the classroom to help in particular projects. In the preparation phase for the work experience placement, individual pupil needs should be identified at the outset through discussion with a tutor or a work-experience co-ordinator. The employer hosting the placement should be informed of pupil targets. Ideally, the company should also be involved in their setting, but time constraints often make this very difficult. Some large companies have their own work-experience diaries providing an opportunity for students to show their aims and objectives to staff in their chosen departments. During the placement every student should be visited at least once and have a named adult accessible as a contact in case of difficulty. Finally work-experience programmes should include a planned debriefing to provide students with an opportunity to reflect on their experiences and identify the learning outcomes. The experience should be accredited in some way.

Such guidelines are often difficult to follow, but they would ensure a personally profitable period in the world of work for pupils in their last year of school where the alternative dual-system approach, as employed in Germany, is not available. It would also provide:

7. A more acute awareness that the workplace demands new skills and new attitudes and a responsiveness to its needs

The nature of the globalized market-place for goods and services has imposed new demands and practices on companies in the industrialized world. In *Lifelong Learning*, Longworth and Davies made reference to Charles Handy's equation $\frac{1}{2} \times 2 \times 3$. Its significance is that our large companies are aiming to downsize their workforces to half the present number, pay these twice as much and obtain three times the productivity from them. Work becomes 'outsourced' to small specialized companies, many of them employing the newly displaced workers, and providing similar services to several companies. Down-sizing, or 'right-sizing', as Lou Gerstner, CEO of IBM, more provocatively expressed it, is now continuing but not at the same level as it did in the early 1990s. It has had a devastating effect upon patterns of employment from which industrialized countries are still recovering.

Equally, the migration of work in the advanced nations towards high added-value service industries, high-skill occupations within the tertiary sector and high technology support systems is replacing traditional notions of work content. It is an extension of the movement from the industrial society, predominantly concentrating on the manufacture of goods and products and using machines as an extension of the hands, to the knowledge society, adding value by turning information into knowledge and services and using computers as an extension of the brain. As Figure 5.3 shows, most forecasts for skills needs show a massive reduction in the need for semi- and unskilled work and a consequent increase in the future demand for 'knowledge workers', management, professional and administrative staff. New skills are shown in Figure 5.2. They are much more comprehensive, demanding a level of understanding and knowledge much in excess of that traditionally taught in today's curricula, and an application of personal skills developed and updated continuously in all age groups.

Learning to learn	➤ Knowing one's learning style ➤ Being open to new learning techniques and new knowledge ➤ Wanting to learn with self-confidence
Applying new knowledge into practice	• Seeing the connection between theory and practice • Transferring knowledge into action
Questioning and reasoning	✓ Being continuously aware of changes ✓ Continually wanting to improve procedures and processes ✓ Never being satisfied with the status quo
Managing oneself and others	❖ Setting realistic personal targets ❖ Recognizing the gap between the current and the target and understanding how to fill it ❖ Continuously developing personal skills
Managing information	❑ Collecting, storing, analysing and combining information ❑ Using information technology
Communication skills	▪ Expressing oneself clearly orally and verbally in formal and informal situations ▪ Persuading others ▪ Listening to others
Team work	➤ Sharing information and knowledge ➤ Receiving information and knowledge ➤ Participating in goal-setting ➤ Achieving common goals
Problem-solving skills	• Creativity and innovation
Adaptability and flexibility	✓ Facing change with confidence ✓ Adapting to the new situations and tasks ✓ Being ready to change personal direction
Lifelong Learning	▪ Continuously upgrading personal skills and competence ▪ Cherishing the habit of learning

Figure 5.2 Core skills for the lifelong learning age

If, as the OECD jobs study says, the new generation now entering work can expect six or more job changes in a working life, the implications for educational organizations are serious. Greater flexibility, adaptability and versatility are demanded both of the people entering the workforce and of those already in it. Careers advisors have a difficult enough job in the present climate. In an environment where 40 per cent or more of year 2010 jobs have not yet been invented it will be impossible to carry on in the same way. Like teachers and lecturers, business-men and community leaders will have to change the content, method and purpose of what they do. The *Kent, Region of Learning*, book states 'the only thing we in this generation know for certain is that we don't know anything for certain,' and this is now becoming a truism.

Preparing people for a life of uncertainty and constant career change cannot be done without wholesale changes in curricula and approach which prepare people to be unleashed on a world of uncertainty and constant career change. This is the dilemma of education. It affects schools, universities, adult education colleges and the education departments of companies, which will have to pick up the pieces if the first three fail. As we have seen in other chapters, and will see in future ones, there are signs that some universities are beginning to appreciate that evolutionary measures are not enough. Some adult education colleges have recognized this for many years. But educational lead times are incompatible with the sort of industrial and societal changes required to keep a country competitive in today's world. Only a rapid and unequivocal commitment to lifelong learning for all can deliver the nirvana of the three great bases of modern society – education, industry, community – working together for the greater good of all.

DENMARK:	– UNSKILLED WORKERS FROM 35%-10%
	– MANAGEMENT AND PROFESSIONAL
	  STAFF (GRADUATES) DOUBLES FROM 15-
	  30% BY 2000

GERMANY:	– 3 MILLION FEWER UNSKILLED WORKERS – 1.5 MILLION MORE H.E. GRADUATES – PLUS 1.3 MILLION MORE SKILLED WORKERS
UK:	– 30% INCREASE FOR MANAGERS AND ADMINISTRATORS – 20% INCREASE FOR SKILLED WORKERS
NL:	– SECONDARY EDUCATION RISES 58-69%
FRANCE:	– BAC+2 or HIGHER - 11-21% INCREASE
PORTUGAL:	– DECREASE 15 TO 10% FOR UNQUALIFIED

Figure 5.3 Lifelong learning and changing skills needs (IRDAC forecasts)

The demand for unskilled and even skilled jobs has fallen dramatically in all the countries shown in Figure 5.3, while the demand for 'white-collar' occupations, scientists, managers and engineers has increased accordingly. For example, according to the UK Green Paper, *The Learning Age*, the peak of 33 per cent of the workforce employed in manufacturing industry during the 1960s has fallen to less than 20 per cent in the 1990s and is falling further. Manufacturing jobs have either become heavily mechanized requiring less labour, or they have migrated to those parts of the world where labour is cheaper. Instead the number of jobs in the high-tech, knowledge and service industries, which require a much greater level of education and a constant updating process, has increased to take up the slack. Women have returned to work in large numbers. They now comprise half the workforce in the UK, while the service industries account for almost 70 per cent of all workers.

This has happened most acutely in the Anglo-Saxon and the North-European world, where strong labour unions were not able to slow down the process. Coincidentally, these are also the countries which have experienced the strongest economic growth in the past three years, but it is too early, and too facile, to state that the one is the result of the other. Those OECD studies that have been carried out are inconclusive on the matter, and separating the empirical wheat from the politically rhetorical chaff is a difficult task.

What is universally true of all countries however is that a constantly shifting industrial and business environment gives rise to the need for education systems to develop more self-sufficient, entrepreneurial, creative and flexible people. These will have to adapt to needs as they change and apply themselves continuously to updating their skills and knowledge in order to remain in employment.

8. More research into new, alternative and more effective learning methods

Alvin Toffler also wrote at length of the need to recognize and understand the new fault lines in society between the industrial, mass-thinking 'second wave' and the emerging more individualistic (in his neologism 'demassified') society based on information, knowledge and the expression of personal preference and growth. 'We are living,' he said, 'in a world of great but exhilarating conflict between those who want to control others and those who do not want to be controlled. The latter have found, through modern communications technology, a modus vivendi which releases them from the need to be accountable to anyone but themselves.' This of course presents its own inherent dangers as the growth of far-right militias in the United States testifies. The 1980s business guru, John Naisbitt, echoed this trend in his biannually updated ten world-changing trends, which found its way onto corporate tables in many places in the developed world. 'The growth of individualism,' he said is one of the most powerful of these, affecting business and society in equal measure.

Sherry Turkle, in her study of the effects of the psychological development of people interacting with computers, from young children to research scientists, describes 'a culture in the making'. Those who work frequently with the machine, she discovered, build an intensive personal relationship with it. The computer becomes more than a tool, it becomes a new way of seeing the world. It provokes also a new way of seeing the self, providing insights into the way our minds work. Both children and adults tend to accept the sort of mental and intellectual challenges presented by the machine, whether they are games or real-life problem-solving tasks that they would not dream of accepting in the world outside of the computer. Identification with film stars or sports personalities has been replaced by identification with much more complex and well-rounded computer characters. Many would see this as a threat to children in particular, but Turkle is not describing the typical arcade game killers of popular imagination in this context, but the world of positive simulation games and problem-solving exercises. The potential for good at least equals the potential to destroy.

The battle is still raging fiercely, but the forces of individualism have increased their influence dramatically. Society has, for many, become a matter of personal choice and action. The number of electronic cottages providing services for small and large businesses has burgeoned, and by extension, so has the number of people hooking into information services around the world. Similarly, it is not only companies and universities providing home pages on the Internet, but also schools and individuals. There is, it seems, a new need to broadcast to the world who we are and what we stand for.

But in this world of change, nothing stays firm. The pendulum is now swinging backwards again. As we have seen, there is now a new counter-movement toward 'community thinking', emphasizing co-operation and team-work and building a community spirit. The ELLILearning Highway forum on Learning Communities has uncovered scores of community-based, co-operative activities based on towns, villages and regions around the world. UNESCO has a similar plethora of references. The UK Learning Cities network has grown from one to more than one hundred in the past two years, and organizations with similar aims and common interests are building up joint strategies. The 1998 European Commission Esprit Research programme on Training and Learning emphasizes organizational and team learning as well as individual learning. These are trends to be explored in later chapters, but it should be noted now that learning change is not only the province of the individual. Sometimes the existence of a collective challenge provides the inspiration and motivation for individuals to act upon their own learning needs.

9. Special programmes to address the problems of learning disadvantage, learning exclusion and learning dropout

It is vitally important that all young people have requisite education, that will offer them access to the full range of life choices and make them fit for independence, through employability, and the development of self-worth and a capacity for sound personal relationships. This will necessitate a reassessment of the traditional school curriculum, especially in respect of education for personal development and well-being. A renewed commitment to overcoming the sense of failure experienced by sizeable numbers of children and proper career counselling, guidance and support, especially for potential dropouts, is essential.

So wrote Chapman and Aspin in *The School and the Community* and they are right. OECD follows this up. 'Particular attention should be given to students with special needs and those at risk of school failure and social alienation,' it says and suggests, as earlier chapters here have done, that one of the answers is a greater integration between school, family and the community. But this in itself is not enough. Chapman and Aspin's reference to proper career counselling becomes less relevant in a lifelong learning world in which employment patterns change year on year. Indeed the word 'career' is itself taking on a new meaning, referring as much to personal lifelong development as much as to the pursuit of a particular metier or job path. Only a combination of curriculum reform, more relevant content, brighter methodologies for learning, failure-free assessment systems and solid and knowledgeable social support systems can alleviate problems of learning exclusion and drop-out. The system should aim to make it attractive enough to encourage drop-in!

Exclusion is not confined to the young or the handicapped. Demography, early retirement and an improvement in health of older people are building up considerable pressure for programmes to keep the aged mentally and physically supple. The University of the Third Age (UTA), in which citizens share their knowledge and expertise with other citizens in a collaborative community venture, and obtain missing expertise from elsewhere when required, has been particularly successful in some areas for many years. Courses often take place in homes. For the most part grossly under-funded, it relies on the goodwill and dynamism of a few leaders in the locality. Where these do not exist or where there is no funding provision, UTA tends not to exist either. There is considerable scope for innovative seeding projects to increase this cost-beneficial form of learning for the older learner. Not only would it pay for itself in illness prevention on a whole community basis, it would create a large cadre of members with purchasing leverage in their own neighbourhood. There is scope too for more formalization (where it is required) of learning in the form of an increase in UTA degrees, mentoring projects, learning centres, e-mail contact and other support systems, such as happens through the University of Helsinki. Here the supply of programmes for old people living in residential homes, service buildings and hospitals has expanded greatly.

Another such system is the Pensioners' High Schools, pioneered in Denmark and now spreading to other parts of Europe. There are now more than 100 of these providing residential courses ranging from ceramics to music appreciation, journalism and computer literacy. Most of them have health centres. For the cost of no more than their weekly pension, pensioners are provided with full board, tuition and activities. Again there is scope for a more formalized structure to enable more people to benefit from the increased access to learning.

Markkula and Suurla (1998) say, 'Through lifelong learning people can be made to detect possibilities where they have not yet been detected. It is not so long ago that we thought an old person is not capable of learning new things or that memory automatically deteriorates with age. It is outmoded and fatally wrong to think that senior citizens need not learn any more and that they can be of little use to the community.' Indeed, the older generation has a great deal to offer and would be delighted to offer it. Lessem and Palsule lament the loss of the idea of 'rites of passage' in western society. In the 20th century, they suggest, we have lost our concept of rites of passage. Traditionally, people in their twenties evoke a search for identity, a pioneering spirit fuelled by competitive energy. In their thirties they settle down and consolidate, raising their children to conform to the norms of the society they have helped to create. In their forties they seek renewal through an explosive release of learning energy and in their later years they give back something to the society which has nurtured and sustained them – a sort of return learning journey. Certainly much needs to be done to tap into the experience and knowledge which the older generation has to offer.

10. Frequent celebrations of learning on a national and community basis and innovative programmes which enhance the image of learning in the public mind – exhibitions, festivals, creative learning competitions, national and local learning days, weeks and years

Appendix 2 describes the Learning Festival held in Sapporo in 1990, as a part of a national series of festivals sponsored in each major city by the Japanese Government. The key image of the visitor was that learning is enjoyable and fulfilling. The booklets delivered to every home, explained how, where and why individuals and families could obtain further information, enrol on new courses and enjoy the benefits of learning. It is estimated that more than 500 000 people attended the learning fair and more than 60 000 responded to the call to take further learning for the first time.

Other cities are imitating this model. The city of St Albert near Edmonton declared itself to be a 'Continuous Learning Community' in 1996. It espouses the five principles of public participation, prosperity, partnering, planet (environment) and society and has developed a sophisticated business plan to implement its many ideas. Each year it has a celebration of its new status. In 1997 it sponsored a one day fun festival of learning which incorporated a conference for professionals from all sectors of the city, a learning fair, and an exhibition into which every organization wanted to contribute, and which gave an opportunity for hundreds of people to contribute to the festival. Its success was measured by a questionnaire and such was the enthusiasm, that almost 100 per cent of people voted for a continuation. In 1998, therefore, a three day event was held, and this was equally successful.

But learning celebrations do not need to be held on such a large scale and they do not need to be in the form of fairs. Learning organizations in industry

frequently find ways to reward the learning of their employees. Some large companies in the UK, the USA and elsewhere for example have a special award session
for those of their employees who have gained degrees or diplomas in local colleges,
universities and open learning organizations, as a public recognition of learning
achievement. St Albert sponsored a quite separate 'Learning for health' celebration. Many universities hold open days to which the public is invited. Schools have
their annual fair or garden party to raise money for essential schools equipment.
Not all of these are celebrations of learning as such – sometimes they are an exhibition of the sophisticated equipment or simple income generation events – and not
all of them extol the virtues, the values and the pleasure to be obtained from it. But
the opportunities are there and one would expect that the approach of a learning
society would stimulate a new focus on these.

There is too the opportunity to include the excluded in learning celebrations.
Lifelong Learning suggested that competitions should be held in each community,
judged by the unemployed, the handicapped, the minority groups. These might be
the best new vocational course, the best new educational communications project,
children's photographic or environmental competitions. Much of this will happen
in a learning community environment, where contribution is encouraged and
enabled. It would have the effect of demonstrating the value of learning to those
who, for whatever reason, are not convinced.

Chapter 6

Learning for all seasons

The fifth group of lifelong learning insights covers the way in which nations, cities and towns can activate the learning of their citizens through innovative initiatives. The premise therefore is:

Lifelong learning is proactive rather than reactive, long-term rather than short-term, outward rather than inward-looking, holistic rather than fragmented. This means:

1. The development of seamless systems of learning into which learners of all types can fit, providing links vertically and horizontally between age groups

As education is seen more as a continuous lifelong process rather than a series of institutional episodes at the early stages of one's life, so the way in which it is delivered and received changes. UNESCO, in its Agenda 21 sees it thus: 'Practically everyone will go through one form or another of higher/post-secondary education, *but at various stages of their lives*' (their italics). 'It will often happen in new and increasingly diverse ways, with increasingly varied and even customised, study objectives, entry paths and chosen course lengths.' Naturally this is seen as a challenge to which 'the only solution will be to see higher education as a place for lifelong learning'.

The result of such a process will be the need to rethink the whole structure of education from cradle to grave. What attributes of mind are needed to enable people to pick and mix and to develop their own learning pathways to an uncertain and constantly shifting future? Certainly flexibility, adaptability and versatility come to mind as coping outlooks, together with the facility to fit easily into a variety of learning milieux. None of these is easily encouraged in rigid and fragmented educational environments. They require equal flexibility, adaptability and versatility in the learning provider, not just at higher education level, but also at school and in adult and further education colleges.

In higher education, this new role has many manifestations already. Christopher Padfield (1997) points out that 'some universities offer to customize Masters programmes to individual students'requirements.' Many US universities based in cities around the world offer such a system. Padfield continues:

> Some provide extensive mentoring services for professionals in industry, helping them plan and reflect upon their learning. Others encourage practising professionals to register for part-time research degrees. If universities *do not* find ways of engaging with the learning of professionals as peers, then to some extent they are accepting a role at the bottom (first qualification) of the professional development system, and they can expect, over time, to lose their pre-eminent status to other institutions.

This is a certainly a concern for those traditional universities whose natural reflex is to look inwards at procedures and protocols, rather than outwards at the educational marketplace. Competition is widening and a glance at the educational pages of the more upmarket newspapers and magazines shows how the effects of distance learning and Internet technologies will offer ever wider choice to the potential learner. Nothing is more certain that higher education in the cities of the developed nations will look very different in ten years' time.

This is also true of other parts of the cradle-to-grave system, particularly at those points where people of all ages encounter some sort of break. Transition between different stages of education is a difficult time for students, especially so at the transition time between school and working life. Despite widespread knowledge that further qualifications lead to financial success, a high proportion of students leave school with the intention of never participating in learning again. This is where the counselling services can act most usefully and where partnership programmes can also help. In the London-based Woodberry Down School/IBM Twinning Scheme, IBM people went into the school to teach interviewing skills to young people about to go for their first job. It was an eye-opener. Some of those children did not even know to wear a tie for a clerical job interview and few had any skills of listening to questions, formulating coherent answers or personal confidence. But the interviewing programme went further than that. It forced the students to think bigger, to see the interview as a stepping stone to further ambitions. And coming from experienced people who were not their teachers it encouraged many of them to consider further education with a set of personal goals.

That is one success story. But where local counselling services are scarce, this sensitive point in a person's life story is the point to concentrate them. In Finland for example, a system of student counselling providing educational and vocational guidance has been created at national, local and institutional level. UNEVOC describes how trained teacher/counsellors are employed in the final year of school under the authority of the Minister of Education, while careers advisers are also available from the locality to supplement advice and persuasion. Each locality also has its own Council of Careers Guidance comprising teachers, advisors and people from industry.

Other countries, for example Germany, with strong apprenticeship schemes operate a dual principle in which the school-leaver spends a high proportion of time in industry during the last school year. The GRETA (Groupe D'établissements) system in France operates in a similar way. According to Yamamoto, a GRETA comprises groups of ten or more secondary schools offering an alternative vocational curriculum with specialization options for those students who require it in the last year of school. It staffs itself with the necessary professionals – counsellors, specialist teachers – equipment, and credit accumulation structures to serve the schools in each GRETA group.

Certainly such programmes help to ease the transition between school and work and to keep young people in the learning milieu, though they will need to keep themselves continuously up to date with developments in lifelong learning practice. In a multi-career world, for example, they will need to know how to inculcate a flexible mindset in their students which allows them to understand when, where and how to change course when necessary.

2. The sharing of educational resources, including courses, between all sectors of the community

The UNESCO higher education conference paper on the *World of Work* identifies six aspects of co-operation between universities and industry:

- Participation of industry in decision-making processes, for example through membership on boards or advisory panels;
- Involvement of practitioners in curriculum development;
- Mobility between academic and professional careers as well as part-time teaching by practitioners;
- Internships for students prior to or during the course of study;
- Involvement of students in research projects sponsored by industry;
- Provision of vocational counselling services for students and placement of graduates.

These very much understate the current and, even more, the possible, collaboration activities between industry and higher education. Nor do they acknowledge the increasingly large part that industry is now playing, both in research and teaching particularly in the western world, and despite the differences between the two cultures.

There are constraints in some countries. The European Round Table of Industrialists in 'Developing Europe's future capacity' points out that in France and southern Europe generally, there are legal and traditional barriers which give universities very little autonomy to respond to industry's needs. Instead the demands are being met by private schools and professional organizations. Many companies in Spain, such as Telefonica, Banesto and Alcatel, provide almost all of their own training at their own institutions.

But the scene is rapidly changing. After centuries of mutual scepticism and distrust, university continuing education departments are developing tailored courses in collaboration with industry, for delivery in one or both organizations. Examples come to mind, like EuroPACE, which provided cutting edge research lectures by satellite to high level European engineers, scientists and managers in industry. The National Technological University still does so in the USA. But these institutions have been around for more than ten years. More recently, the outsourcing policies of large corporations have presented opportunities for universities to take over large parts of the delivery of pre-competitive courses for industry. The Southampton University Management School, for example, negotiated with IBM UK to deliver several thousand student hours to IBM personnel. Other examples abound, particularly in the United States where technological capability tends to be so much greater and courses delivered at a distance. Globalization will intensify this trend.

As discussed at length in *Lifelong Learning* however, the teaching demands of industry are high, requiring constant feedback on the quality of the teaching, the content and the delivery method from the student. This has, in many cases, been a stark learning experience for universities, as much as it has for industry. As the UNESCO *Higher Education World of Work* paper says 'the less an individual institution of higher education controls the education provided, the more it is challenged to reflect and purposefully shape its part in the process.'

Neither organization type yet implements the sort of lifelong learning methods recommended in this chapter. Didactic classroom 'yak and track' methods still deliver three-hour long lectures, expecting no more than 50 per cent to stick. Learning conferences are full of two-hour long 'wise monkey' panel sessions, partly delivered with little more than an overhead projector and usually not even that, and certainly with no opportunity for debate, discussion, feedback or audience ownership of the topic. In many cases the opportunity to speak is the only way in which an academic can attend the conference in the first place, which is a revealing statement about the perceived value of conferences for learning. But, though progress is slow, new perceptions about learning efficiency are now leading to the need to consider new ways of involving the student or audience in the presentation of the course or lecture. This is particularly true where industry is persuading universities to develop distance learning tools and techniques and open learning courses.

An example of good co-operation between industry, universities and the media comes from Italy. The NETTUNO Consortium is a partnership between higher education institutions, companies and TV channels in the Naples area. It uses the sort of technical and pedagogical resources which can give students the ownership of their own learning at their own pace and according to their own needs. Courses and curricula are developed jointly by university lecturers and company experts and are delivered through a variety of means – satellite TV, video-conferencing, multimedia software and distance teaching. They can be accessed at home, in the university, on company premises – wherever the learner requires it. Tutoring facilities are available through video-conferencing. This is an excellent example of university–industry co-operation in course development and delivery tailored to the needs of the user. It can be improved even more through a more effective use of the Internet and the new planning and delivery software it offers.

There is just one more strand to this theme of co-operation. Many large companies have excellent dedicated education facilities, with classrooms equipped with the full range of twin overhead projectors, barco, PCs, flip-chart stands, white board and slide and film projection facilities. Break-out rooms, videoconferencing rooms and residential facilities are also available. The IBM International Education Centre situated in beautiful countryside at the forest of Soignes at La Hulpe, near Brussels, comes to mind, and there are many more around the world. Universities too have out-of-campus educational sites, though not always, outside of the USA, so well endowed with technology.

These are physical resources specifically designed to proclaim the importance of learning and the ease through which it can be carried out. Many organizations in the State system would give their eye teeth for such an array of learning splendour. What, for example, could a weekend between teachers and students of a school at such a place do for the lifelong perceptions of those fortunate enough to experience it? How could a university exchange the comforts of delivering courses in such an environment for the use of some of its sophisticated scientific equipment by industry? How can Adult and Continuing Education combine its courses with those of industry to make full use of such facilities? What is the role of a third party, such as a learning city? The opportunities for full use of industry and university facilities, for competitions, learning celebrations, new insights for disadvantaged learners, demonstrations of the power of learning, are legion. This would be another manifestation of the sharing, caring learning society of the 21st century.

3. The cultural and physical re-orientation of higher education to act as a central resource for everyone in the community

The universal university is now a vogue phrase. Many sessions from Government, higher education and the NGOs echoed the message at the UNESCO Conference on Higher Education to decide directions and principles for the 21st century. 'The universality of higher education implies universal access for all those who have the ability and motivation (access and merit) and suitable preparation at every stage in life,' says one of its key documents, and goes on to propose other universalities, including:

> *The universality of higher education implies the use of varied forms of intervention in order to meet the educational needs of all at all stages of life.*
> By this is meant that universities are a crucial part of a system of continuing education and training. Lifelong learning adjusts to the individual characteristics and circumstances. The facilities they can provide include modifying its approach to individual needs – part-time courses, linked work and training, distance learning, modular courses, virtual delivery methods and the decentralization of training groups. If universities exist to serve individuals, they have to be prepared to take risks, try out new systems and processes, and make full use of the potential of new technology and distance learning.

> *The universality of higher education implies that its function is not only to train but also to educate.*
> This implies that universities have a mission to create the conditions for learning in the longer term. It includes education for personal development and the way in which individuals can contribute to social and economic development as citizens of a city, region or country. This contribution extends to the development of human potential in all its aspects.

> *The universality of higher education implies that its functions include vigilance and consciousness-raising.*
> Universities can make their intellectual resources and independence of thought available to increase debate about, and consciousness of, the many social issues arising in the community, nationally and globally. Paramount among these are those which affect the future of society and are most likely to build a better and more sustainable development.

> *The universality of higher education implies that it should have a guiding ethical role at a time when there is a crisis of values.*
> This signifies several things, including the preservation of human rights. While these are fundamentally sacrosanct, at the same time they have to be placed in the context of history and the times in which universities operate. Globalization is a fact of the late 20th century, as is the triumph of capitalism. But there is still a need for a set of universal values in which, in the words of the document, 'the universal

"We" takes precedence over "I", in which science and technology are employed for the benefit of all humanity and not in the selfish interests of various powerful parties'. Such a role begins in the higher education institutions themselves, in their method of organization and in the relationship they build up with the communities in which they operate.

The universality of higher education implies that it must develop a management method based on the dual principle of responsible autonomy and transparent accountability.
Higher Education has tended to cultivate an ivory tower image to those who do not know it. While the universal university needs to ensure the principle of academic freedom in a free society, it also needs to develop new relationships with local and national political authorities which may be responsible for proposing development projects. But academic freedom demands academic responsibility and visible accountability. The involvement of the community in its management and its projects would go a long way to dispelling the mistrust, envy and uncertainty surrounding its activities.

If the Higher Education sector is serious about implementing these universalities, we can look forward to genuine lifelong learning leadership in the local community. It should not, but it may if the interpretation of lifelong learning is a narrow one, be dependent on the availability of additional money.

4. Preparing people to meet the future by developing life skills and attributes at all stages and by encouraging self-esteem and self-worth in everyone

Those governments which have formulated lifelong learning strategies are well aware of the effects of internationalization. Finland's strategy is predicated on the need of a small country to create an educational system looking outwards to the world in order to survive. As we have seen it sees itself as the European laboratory for information society activity, related directly to globalization opportunities around the world. Its national lifelong learning strategy is based on the development of outward-looking vision. 'Learning is a source of joy,' it says:

> What is learnt unhappily, is happily forgotten. Sometimes life can teach you a hard lesson. Yet the basic message of lifelong learning is not to plod compulsively throughout one's life as a reaction to mounting demands. Learning, and particularly learning together, is fulfilling when it helps solve genuine problems and when it helps to develop the good life, creativity and cultural skills, improved abilities and a strong sense of citizenship.

This is a strong signal to educators to develop the whole person with a well-rounded personality and a feeling of self-worth. The English, Welsh and Scottish strategies place a heavy emphasis on Industry and Education working together to meet the challenges of a globalized world as a matter of survival. This is where the use of life skills is at its most significant. The University for Industry, by far the most forward-looking, and expensive, recommendation pours, with European help, many millions of pounds into its implementation. 'The information and knowledge-based revolution of the 21st Century will be built upon the intellect and the creativity of the people,' says the Green Paper, while the Fryer Report on Lifelong Learning, which spawned the Green Paper, supports this thesis, calling upon individuals and enterprises to combine in taking charge of their own learning. 'This country (Britain) needs to develop a new learning culture, a culture of lifelong learning for all,' it says. 'It is essential in order to help the country and all of its people to meet the challenges they now face, as they move towards the 21st Century. Establishing such a culture represents a major task for everyone in this country, especially for the Government and those people whose job it is to fund, promote or provide learning. They will all need to modify their approach and behaviour.'

That some governments and some industries have understood the message of the new workplace is not in doubt. Making lifelong learning happen, though, is, as Bob Fryer acknowledges, a far more difficult task, and will depend on the ability of the education providers themselves, the schools, universities and further education colleges to update themselves in the new methods, philosophies and procedures of a Learning Society.

It is not just a question of new curriculum, content and methodology. New life skills emphasizing reflecting and thinking, studying and learning, co-operating, entrepreneurship and communicating become more crucial if people are to reap advantage from the new technological empowerment. If they are not fostered, opportunities for growth will suffer. Nor is it a question of new, better and more information services. To illustrate that, it is perhaps worth repeating the message of the Learning Ladder, shown in Figure 6.1. This demonstrates a model progression from data to wisdom in the individual which education systems might try to emulate. The widening rungs confirm the widening difficulty of achieving the next stage but the progression is a logical one and constitutes the challenge for each person. It is sad that much of our current education, particularly in the schools, goes little beyond the information rung and, moreover, is not actually designed to do more than that.

The British Prime Minister's assertion that the way to the future is labelled education, education and education shows some insight into the needs of countries. He might have improved this by making it learning, learning and learning, but at the time lifelong learning was not strongly on the political agenda. But he knew this, as does every thinking leader whether he be in national or in local government. An under-educated public, out of touch with technological progress, fearful of new ideas and opportunities and uncertain of its ability to cope with change can and will hold back the competitive development of industries and nations. The Finnish National Strategy believes that this starts at the school. 'The methods used in young people's basic education are critical for the development of self-esteem, learning motivation and learning skills, it says.

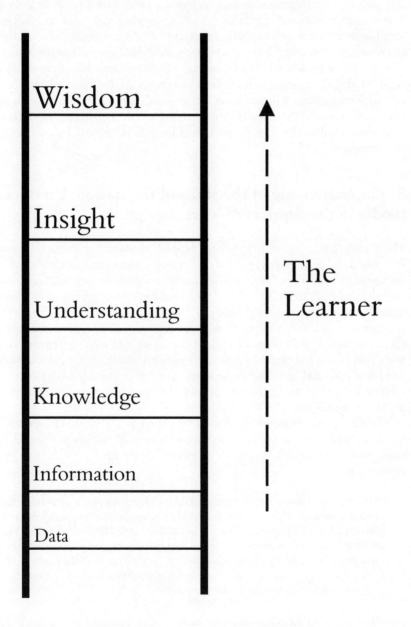

Figure 6.1 The learning ladder: a personal voyage from data to wisdom

The UK Confederation of British Industry proposes a new curriculum after the year 2000 divided into a different permutation of core subjects than at present. Within the core it suggests should be included a whole new set of skills and values. These include personal development skills, learning skills and self-awareness, social skills, problem-solving skills, awareness of values, attitudes to work, oneself and to others. This it says will provide the foundations for employability in the 21st century. The question 'why wait until the year 2000 in order to implement such a badly-needed skills base?' is an obvious one. After all, the first children to begin that new curriculum will not leave school until 2011, and that will be into an entirely different world in which employability will depend heavily on the owner-ship of such skills and a high proportion of the jobs which will be available are as yet unknown.

5. The harnessing of the skills of the national and local media in the support of learning

The media have a powerful effect on people's thoughts, opinions and actions. Effectively and imaginatively used, they can play an important part in changing the culture of a nation into a Learning Culture. Where they see their mission mainly as an instrument of entertainment they tend to address the lowest common denomi-nator in the search for audience and can, by trivialization and lack of depth in real issues, reduce the ability of people to make informed choices. In some countries they act as agents of propaganda and deprive people of a basic democratic right to understand truth and exercise choice. But where they can strike a balance between entertainment and intelligent comment which encourages intelligent and informed response they perform a service both to a nation and its people. They help to create a learning culture.

The final policy report of the high-level expert group to the European Com-mission, *Building the European Information Society for us all* recognizes this and, at the same time, expresses a legitimate concern about media concentration and democracy:

> The media have always had an important role to play in supporting pluralism and open government. We are concerned, however, that the internationalization and simultaneous concentration of the media could create a democratic deficit. The internationalization of media operations increasingly transcends the regulatory capacities of national administrations, and the concentration of the media could leave a privileged group of effective lobbyists and political actors in a position to channel media – and thereby public – attention.

They go on to say that public access to high-quality, neutral information is neces-sary for the proper functioning of democracy. Without unbiased news on affairs in the community, the country or the wider world, citizens cannot play an active part in the governance of society or make informed choices in elections. There is a concern here. The information we receive is not always delivered in a totally neutral and transparent manner. Ownership of the media is becoming increasingly concentrated: one media conglomerate may control a range of newspapers, television stations, news programmes, etc. With only a few organizations deciding what information the public should be exposed to and the lack of transparency about who owns what in the media, the result could be detrimental to cultural and political pluralism.

However we should recognize that, for good or otherwise, the media have a crucial function in a Learning Society. They have access to the hearts and minds of whole populations and can help to transform them into dynamic, well-educated and flexible lifelong learning societies. While the aims and objectives of the media differ from country to country, there is evidence in some of an increasing realization that people are sentient and intelligent human beings, ready to be mentally stimulated by quality programmes and thought-provoking debate. In UK television, the BBC Learning Channel, although relegated to the early hours of the morning, contains diverse and excellent material, while many viewers switch onto the Open University programmes, whether or not they are registered on the courses. Other channels, too, offer late night education. In many countries the emergence of popular knowledge channels devoted to programmes on environmental or historical material has uncovered a latent and unexpressed demand for visual material to exercise the brain rather than entertain the brain-stem. In Finland and other Nordic countries, television channels broadcast Continuing Education programmes from universities to industry.

Newspapers tend to be more circumspect, taking care not to offend their readers with material they may not want. But there are exceptions. Again in Europe, many of the broadsheet newspapers include a weekly education page, and, though they tend to deal mainly with chalk-face and a narrow range of curriculum issues, sometimes lifelong learning gets a mention. The increase in human interest stories based on learning may encourage more coverage in the future.

However, while global television news channels bring world events into the living room, we are all experiencing the information assault course. The real challenge lies in our ability to cope with this new mental invasion. Few of us have been given the skills and competencies to interpret the bombardment of ideas, facts, opinions and sensations into useful knowledge, or to turn it into insights. Without this ability, such an overload can desensitize, rather than enrich, us. The lifelong learning culture, which would encourage such skills as a basic requirement, advocates a new look at school curricula to address these issues.

These are global, national and local issues. At the local level particularly, the opportunity exists to influence the media to participate in helping to build a strong learning community and to involve the people in sustaining it.

6. Special programmes to encourage people to care for their own environment

The less fortunate parts of the world are constrained by several factors. UNCTAD projections indicate that the number of human beings on this very finite planet will rise from 5 billion to 11 billion by the mid-21st century, the majority in areas which are already overcrowded and underdeveloped in technological terms. The dangers are environmental, nutritional, educational and moral and they have the potential to spread instability throughout the whole planet. In such conditions, lifelong learning becomes a luxury for people destined to live at subsistence level and below. However, despite the problems, it is still a goal to aim for, and organizations such as the World Bank have recognized that improved learning is a necessary condition for the provision of basic services and infrastructures in the developing world.

But the major effect of excessive population growth will be on the environment, and this is where the need for lifelong learning takes root. The survival of human beings on the planet depends upon proper management of global and local environments. Mankind, in its ignorance, cannot much longer deplete resources and destroy ecosystems. The razing of forests in the tropical regions affects everyone who lives on the planet. And so does the over-toxification of crops through the injudicious use of chemicals, and the continuous manufacture of nuclear waste for which burial holes and containers made of materials lasting for several thousand years have to be found.

Environmentalists have tried to raise consciousness and people have responded in their millions. But there are millions more who have not yet heard the message or, if they have, ignore it for personal or corporate gain. Nor is this just a problem of the developing world. Sensitization to the maintenance of what Jonathan Schell (1982) calls 'our only planetary habitat' has to involve as many informed people as possible in active caring projects at local level. For our survival, little is more urgent than this.

But while OECD, UNESCO, Governments, cities everywhere and the European Commission are redefining their missions with a new, expanded vision of lifelong learning as a central unifying theme in order to solve environmental problems, what of the role of local government? 'Think globally, act locally' has been an environmental slogan for a long time, and the sort of actions which the community can take to care for its own trees, rivers, birds, plants depend on effective co-ordination of awareness-raising exercises for citizens of all ages. Some examples are described in Chapter 21.

7. The transformation of schools, higher and further education institutions, local government offices and companies into 'learning organizations', with guidelines similar to those practised in the best industrial companies but tailored to suit their own cultures

Longworth and Davies in *Lifelong Learning* discussed the characteristics of learning organizations in some depth, and provided a case study of the Rover Learning Business as an example. Since that was published, new insights into the role of learning in company development have attracted more and more companies to the concept. Many small and medium sized enterprises are also becoming learning organizations. Take the example of an SME employing about 300 people based in the north-east of England and with an export market to the rest of the world. Its visionary chairman, Ian Harris, sees no other survival option than to aim for world-class status through the learning development of the people who work for the company. The short case study below serves as an example of the way in which lifelong learning is put into practice in one small company, and as a guideline for other organizations which want to understand the issues.

'Getting to the future first, and thereby having control over it, is largely a matter of paradigm shift; in plain language, altering mindsets,' says Harris, and he does not mean only the mindsets of his own workforce. 'The question facing us is not whether there is a business advantage, which it is patently obvious there is, but how to get people steeped in the adversarial paradigm to give of their best, and to become lifetime learners; both those who think that necessary education ends with a piece of paper, and those who are relatively uneducated.'

Harris quotes four central points over which the company has control for its continuing success. He can do little about such external factors as exchange rates, economic meltdowns or international incidents:

1. *Focus*. The Bonas human resource policy core is to align corporate objectives with people development. The company has learned to recruit on the basis of attitude rather than experience or paper qualifications. It is a rigorous selection and induction process looking at the whole person, not just that part which is able to perform the task. It looks for people who are capable of responding to proper training and development, people who should be able progressively to raise their own horizons and thereby to realize their full potential. Often this potential is unforeseen by the persons themselves. Managers are urged only to hire people who are better than themselves and then to make their own judgements about how well and how far the company is able to develop them.

   In training the company concentrates on process rather than result. It creates non-adversarial relationships, based on team-work and shared learning experiences, with the focus on understanding both internal and external customer requirements – customers as 'us' not 'them'. The aim is to develop people who recognize and attempt to solve problems, rather than those who present problems for others to solve – that is an empowered organization, where continuous improvement is on everyone's agenda. Training tools and techniques, language labs, PCs, etc are continuously available on site.

2. *Vision*. This refers to the objectives and goals of the company as a whole and the way in which people relate to it. Harris says 'a vision is only effective if it is shared.' To this end the company launched a programme of involvement for everyone in continuous improvement with the goal of being 'World Class' by 1999. World Class is defined as being the best in its industry, as measured by comparative benchmarks. It is again rigorously demanding. In a Learning Organization, the details of the vision become changeable with time, which is why the company has engaged in an extensive 'Hoshin' planning exercise, based on the European Foundation for Quality Management model, to take the company through to 2003.

3. *Communication*. If the goal is to make people development an integral part of every business objective, then its successful achievement depends upon communication. This, Harris says, is a key area where management has a traditional mindset problem. Staff surveys after a system of daily briefings had been installed indicated that messages simply had not got through. So the drivers of change, to which every individual can relate, have to be central both to the shared vision and the communication process, with the intention of relating individual actions to corporate goals.

Typical of the range of programmes for staff/company development are:

- 'Radar Charts' – displayed throughout the company, and tracking tangible issues, with monthly targets for each objective. These not only keep the workforce up to date with the company's progress but involve them with it, creating understanding and giving ownership to the individual;
- A personal learning index – displays of the number of individuals studying for a recognized qualification and the progress they are making, clear for all to see, including customers and suppliers;
- Corporate Objective contributions – identified by every function or team and refined into specific individual tasks. This is the Hoshin element;
- Corrective Action teams – cross-functional groups to deal with non-standard situations, participation in which provides leadership opportunities. The habits engendered in these cause people to seek better understanding and better analytical tools – that is a virtuous circle of educational development;

- The Kaizen programme, where any process operator can recommend an immediate improvement to his or her team leader, and is then given the time and resources to try it;
- Two-day method improvement reviews – time allowed for a complete team to tackle an often ambitious objective that they themselves have determined.

These continuous improvement programmes are designed to engender interest, commitment, and a rising skill-base. They make both education and training relevant and personal, and produce competitive advantage for the company.

4. *Involvement.* How to keep the process of continuous improvement going. The following have produced results:

- An open, fair and appreciative environment;
- A display of the daily outputs of each job, charting the incumbent's proficiency and progress. This may begin from a starting point of 'no knowledge or experience' even though he or she may have the core skills, to 'can train others'. It plays an important part in the six-monthly full appraisal;
- A monthly appraisal system conducted by the team leader. This measures 14 behavioural criteria, grouped under seven headings, and is termed the 'Philosophy of Work'. It was the product of a shop floor corrective action team, which had been tasked with raising the profile and relevance of the appraisal process. Monthly score sheets remove subjectivity, while the sum of these measures gives a monthly score out of 100, and the overall index is tracked on the Corporate Radar Charts.

People are encouraged to conduct a personal SWOT analysis. How will they be positioned when this job no longer exists? The objective of this policy is to make this continuous personal improvement irreversible. To assist with this every employee has his or her own personal tutor to debate, counsel, and to deliver the appropriate learning package in a seamless, classless way.

The company is an accredited NVQ provider, ie it undertakes to provide courses to a certain level equivalent to a national UK standard. As such it can tailor the material to the learner. It trains all its people in problem-solving skills; raising everyone to a minimum of an NVQ level 2 by the end of 1997, and then to level 3. A level 3 qualification in process management is in place for those willing to commit to it. 'It's a modest start', says Harris 'But we are aiming much higher.'

Harris relates the following anecdote as an example. Three years ago, a contract cleaner, Jim, joined the company in direct, low paid employment. He underwent the usual induction training. He did well and later he was tested for, and given the job of team leader. Last year, he completed an NVQ3 in supervisory management, and his tutor stated that his final year project was among the best he had ever seen. Incidentally, it produced savings of £6000 a year. When he joined the company he had 3 low grade CSEs (A former qualification in the UK for 'non-academic' pupils, it was discontinued in 1984). Never in a million years did he expect to obtain any other academic qualifications. The last three years have revolutionized his thinking and enriched his life. His mindset has switched to personal develop-ment, because crucially, he can visualize the process and the benefits.

This story and the case study of which it is a part is indicative of the way in which industry is preparing itself, through learning, to meet the challenges of a competitive world. Some countries are well ahead of others in this. But what of other organizations outside the business and commercial field? Universities and schools in particular. Can they learn anything from this example?

Perhaps several criteria do not apply here, since the cultures and the goals are different. But what of the central tenets of the study? The need for staff to stay con-tinuously updated as a matter of professional practice is as much a function of a school as it is of a company – and even more of a university. The need for staff to improve their personal skills is similarly universal. This is not a matter of going on a course every few years – the process and the method is one of continuous improvement. The need to keep everyone in the organization up to date and involved and committed to a philosophy and a plan, and to give everyone in the organization the opportunity to contribute to its continuing development, is a basic tenet of the learning organization. In an educational establishment this would include the students. Open and visible personal progress charts, Kaizen techniques, personal learning plans, teamwork development, problem-solving skills, radar charts, appreciative environments. Some of these are relevant too, though it is understandable that schools may not wish to lower the self-esteem of some by raising that of others. But personal targets, as they are successfully carried out in the schools of Birmingham, England, are a variation on the same theme. Nor can we ignore the undoubted political, social and economic problems faced by many educational institutions. But, while finance plays an important part in the maintenance of a learning organization, attitude, vision and the application of cre-ativity are much more significant – management and staff attitudes to organiza-tional and personal development, a clear and evolving vision of where the organization and the individual is aimed, and the opportunity to be think, speak and act creatively, for example.

Of course there are pockets of good practice in all establishments, and these should be celebrated, but there is a long way to go before education catches up with industry both in its application of the principles of learning and in its appreciation of the conditions conducive to its successful accomplishment. Figure 6.2 provides a check-list of transformations towards a Learning Organization.

Becoming a learning organization involves the following transformation:

From	To
Functional departments	process teams
Hierarchical structures	flat structures
Discrete tasks	multidimensional work
People following instructions	people doing what is right
People waiting to be given work	people using initiative
Management	leadership
Supervisors	coaches
Training courses	continuous learning
Activity-based compensation	results-based compensation
Vertical advancement	horizontal broadening
Policy-driven systems	customer-driven systems

Figure 6.2 Transformations

All workplace organizations, Learning Providers and Professional Associations can learn a great deal by incorporating these into their own awareness systems.

Chapter 7

Summary of part 1

Below is a summary of the five key themes and their sub-themes discussed in this chapter. They try to encapsulate the philosophy, vision and the actions to be taken to make lifelong learning a reality in the 21st century. Because many of them have pointed to the idea of a learning community as the engine of the learning society arguing that the axiom 'think globally, act locally' is the real key to making lifelong learning work, part 2 of this book discusses just how such a community – a city, a town or a region – can change its thinking to implement lifelong learning principles in all sectors of activity.

1. The lifelong learning focus is on learning and the needs and requirements of learners

This means:

- the learner is now the customer whose needs are paramount. The learning provider becomes more accountable and, in order to facilitate better learning, it should take into account the learning styles and preferences of each individual and tailor the course to these;
- the learner will have a greater involvement with the content and methodology of his/her own learning and a more developed sense of ownership of it;
- in being more responsive to individual learning needs teachers will develop a more versatile range of skills and competencies. They would become 'learning counsellors', with a knowledge of the best use of learning technologies, the development of leadership skills and the tools and techniques of lifelong learning – a much more sophisticated and complex set of abilities;

- teacher training organizations will not teach teachers how to teach, but how to stimulate learning and confident self-development in people of all ages – empowering others to learn. Learning counsellors will be equally at home in all parts of the learning system;
- the skills, talents and knowledge available in the community at large will need to be mobilized in the service of learners;
- education technology tools and techniques will be increasingly used interactively as both learning stimulators and content presenters;
- curricula in all parts of the formal education system will emphasize the acquisition of skills, values, and turning knowledge into understanding, rather than information content and memorization.

2. Lifelong learning is more holistic. It is an economic, social and cultural, as well as an educational, philosophy

This means:

- exploiting the relationship between high levels of education, economic success and low social costs. For example, education's positive impact on environmental quality, crime and health;
- re-assessing and re-designing financial programmes at national and community levels to take into account the interdependent social, economic, educational, fiscal and cultural nature of lifelong learning;
- introducing lifelong learning programmes across and within all sectoral and departmental responsibilities in national and local government;
- special fiscal measures to encourage and reward learning;
- a proactive information and promotion campaign presenting the benefits of learning to the nation, to the community, to organizations and to individuals;
- regular learning audits of the present and future learning requirements of all citizens, carried out in each community. Databases constantly updated and maintained;
- the encouragement of towns, cities and regions to declare themselves as 'Communities of Learning' and to develop and implement strategies which develop their human potential;
- schemes to develop partnerships for sharing resources, including human resources, between sectors of the local community.

3. In a lifelong learning world, examination and assessment methods are used to confirm progress and encourage further learning for everyone rather than to highlight success/failure in the few

This means:

- individual target-based assessment structures which present a progressive series of achievable challenges within national and regional systems;
- equal value for practical/vocational and academic achievement and a system recognizing late development, multiple abilities and different approaches to learning;
- credit for non-standard experiential learning through Assessment of Prior Experience programmes;
- schemes and strategies to include the excluded by enhancing the attractiveness of learning;
- greater portability of degrees and diplomas to reflect the increased internation-alization of the employment market;
- more partnership programmes between industry and education to break down the stereotypes and create co-operation and understanding on evaluation methods;
- the development of credit-based, linked modular education systems into which everyone can be accommodated wherever, whenever and however they wish to study;
- a new look at the purpose of examinations as a non-threatening part of each individual's learning process.

4. Lifelong learning proactively encourages the development of the habit of learning in everyone rather than reactively responding to specific needs at specific times

This means:

- improved positive encouragement and feedback to all learners in national and local education systems;
- deploying similar techniques to those used for the promotion and advertising of goods, products and services to promote and advertise the value and pleasure of learning;

- political acknowledgement that learning is important to national prosperity, and non-political multi-sectoral programmes to increase the incidence of learning in the community;
- more interesting and exciting teaching methods which can compete with the sophistication of the media, which do not turn children off learning and which give them the habit and skills to learn for life;
- the encouragement of learners to look outside of themselves for learning stimulation and to understand themselves and the value of their learning. These might include:
  - bringing new experiences into the classroom through the use of new open and distance learning technologies;
  - using networks creatively for collaborative learning strategies between people of different cultures, creeds and colours to enhance both international understanding and learning performance;
  - using the talents and experience of people in every community;
  - more work outside the classroom through partnerships and work experience programmes;
  - positive action research programmes to make learning more enjoyable and pleasurable rather than difficult and threatening;
  - more research into new, alternative and more effective learning methods;
  - special second-chance programmes to address the problems of learning disadvantage, learning exclusion and learning dropout;
  - a focus on the development of new skills and attitudes more relevant to the workplace.
  - the development and use of personal learning plans and mentoring programmes nationally and in local communities.
  - innovative programmes enhancing the image of learning in the public mind.
- frequent celebrations of learning in the community – learning exhibitions, festivals, creative learning competitions, national and local learning days, weeks and years.

5. Lifelong learning is long-term rather than short-term, outward rather than inward-looking, holistic rather than fragmented, proactive rather than reactive

This means:

- vertical and horizontal links between age groups and seamless systems of learning to smooth out the problems of transition;
- educational resource sharing, including courses, between industry and the education sector;

- a cultural and physical re-orientation of universities to function as a central focus for local community development;
- more emphasis on self-esteem and self-worth, and the development of life skills preparing people to meet a different future;
- harnessing the skills of the media in support of lifelong learning;
- encouraging people to care for their own environment as a lifelong commitment;
- the transformation of schools, higher and further education institutions, local government offices and companies into Learning Organizations, with guidelines similar to those practised in the best industrial companies but tailored to suit their own cultures.

Figure 7.1, opposite, encapsulates many of these ideas.

	Education and Training	Lifelong Learning	Difference
1.	Teacher rules and decides. Ownership of the need to learn and its content is with the teacher	Learner, as customer, rules. As far as possible ownership of the need to learn and its content is given to individuals	Variety of techniques and tools to be developed to fit in with the individual's needs, demands and learning styles
2.	Compartmentalized according to age	Lifelong in concept and content, providing links vertically and horizontally between age groups	A seamless system providing learning support from cradle to grave, from 0–90
3.	Knowledge and Information based – what to think	Skills and values based – how to think	Empower people to carry out a wide range of activities in all walks of life and work
4.	Based on the needs of the organization, nation or society	Based on the desires of the individual and the need of organizations and nations to develop their human potential	Encourage and stimulate people to recognize the power of their own human potential and develop it
5.	Authority decides where, why, when and how	Learner is empowered and mentally enabled to decide where, why, when and how	Alternative learning methods. Learning taking place everywhere – home, school, work, pub, shops, etc
6.	Validated to separate failures from successes	Validated to confirm progress and encourage further learning	New non-failure oriented examination and accreditation systems
7.	Reactive – meets identified needs of organizations and some people	Proactive – encourages the habit of learning in all people	Audit learning needs of the whole community and nation. Learning Counselling
8.	Each sector of society determines its own needs	Holistic – encourages each sector of the community to cooperate	Combines and uses whole community human resources for the benefit of each part
9.	Educates and trains for employment and short term need	Educates for employability in the long-term	Development of personal skills and competences
10.	Work-based	Life-based	Work and life outside work as part of same human need
11.	Inward-looking – to satisfy specified needs	Outward-looking – to open minds, encourage broader horizons and promote understanding of others	People understand other creeds, cultures, races and customs through learning and technology
12.	Satisfies the present	Prepares for the future	All people can meet future confidently and creatively
13.	Learning as a difficult chore and as **received** wisdom	Learning as fun, participative and involving, and as **perceived** wisdom	Frequent celebrations of learning by individuals, in families, in organizations and in communities
14.	Education as a financial investment for organizations and nations	Learning as a social, personal and financial investment in and by people for the benefit of nations, organizations, society	By a nation in its citizens, by a business or government organization in its workforce, by educational organizations in the students' future; by people in their own worth and happiness

Figure 7.1 From the age of education and training to the era of lifelong learning

Part 2

Learning cities, learning towns, learning regions – making lifelong learning work

Part 1

Chapter 8

Introducing the learning city

A Learning Community is a City, Town or Region which mobilizes all its resources in every sector to develop and enrich all its human potential for the fostering of personal growth, the maintenance of social cohesion, and the creation of prosperity.

ELLI definition

The information society and the learning society

The Information Society is already having a powerful effect on the City. As the 20th century gives way to the 21st it is evident that information technology (IT) will dominate the way things are done in all sectors – business and industry, schools, universities, local government. IT will act as an extension to human capability like no other tool before it. Little wonder that information has proliferated. White Papers, reports, conferences, books, strategies are published regularly spelling out its opportunities, its pitfalls, its characteristics, its dynamics and its consequences for the human race. The information superhighway rolls inexorably past the front doors of all citizens; television, satellite and cable channels present to them continuously and ceaselessly the best, and the worst, of civilization's creative genius; the Internet binds them all into a single communicating organism through myriad invisible electronic tendrils. For the technologically literate it is POWER ie Progress, Opportunity, Wealth, Excitement and Resource. They are the members of the Learning Society which must inevitably accompany the Information Society in order to assist and support its development.

That is for those who are a part of the excitement. Many citizens are encumbered by the seven Is – Ignorance, Incomprehension, Inability, Incapacity, Impotence, Incompetence and Inadequacy. They are in vastly superior numbers. They are the new excluded. They have not been born with learning, nor have they achieved it. Many have not even had learning thrust upon them. Clearly, for people to obtain the benefits of the information revolution with confidence, creativity and enjoyment, it needs to be matched by a learning revolution, a step increase in the learning capacity of whole cities. The evolutionary alternative imposes an unacceptable time delay.

But how can this learning revolution take place? How would it be financed? What sort of infrastructure needs to be built around it? Who would be its targets? What resources would it need and where would they come from? These are the questions facing city leaders in the dash for economic viability in the Information Age. One response comes from the world of the environment. The phrase 'think globally, act locally' is written large into environmental jargon. Action takes place where the people are and not always at the behest of governments or non-governmental organizations. So it is in the building of the learning society. Governments have a major role in setting the agenda and the vision, but it is in the cities and towns and villages that the action will take place.

This synergy between government recommendation and community action is described by the European Round Table of Industrialists in its booklet *Education for Europeans – The integration of Technology into European Education*. In describing new resources for learning as an investment, it says, 'We are convinced that if we Europeans do not keep pace with our international competitors and do not make these major investments now, Europe will suffer a serious economic decline in the future. These investments have to be made by governments, industry and citizens. New forms of creative partnerships have to be sought.'

It is in the latter part of this that the community comes into its own. This is where the creative partnerships will take place and where the motivation lies for individual citizens.

Learning cities and learning communities

The concept of the 'learning community', 'learning city' or 'learing region' is rapidly becoming accepted in the population centres of many countries. To avoid confusion with the other meaning of community as a group of people with common interests, the second term will be used. It is thus here used as a geographical concept, and encompasses towns, regions and even villages, which harness and integrate their economic, political, educational, social, cultural and environmental structures toward developing the talents and human potential of all its citizens. A learning city provides both a structural and a mental framework which allows its citizens to understand and react positively to change.

As cities grow into lifelong learning cities, the interactions and interdependencies between the different sectors will become more marked, more urgent and more fruitful. The process of creating a learning city potentially offers substantial benefits and opportunities for every citizen, but it needs inspirational management and a communicated sense of purpose and direction, preferably using modern communications technology and media support. A symbiosis of mutual interest lies at the heart of the learning city. It promotes productive partnerships and the development of projects aiming to improve learning opportunities. Thus, lifelong learning encourages interaction between international and local, public and private, educational and industrial, governance and people as essential components. They need to be nurtured and fostered with care, commitment, co-operative intent and enlightened education for all within a caring community.

True learning cities are outward looking. People moving from one city to another should be able to recognize in each the ambience of learning and use it as a means of integration. Similarly, no one city will have a monopoly of knowledge. It is not closed – it enriches itself through experiences, knowledge and insights drawn in from other places, other continents. The new networking technologies help in this, such as the ELLI 'Learning Highway' network which provides lifelong learning courses and contacts as well as electronic mail and discussion forums mail for learning cities. These have existed in business and industry and universities for some time. Their expansion into links between third age pensioners, children in schools, professional organizations, environmental interest groups and town councillors, to name but a few, will help break down cultural and age barriers. Such links are exciting and innovative, and they open up real possibilities for understanding and co-operation, but people will need some help and encouragement from specially trained leaders. Electronic travel, like the real thing, will broaden the mind, but only so long as the traveller leaves the door to the mind open.

In the UK, 'Cities of Learning' have proliferated in a very short time. While Edinburgh was one of the original 'Educating Cities' participating in an OECD project in the 1980s, it has now been joined by Liverpool, Glasgow, Southampton, Norwich, Sheffield and more than 100 other cities and towns in other parts of Britain. Meanwhile, the Educating Cities organization based in Barcelona holds an annual conference for its members from around the world, and the ELLIcities network, based on the European Lifelong Learning Initiative, provides electronic facilities and forums, holds seminars and develops workshops for a growing number of European cities. Similar organizations exist in North America, Australia and Asia.

But any city can call itself a learning city without necessarily doing a great deal beyond satisfying its basic responsibilities. The development of guidelines by which learning cities can be judged is another fast-growing industry. ELLI, reverting to the word community, has another definition, shown in Figure 8.1 below.

A Learning Community

is a city, town or region which

goes beyond its statutory duty to provide education and training for those who require it

And instead

creates a vibrant, participative, culturally aware and economically buoyant human environment

through the provision, justification and active promotion of learning opportunities

to enhance the potential of all its citizens

Figure 8.1 The ELLI Learning City definition

In this, each word has, according to ELLI, a definite meaning.

City, town or region – A learning community can be large, medium-sized or small. The smaller it is the more easily established is the community. A city or region may comprise several interacting learning communities, based upon smaller geographical units.

Statutory duty – each local authority is required by law to provide a basic level of education for its children and opportunities for higher learning through universities, further education or adult education colleges. These are laid down by Government.

Education and training – describes the past and the present. In a true learning community these words are gradually being replaced by 'learning' or 'lifelong learning' to emphasize the new focus on the needs of individual learners.

Vibrant – a dynamic environment which hums with co-operative activity and vital, spontaneous energy.

Participative – this is part of the stakeholder vision in which citizens are encouraged to actively participate in the development and growth of their own communities and to establish links with other communities.

Culturally aware – not only being aware of their own identity *vis-à-vis* the cultural heritage within their community, but also aware of, and comfortable with, the effects of change on their, and the community's, future.

Economically buoyant – most research demonstrates a strong link between educational growth and economic health. A learning community will be well in tune with the wealth-creating aspects of its activities.

Provision of learning opportunities – this sets the agenda for a future in which learning replaces education and training.

Justification – so that every citizen knows why learning is important both to him/herself and the well-being of the community in which he/she lives.

Active promotion – and in which the community itself encourages and animates its citizens to take advantage of the learning opportunities.

Enhance the potential – each citizen has enormous potential to learn, develop personally and contribute profitably to the community.

All – perhaps the most important word. A learning city is not for the favoured few but for every citizen to donate skills, talents and knowledge for the many and receive the learning to which he or she is entitled.

Co-operation and interaction between all the sectors making up the city – business and industry, primary, secondary and tertiary education, social services, the voluntary sector, special interest groups, professional bodies and others – is important. As cities grow into lifelong learning communities, interactions and interdependencies are built up between them and in time they become more dynamic and more profitable for all partners. Figure 8.2 below illustrates this process. This symbiosis of mutual interest between dissimilar organizations provides a central focus for the growth of the learning city.

Working together in the learning city

The essential glue binding all of them together is learning. It stimulates and improves personal development opportunities for citizens of all ages. It promotes a stakeholder society in which everyone participates. It is a holistic concept.

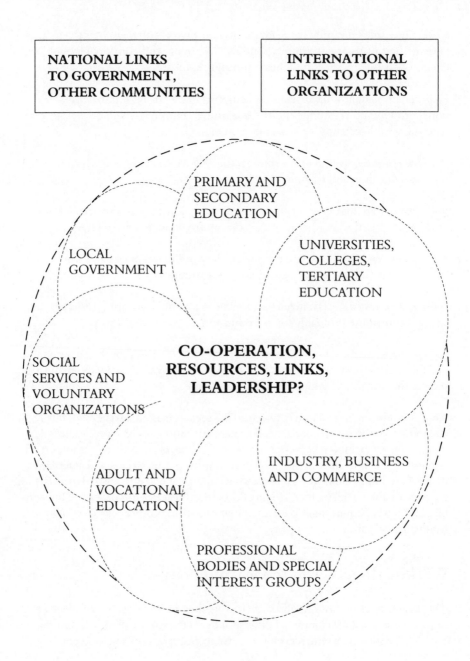

Figure 8.2 Working together

Leadership and co-ordination are both problems and opportunities. In some circumstances, different sectors will take a position of leadership over that aspect of the learning city in wh:cn they have expertise. But projects, initiatives and strategies will need to be co-, ,t 'nated and few sectors are willing to expend the resource needed to carry out such a large task. Longworth and Davies (1996) suggest that universities, as universal organizations at the he: t of the learning revolution, are ideally placed to take this position of leadership. Such a responsibility would encourage them to adopt a more community-oriented mission, both in their research and their teaching, while retaining their national and international links. But, though there are examples where individual departments offer facilities, expertise and a dynamic for community development, there is little evidence that they are ready, willing or able to take on a true leadership and co-ordination role.

Local government can also carry out this task, but which part of local government? There is some evidence in places like Glasgow and Birmingham that the City and Regional Development Agencies now see the creation of a learning city as a legitimate aim, arguing, with reason, that the economic future of the city depends upon creating interlocking and interdependent structures based on lifelong learning principles. Although their remit is not overtly educational, they have the resources and often a vision of the paramountcy of learning, which education departments do not necessarily have, to initiate and monitor progress. They also have the budget.

But the concept of a learning city goes well beyond economic considerations. It will also be a caring city. It will have to make special provision for the excluded, the slow learner and the late developer, the eccentric and the deranged, the damaged and the desperate. In time greater knowledge and better remedial help and support programmes will reduce the number of those with special needs and difficulties, as, it has been argued in Part 1, will crime itself.

Meanwhile many cities are struggling to understand the nature of the task ahead of them and the practical actions they need to take in order to create the city of tomorrow within the financial, political, cultural and social restrictions of today. The rest of Part 2 therefore explores the essential characteristics of the learning city and relates it to where progress has already been made. While local cultures, circumstances and perceptions may differ, several generic aspects in lifelong learning are common to all cities, and each chapter describes a distinct operational focus.

Chapter 9

Leadership in the learning city – making things happen

A learning city links its strategy to the development of leadership and learning counselling skills in and for the whole community.

The concept of leadership is changing. At a period in history when such skills as decision-making, problem-solving and communicating instructions are passed down the line to the most appropriate point in industry, empowerment is a more fashionable, and appropriate, word. The process of renewal and regeneration of the learning city, and participation by large numbers of stakeholders, becomes self-sustaining over time. But such a happy state lies a long way ahead in most cities. In the primary stages of the development of any new project or system, ideas, solutions and procedures are imparted by the few with the insight and the energy to take the leadership role, to the many. The sensitivity and innovation with which this leadership is exercised can be the difference between success and failure in these circumstances. It is a process of empowering as many people as possible to play a responsible role in learning city development, in a cascade model of growth, so that the city itself becomes a learning organization.

Paul Elsner comments on the new vision of leaders in a long and fascinating Internet article on the journey of the Maricopa Community Colleges Network towards a 'new learning paradigm'. Maricopa is an American schools district containing as many as ten Community Colleges with links to universities and other schools. It commenced its journey to becoming a learning organization in 1994. Under the title *A Redefinition of Leaders* Elsner writes:

> Several hundred Maricopans began to become qualified as learner facilitators. We began to learn not from the Chancellor, the Vice Chancellors or the Presidents,

but from students, classified staff, faculty and anyone who happened to have obtained certain expertise from the facilitation and training processes. This is one of the characteristics of the desired learning paradigm: we learn from one another. Learners are leaders. Leaders are learners.

He continues to describe how such new perceptions resulted in the lowering importance of hierarchies, a more open communication between people at all levels, vastly greater collaboration between organizations and people in the whole school district and a 'quantum leap' in understanding and contribution. Authoritarian structures melt away and co-operation increases. 'The most recent illustration occurred,' he says 'when three colleges, and potentially all ten, began to examine the possibility of multiple uses of a new midrise tower acquired for Rio Salado Community College. This college, a non-traditional institution that relies heavily on outreach and distance education, proposed a state-of-the-art technology-production centre in a new building. In the spirit of collaborative planning (a learning organization behaviour), the President of Rio Salado invited other college staff and presidents to participate in a day of dialogue and planning. A staff assistant, quite far removed from the executive responsibility for high-level decision making, facilitated the day's discussion. Everyone in the room was a high ranking executive within the Maricopa Community College system, yet this staff person led the discussion and facilitated communication among presidents, deans and technology experts. These processes are consistent with the new desired learning paradigm.

Elsner expresses surprise at such a reversal of roles, but the experience of every business that has gone down this route demonstrates the same syndrome. Skills of leadership are present in many people, and above all in those learners with a confidence in their own knowledge and expertise. New leaders are both empowered and empowerers. Such stories illustrate the importance of similar leadership development strategies in the education departments of learning cities. They do not however say what the city should do to start the process of developing leaders who will in turn help develop the city into a learning city. For this a specific set of actions is necessary, and some suggestions are given in Chapter 24. Of course, many cities are already running courses for community leaders, but these often tend to be in the more narrowly-defined areas of voluntary community development and social deprivation. Something more is required.

One of the first steps a city can take is to organize courses to develop the learning leaders who can help achieve common goals. These should not always be the obvious candidates of teachers, social workers, managers and councillors. Leaders can, and should come from anywhere in the community, from any background – from industry, voluntary organizations, education, perhaps even from the ranks of the unemployed. They need to be given the vision of a learning city and invited to participate in its development, inserting their own ideas and practical advice. This is the learning city as a learning organization, an exercise in participation and commitment with the aim of eventually involving everyone in the city in the common objective.

Leaders should be immersed in the skills of creativity and, just as important, how to develop creativity in others. It should be a cascade process, each member of each group developing another group. They should run brainstorming sessions with local government officers, schoolteachers and children, the disadvantaged and disabled, higher education lecturers, special interest groups. These, in themselves, would inspire new solutions to old problems. They should be encouraged to use all the resources of the community around them – the buildings, the streets, the parks, the theatres, the shops, restaurants and public houses to spread the message of learning and to involve people in projects to enhance it.

Glasgow's progress towards a learning city is master-minded by the Glasgow Development Agency. Within its 'Learning Inquiry' strategy, still at an early stage, its leaders are the members of four 'themed action groups'. These comprise 12 'experts' to develop plans, solutions and activities within four overarching themes:

- How to get more organizations involved in developing their people, especially SMEs.
- How to encourage institutions to improve quality in the supply of access to training and how to evaluate it.
- How to stimulate personal motivation to learn, especially where traditional learning achievement is poor.
- How to surmount 'Barriers to Learning', a topic to be addressed by all groups.

Within their remits are such issues as new ways of learning, citizen involvement, developing learning cultures, wealth creation and identifying best practice.

Each group will be supported by a facilitator who will advise and help put into action the workplans. The facilitators work together, consulting and using the staff within the city's lifelong learning directorate, also based at the Development Agency. While much is employee-oriented toward improving industry performance and the continuous training of the workforce, the strategy does recognize that 'regeneration and a culture of lifelong learning cannot be accomplished by any one agency alone. All organizations have a unique contribution to make, but they must work together to produce added value.'

Another example comes from Japan. As long ago as 1994, more than 53 per cent of Japanese cities had a lifelong learning committee. Eighteeen per cent have lifelong learning departments and 28 per cent were actively promoting the concept, not just within the education departments but right across the city administration. Yashio city in the East of Japan has, through this mechanism, originated more than 70 lifelong learning programmes for its citizens from kindergarten to third age. Its staff members work as lecturers and go everywhere where they are asked to. They are the new leaders.

The Campaign for Learning, already mentioned in Chapter 2 as leaders of learning development in the United Kingdom, especially for those for whom learning is an unfamiliar concept, have taken the message right to the people. They encouraged *The Daily Mirror*, a mass circulation tabloid newspaper, to print an eight-page supplement on Lifelong Learning in one of its March 1998 issues. The format and content is particularly interesting. Among other strategies, it uses articles by national folk heroes, who have learned to learn after bad experiences at school, in order to pass over the message of learning to a readership not notably switched on to the subject. In other sections it describes how television and soap stars have to continuously update their techniques and skills in order to remain in employment, festivals where learning has been presented as a fun activity and the changes made in the workplace which entail new learning requirements for workers. The objective was to switch readers into understanding the value of learning by identifying with the people they admire for their success. The 'you too can do this with more self-application' approach.

There is probably great scope for regional and local campaign organizations along the same lines. But this story does highlight another aspect of leadership in the notion that lifelong learning progress in a city needs to have a driving force, an organization with ownership of the task of making it happen. Most cities setting out on the path of becoming a learning city have started by setting up committees of all the interested parties. In some they are huge. Every organization feels it cannot afford not to be a part of this great venture, and every organization wants to insert its own set of opinions, prejudices, viewpoints and advice into the melting pot, irrespective of whether it has experience or insight into the very different nature of lifelong learning.

Such committees are necessary and can achieve much, but political considerations – treading on coals in order not to offend this or that type of organization, obtaining full agreement from member associations, an inability to take hard decisions – do throw up obstacles and slow down action sometimes to stopping point. Everyone who has tried to create action from idea through large committee structures will recognize the syndrome. Committees cannot run operations, though they can expand the number of supporting projects through their influence. One organization, or one sector, should be given the responsibility to implement the lifelong learning strategy. This is not to advocate a dictatorship of the process. It will need to be done through democratic means. But the handing over of responsibility to a driver of this type ensures that ideas, projects and processes are marketed to other players with enthusiasm and commitment, and that there is a line of accountability for implementation.

Nor is the driver necessarily the executor of everything. Too much will need to take place in the passage to a lifelong learning city for any one organization to take that role. But it will need to persuade, cajole, lead, inform, teach, educate and develop understanding in other organizations that lifelong learning is different, holistic and learning-oriented and that they too will have to become learning-oriented with all that it entails. It therefore will need to be a respected organization with links to all other sectors.

Which organization can perform this task? In Glasgow and some other cities in Britain it is the Development Agency which leads the pack. And this is reasonable, since Development Agencies have a commitment to change things, a budget to allow them to do it, a staff which can focus on the task and a healthy distance from the vested interests. They need to be convinced that their work will be in vain if the vision of a lifelong learning city does not happen. However, other cities may choose differently. Business and industry has the marketing and development know-how and, particularly in France, strong Chambers of Commerce may be the new leaders.

In Japan leadership is with the centres of lifelong learning. According to the NIER comparative study, the country boasts more than 18,000 'citizens' public halls' for lifelong learning. The lifelong learning centre in each prefecture has six major objectives:

- to provide information and enhance knowledge;
- to research people's need for learning, develop appropriate programmes and conduct studies in them;
- to co-operate with other organizations and outsource learning where possible;
- to train leaders and advisers;
- to evaluate results; and
- to run classes for the community.

The fourth point is the relevant activity in this context, while the others are discussed in later chapters.

In other places universities may be an acceptable central focus of community involvement. In *Lifelong Learning* and subsequent papers, we proposed the vision of a 'universal university'. 'Instead of an institution for educating an elite of highly intelligent undergraduates and researchers,' we said, 'the university of the 21st century would become a universal university, open to all irrespective of background, of qualification, of age, of subject. To create the sort of society in which learning is natural and pervasive, that is the way the traditional university must go.' Thus the mission of the university as the place which adopts a leadership role in the local community, serving it and involving its citizens in the research it carries out, would see the community as a huge learning research laboratory. It would act as a conduit to the rest of the world through its national and international dimensions and contacts, importing and exporting new knowledge and ideas from and to it. By involving the people it would disseminate valuable knowledge, understanding and insights to the whole community.

The *Mumbai Statement on Lifelong Learning* (UNESCO: 1998) supports this view:

The transformation to lifelong learning institutions requires a holistic approach which a) supports the institution becoming a lifelong learning community itself b) integrates academic, financial and administrative elements c) provides structures which are responsible for organizational staff, students and curriculum development and community engagement and d) aligns the various supportive structures such as academic information systems, library provision and learning technologies to the new mission of universities in learning societies.

This all-encompassing view of the university with a mission to serve the community in which it resides is not new. Land-grant universities in the United States of America have had that responsibility for many years. But it is now a guideline for all universities all around the world. Certainly local authorities in cities which aspire to become learning cities would be interested in discussing how that would manifest itself in reality.

Chapter 10

Employment and employability in the learning city – making learning work

---

A learning city effects plans to define and develop the skills and competencies which make all its citizens employable.

The European White Paper *Teaching and Learning* stresses the importance of employability. 'Work environment and organization are much more demanding than before,' it says, 'the pace of change is accelerating significantly. People have to adapt to constant upgrading and improving of their personal skills and knowledge.' The same White Paper points out that 'long-term unemployment continues to increase and the spread of social exclusion, particularly among young people, has become a major problem in our societies.'

So how can the city help its organizations large and small, in every sector of activity, to recognize that lifelong learning is the key to an employed future? Cities, towns and regions are in the front line of the battle against exclusion produced by unemployment and have to devise plans to combat it. But this battle demands four new approaches.

First, it has to be *innovative* – traditional formulae which have failed in the past don't often get a second chance to succeed. Learning environments and methods will have to change in order to attract those who, for whatever reason, have had bad experiences in education.

Second, it has to be *sensitive* – for those involved, the barriers are as much psychological as well as economic and social. Often the excluded do not believe that they are employable. They either have skills which they thought were for life and have been made redundant, or they have no skills at all, and it is a delicate process to bring them to understand that they are able to develop new skills.

Third, it has to be a *partnership* between different agencies in the city and co-ordinated into a city strategy – employability is not restricted to one single industry or sector. It is only at the city level that the overall vision exists to co-ordinate the various strands of need from school to university and from community to industrial education.

Fourth, it has to be well and positively *publicized* – hearts and minds have to be focused on the benefits of eventual success. While these may seem to be obvious they are not always collectively appreciated.

Every city has its flagship project to address these issues, and every country has national strategies to encourage re-training and re-skilling. The difference at the end of the 20th century is that these are now constants. The flagship project and the learning strategy must become the norm and must increase in number and in quality. Not only will this happen more frequently for more people but also the level and complexity of skills will have to increase over time. Many retraining courses are unfortunately specifically skill-based and the opportunity to transmit the message of lifelong learning is lost.

For many people courses will have to start at the very basic level. In Edinburgh, the ethos of community is very strong. Community Education Centres have been established in the more deprived areas of the city to 'help people gain access to education and employment' as their leaflet *Building Strong Communities* describes it. The Platform Adult Education Centre is one such. Platform doesn't run classes, it has groups. It offers free child care for people with families and the courses themselves are free. It doesn't push qualifications, but they are there if group members want them. It presents itself to potential learners through an attractively-written leaflet, sympathetically worded and aimed at making them believe that they can learn in a relaxed style. It offers individual guidance for each learner and the groups are small.

Platform operates in the Wester Hailes ward of the city, where a survey showed that the local average of people with numeracy and literacy difficulties was double the average for the UK. It therefore operates sensitively to the population it serves and attempts to overcome the barriers to learning existing in that part of the city. It offers courses on learning to learn, computers, confidence building and self-development, and elementary communication as well as more traditional courses such as English, Maths, Scottish History and Philosophy. It invites members of the public to become tutors and to offer courses in their own expertise. It explains that much of this can lead onto higher qualifications, but only if the learner wants to.

Platform is an excellent example of a city supporting an understanding centre, based in the community it serves, starting at the learner's level of comprehension, identifying potential barriers and leading its learners gently to confidence and success. More than 4200 volunteers support Community Education activities in the city, and over 34 000 people attend the courses. Second chance education towards the development of employability starts in places like these.

An innovative community project to address the unemployment situation comes from Wales and is a story from *The Observer* newspaper on September 1998. 'Jobless people are to be recruited as classroom assistants to help children with reading and maths,' the reporter Martin Bright claimed. 'The plans have been drawn up by the Welsh Office minister as part of the government's welfare-to-work scheme. The scheme for the young unemployed was announced in April and extended in September to those over 24 who have been unemployed for more than two years. Under the plan, thousands of jobless people could be signed up to help with the government's drive to boost the basics. They would also help with administrative tasks presently carried out by teachers. Schools would receive a subsidy to take on the assistants, who would be given the opportunity to go on to gain teaching qualifications. The proposals have won the approval of the Department for Education and Employment and will he extended to England if the Welsh scheme, expected to be launched next year, proves successful.

There was a semi-predictable response from the teacher's unions. The head of the National Association of Schoolmasters and Union of Women Teachers said, 'People need to be properly trained to help in schools. This cheap and nasty so-called solution doesn't show much respect for children or for the professionalism of teachers.'

As in the rest of the UK, Wales is suffering a teacher recruitment crisis. The Unions say teachers are leaving the profession because they are being forced to spend too much time on non-teaching tasks, chores that the scheme seeks to ameliorate. The Welsh Office minister disagrees. 'There is a perfect symmetry to my scheme,' he said. 'It is meeting a real need to improve reading, writing and maths, while getting people off benefit and into work. It will also give people a taste for teaching.' He added that candidates would be carefully vetted and that many well-qualified graduates were already entering the scheme. The secretary of the National Union of Teachers welcomed the initiative. 'We would have no difficulty in having more paid classroom assistants to release qualified teachers from some of their tasks as long as it was not imposed on schools. But we would want to make sure they weren't being used to replace existing assistants,' it said.

No project is 100 per cent good or bad and one has to make judgements about the shades of grey in-between. The teacher unions do of course have a legitimate objection within the prevailing mindset about the organization of schools. In that context, protectionist attitudes are perfectly understandable. But in a lifelong learning world, the system is examined in the context of 'who benefits' and 'what can work' from the point of view of the learner. It is looking for a win-win situation. If innovative schemes such as this can produce new insights and new learning opportunities, then it should not be dismissed on the grounds that it does not fit the existing paradigm. This book has argued in several chapters that schools need all the help they can get, and that resources to provide that help exist in all parts of the community. To deny learners the resources to help them learn is the opposite of learner-focus. This is particularly so when employability is one of those focuses.

Two excellent examples of the municipality creating employability come from Göteborg in Sweden. At national level the government started a scheme called 'Knowledge Boost' to increase the knowledge and skills of people under threat of unemployment. Every city and sizeable town participated in its own way. Göteborg initiated a project called 'Competence in Göteborg', which became the largest municipal training programme in Sweden. It was a formidable challenge and its cost was some 250 million crowns (about $35m).

The main objective of 'Competence in Göteborg' was to offer training to employees risking redundancy or to retrain them for new assignments. A large part of the scheme targeted persons who were on the verge of redundancy due to their lack of deeper or wider competence. 17 000 municipal employees of the city who were at risk of unemployment, were offered the opportunity of either preparing themselves for new jobs or assignments, for which they lacked skills, or preparing them to move on to other employment. Many of the courses designed for the project were on-the-job courses and taken during paid hours. Half of the financial burden was borne by the central government on condition that the City of Göteborg did not terminate any employment contracts during the project, a condition which the city also fulfilled.

The project had some very notable results. Women with low previous education were given a considerable lift by the scheme. In the evaluation survey 88 per cent of them made very positive remarks about their courses, especially with regard to personal satisfaction and said that they had been spurred on to further improvement of their own skills and competencies. Not surprisingly the city itself obtained some benefit by demonstrating its interest in the development of skills and further training in a programme established on its own initiative.

Another notable effect was that it speeded up the discussion of the city as a Learning Organization. Public bodies tend to be hampered in their development as learning organizations by the weight of their own rules and regulations. In Göteborg, there are clear indications that a shift from hierarchical structures, with several levels of management and decision-making, is taking place towards more horizontal patterns of organization.

Even the Council Department of Education became heavily involved in the training courses.

The second scheme – 'Competence development of skilled labour' – gave an insight into the benefits of public-private participation organized by the city itself and covers the preparation of young adults for the workplace. It is a network programme linking both existing and new projects for industrial development with a major theme of Lifelong Learning, and the objective is to develop and test models for competence development in close connection with production processes in companies. The major question to be asked was 'how can we create conditions beneficial to learning?' It presented another challenge to find practical methods to assess future demands on the workforce and measure the competence required. The programme is being run in close collaboration with companies in larger Göteborg and is expected to strengthen the competitiveness of industrial enterprises in West Sweden.

The involvement of teachers has a positive spin-off on both schools and their students. It is important that the industrial community sends out clear messages about the bright future of industry as an occupation for bright youngsters. And industrial companies in the region of West Sweden, especially Volvo, have in fact succeeded in doing so. In autumn 1998 Göteborg opened a new type of upper secondary school for industrial technology in co-operation with Volvo. The school will formally fit into the public school system. It is a win-win situation for the company and the city. For Volvo as co-founder there is a vested interest in securing qualified competence for the company in the long term. The Education Department on its part will be able to design modern courses, for use throughout the city, which form the basis for the students' future employability and qualify them for higher studies. There are already 350 applications from 9th grade students for admission to the first 90 places but there are plans to raise the number of places by 270 students by the year 2000.

As Lars Franson (1998), the city's Director of Education, says, 'The speed of technological change in industry poses an ever-growing challenge to education in our upper secondary school. Education itself has to be a link in the chain of lifelong learning. The knowledge acquired there by young people must be applicable to the requirements of industry today and tomorrow.'

If the objective is employability, many cities will be experimenting with lifelong learning projects of this kind during the coming years. The challenge is to develop a strategy around which all young people and adults can benefit. Partnerships with employing organizations will be an essential component of those strategies, as will new skills-based curriculum development, new resource deployment and any project which makes citizens more aware of, and comfortable with, the need for continuous updating.

Chapter 11

Aspirations for the learning city –
raising the sights

A learning city activates the creative potential of its citizens through a strategy for encouraging the use of personal learning plans, mentors and guides in citizens of all ages.

Sometimes the development of a citizen's human potential and creativity relies on a more formal array of tools and techniques to aid lifelong learning. It gives a stronger 'why' and a more structured 'how'. It also helps to have a friend or an acquaintance as a mentor to discuss and update the plans and recommend ways of achieving the objectives. 'Personal learning plans' are one example of the former and are increasingly used in industry, as is the system of guides and mentors. Individuals respond more positively when they have articulated their own personal goals and learning ambitions. This can be done with the assistance of a Learning Counsellor (see Chapter 2) or with another person with the skills to ask the right questions and understand the significance of the answers. A personal learning plan can chart learning goals for the next one, three and/or five years in three domains – personal development, skills for work and skills and knowledge for leisure.

Make it Happen is a Personal Learning Action Plan available from the UK Campaign for Learning. It starts with the individual and tries to get him/her to think about life, work and change. It encourages the plan owner to take more control of the future by considering:

- what you have learnt and achieved;
- what you have enjoyed learning;
- what you are proud of having achieved;
- what you can do now that you could not do before.

The language used is comprehensible and non-threatening, trying to penetrate the thought processes of the owner, and particularly the individual who, for whatever reason, may have doubts or misconceptions about learning. It stresses that this is a voluntary activity.

The preliminary section prepares the way. Under the 'What have I learnt' section plan owners are invited to write down five experiences about what they have learnt in the past, when it was, what helped and what hindered. They are then led to explore further what has helped in the past to reinforce what will be useful in the future, and why they may wish to return to learning.

The next step articulates a personal wish list. It involves 'looking forward into your life and identifying personal goals, comparing all you have learnt and achieved already with what you hope for the future'. Thus plan owners are encouraged to consider what they might wish to learn in six different individual environments:

- as an individual;
- as a member of a family;
- in relation to work, or sometimes lack of work;
- in relation to future work or retirement;
- in relation to leisure activities;
- in relation to the community.

They are also encouraged to estimate how long each wish may take to fulfil. Hints are given. Past and future learning can be achieved through a variety of means – self-study, experiential learning, skills development, personal improvement – and within a variety of fields – improved teamwork, better communication, as a parent or a club secretary, in music, or financial management (including family budgets), do-it-yourself activities – and with a variety of recognitions – certificates, degrees, diplomas, testimonials or none of these.

Next comes thinking about the hit list for future development – for personal improvement, for work, for leisure, for family. Does it involve doing something, reading something, communicating something, for qualification or not, impressing someone, formal or informal learning? And this is followed up by reflecting upon who could be of help – job centres, libraries, careers offices, managers, friends, Adult Education Centres, the media, universities. Here is where a Learning Counsellor in the community would be particularly useful. A helpful matrix is presented with personal development, home life and work life along one axis and technical learning, personal learning and conceptual learning along the other.

Having put together a plan along these lines, the plan owner is encouraged to take action and given guidelines on how to monitor and review their progress at fairly frequent intervals. Potential obstacles are identified such as unrealistic goals, low motivation, lack of confidence, lack of support so that they can be seen as problems to be overcome rather than unexpected barriers to learning.

This may too large and complex for some and insufficiently structured for others. For yet others, a trip through the processes and questions might be enough without the need to develop a formal plan. Flexibility is a necessary virtue. However, it is an example of how learning needs can be articulated and encouraged and highlights the opportunities for the exercise of leadership skills in all parts of the community. At the present time the European Lifelong Learning Initiative is developing a template for a flexible European Personal Learning Plan through its 'Eurotoolls' project based on funding from the European Commission's Socrates programme. This will be available for downloading from summer 1999.

Mentors and guides are also useful for stimulating learning development. The classical definition of a mentor comes from the story of Telemachus who, during his many necessary voyages away from home, asked his friend Mentor to be available as a friend for his son, a task which he willingly and successfully accomplished. In the modern day, mentors can be friends, teachers, managers, or even someone unknown to the learner. They may even be people in another town or country. Mentoring can be carried out through individual contact, through e-mail or over the telephone. A register of mentors might be established at community level.

Indeed such a register is already being developed in the 'Learning Jamat' project, an initiative to develop a Learning Community within one Muslim sect with members in Portugal, France and the UK, and led by the author. This incorporates a learning audit (see Chapter 15) with a double aim. Members of the 'Jamat' (loosely, Community) have a long tradition of contribution to others within their own community and are diligent seekers after knowledge and personal and family improvement. In the audit they are encouraged both to express their needs for learning and their potential contribution to the learning of others. From this will develop a personal learning plan for each of the participants with a register of mentors so that each has the support and guidance of another person in the pursuance of explicit individual goals.

Learners may wish to have several mentors for several subjects. Equally each learner would benefit from being a mentor to someone else on a different topic. These ideas work well in industry and could work equally well at the community level. Another example comes from a Vocational Adult Education Partnership in Finland and reported in a report by Markkula and Suurla (1998). Four organizations took part:

- Tekmanni, a constructional engineering enterprise;
- the vocational Adult Education centre;
- Helsinki Bureau of Apprenticeships Contracts;
- Federation of Finnish Metal Engineering and Electrotechnical Industries.

The aim of the project was to find new ways of combining education and work, and to use existing human resources in the enterprises as trainers, mentors and tutors. A training course was developed using a variety of methods – e-mail, tutor visits, teamwork exercises, video-conferences and distance learning assignments. After this, employees worked in teams of two, three and four, acting as mentors for each other using the same methods as on the course. Thus mentors could act as such without being in the same physical location, and everyone in the workforce became a learner. The project, which completed its first phase in 1997, was so successful that it is being extended to other organizations in Finland.

Mentoring is already carried out in some schools. *Bringing business into learning – a practical guide for schools* (Schools Council Industry Project 1997) contains guidelines for the development of mentoring skills. It describes the role of the mentor as using the particular talents, skills and resources of the mentor to support the particular needs and abilities of a student. Current schemes cover all ages from primary schools to higher education, but all of them share the common aims of helping the student to achieve identified learning goals by implementing a strategy, providing support and carrying out on-going reviews.

All mentoring programmes, it says, have certain features in common which can be applied to any school or college seeking to set up a scheme. The co-ordinator must always ensure the commitment of the senior management team and establish a support team to run and monitor the scheme.

First it is essential that everyone, mentor and student, is clear about the programme and its aims. In the context of the school or college, there may be a 'needs assessment' exercise, based on transparent criteria. These would include such items as attendance, time keeping, attitude to school/college, coursework completion, personal confidence and self-esteem, career aspirations, examination expectations and individual subject performance.

Secondly, the scheme needs an objectives policy identifying the evidence to be used to evaluate its success, and thirdly, mentors should be chosen carefully and sensitively to optimize success. For example, a scheme aimed at developing positive attitudes to school and work among black boys will use black males in employment as role models and mentors. Or a scheme to tackle lateness and absenteeism in Years 9/10 could draw mentors from local industry and business, while a scheme for Years 7/8 to foster positive use of leisure time and discourage crime and drug-related activities could use mentors from the voluntary sector.

A Mentorship training programme is advisable. Training should include:

- familiarization with current educational practice;
- an understanding of the ethos of the school or college;
- knowledge of how the school or college normally deals with the problem the scheme seeks to address;
- issues of confidentiality for both student and mentor;
- the development of listening skills by the mentor.

Equally, the students need to commit themselves to the project, and to understand what is involved in the mentoring process. They need also to explore their expectations, opportunities and constraints.

Matching students to mentors is a careful and sensitive task. Opportunities for withdrawal by either side should always be available and a backup plan should always be in place. Both student and mentor should understand the commitment they have made and have realistic expectations after the initial enthusiasm. Disappointment for both student and mentor can be counterproductive. Equally, in this context, the scheme will need to be supervised – a sort of mentoring of the mentors.

There are hundreds of possibilities and opportunities for good mentoring programmes as a support for learning within a learning city, at all ages and within all sectors. A learning city may wish to develop a personal learning plan and mentoring programme for its own citizens so that it fits the culture of the city. The university would be able to assist with the plan development in association with colleges and schools. It should consider also a two-part plan which includes not just the learning requirements of each citizen, but also some questions about what that citizen can do to assist the learning of others. Learners gain great confidence in their own learning by doing so.

Chapter 12

Resources for the learning city – increasing the assets

A learning city releases the full potential of community resources, including human resources, by enabling mutually beneficial partnerships between public and private sectors.

Those who advocate lifelong learning recognize that vast sums of money are not going to be made available to implement it. And yet they know that new resources will need to be made available. Where are these resources to come from? This book has already provided some indicators in Chapter 3. Resources will be released through such devices as integrated budgets, more efficient use of existing plant and equipment and sharing programmes. But, above all it is through the identification of new, unused, unappreciated and untapped resources already existing within a learning city. Chapman and Aspin (1997) give a clue. 'Schools are a community resource,' they say. 'They are funded and supported by the community, and part of their responsibility is to be open, available and accountable to the community.' This means that schools need to consider being open for many more hours, making their facilities and skills a general community resource, serving the community of which they are a part.'

This is just one example of underused physical resources. What about human resources? In *Lifelong Learning*, Longworth and Davies describe the benefits of a close partnership scheme, 'twinning', between a school in inner London and IBM in much detail. The rationale is simple. Making available the resources of each organization for the benefit of each other greatly enhances the learning and the active participation in each. Skills, talents and knowledge become a common resource to both. The reputations of the organizations are also considerably enhanced as a result. The availability of 700 highly trained professionals in an inner-city school for an hour a week not only broke down stereotypes but also transformed the perceptions, the understanding and the motivation of staff and students alike. And this was a two-way process.

This is just one example of positive symbiosis arising from the sharing of human and physical resources between apparently dissimilar organizations. In the United States of America, many companies have joined the vogue to help schools. Adopt-a-school (see Chapter 3) is commonplace in many cities, although the label tends to pre-vision a one-way transfer of knowledge and resources, rather than a mutual exchange of understanding. Each project has its own objectives. In one, mentoring programmes in which a company employee will act as an advisor and friend to a student are one example of activity while in another company management courses for teachers might have more appeal, though the range of operations in most programmes is wide and responds to expressed needs. Some, like the Chase Manhattan Bank in New York, concentrate on one topic with business students, while others cover a wide variety of social, as well as curriculum, needs.

One enterprising, in every sense of the word, example of public-private partnership comes from Edinburgh. In the words of its policy document:

> Lifelong learning is more than a concept. It is a way of looking at education and training throughout life where the influences of science and technology, the restructuring of industry and economic imperatives, the changes in the nature of work, environmental requirements and education for a wider role in a democratic society are all critical factors. Lifelong learning provides an approach to achieving the objectives set out in the Council's City Strategy; its regeneration strategy and Edinburgh's Economic Future.

These are ideals recognizable to every city already on the road to becoming a learning city, but Edinburgh is setting about implementation in a different, and modern, way. It will establish a company limited by guarantee, with a board of directors consisting of founding partners. The Company will have revenue-raising powers from annual subscriptions, covenanted donations and sponsorship from businesses and organizations across the city and grants from the city council. Its operation will be financed through contributions from the partners from the public, private, business, voluntary and community sectors of the city. It builds on the existing strengths and achievements of education and training provision and takes them forward into a lifelong learning future. The remit of the company is to:

- provide a coherent framework for the development of lifelong learning strategies;
- create a learning culture within the City;
- develop collaborative work between sectors and organizations;
- improve and increase access to existing learning opportunities in and out of the workplace;

- identify and disseminate good practice and thus improve the quality of learning for all;
- promote lifelong learning within individual organizations and sectors;
- attract new resources for the promotion and development of lifelong learning activities in Edinburgh.

By developing and implementing strategies and projects to unite all the social partners and organizations in the city – school and post-school sectors, further and higher education establishments, libraries, museums, societies, business and industry – into a coherent and co-operative effort, it will address and progress lifelong learning issues, including the fight against exclusion.

It thus becomes, under one organization, a shared responsibility between private, public, business, voluntary and community sectors, and is intended to achieve benefits which otherwise could not be realized through individual effort. It will also work with other local, national and international partners.

More particularly, the company will concentrate on:

- regular, targeted information to the public about education and training opportunities in and out of the workplace;
- development of networks to improve quality of information and guidance;
- identification of collaborative arrangements to ensure access for all;
- identification and development of the role and place of information technology in a learning city;
- involvement of local people in regeneration initiatives;
- improvement of links between small to medium enterprises and education and training providers;
- strengthening the links between business and community;
- participation in European projects to extend knowledge and understanding of lifelong learning policies and practice;
- strategies to enable the National Education and Training Targets to be achieved;
- promote community-based flexible approaches which overcome barriers experienced by disadvantaged groups.

Moreover, the company now has an international dimension in that it houses the administrative headquarters of the European Lifelong Learning Initiative.

This presents a different view of the leadership problem posed in Chapter 9. No one sector now has the responsibility of using its resources to direct the effort, often within its own image and interests. It is the responsibility of all to co-operate, and to draw strength from others, within the aegis of the company.

Another example comes from Göteborg in Sweden. The island of Hisingen is a former shipbuilding community, which now houses high-tech industries, mostly small and medium-sized businesses specializing in all aspects of the information and communications industry. More recently university departments have moved in to help create a formal partnership between industry, research and teaching through the establishment of a learning centre on the island. Not only this, but, through the Goteborg City Education Department, the schools on the island also have access to the learning environment so developed. Chambers of Commerce and Trade Development Associations also help to maximize the export and distribution potential arising from this fusion of expertise.

The learning facility, Lindholmen Knowledge Centre, lies at the heart of a renewed shipyard area, a set of former warehouses tastefully redesigned and equipped with the technology to provide both high-class teaching and world-class research. It functions as a meeting place between education and industry. A constant dialogue about the companies' needs and the content and methodology of education is created, and this results in courses tailored for particular companies, workplace training and education aimed at increasing personal competence and technical skills. Smaller companies get help with product development and can test new products in a laboratory. Among the futuristic resources for better learning is a Virtual Reality facility, in which new technologies can be demonstrated and developed in co-operation between educators and companies.

Five pre-university level gymnasia (schools), the Hisingen Gymnasium for Adults and other adult-education facilities, Chalmers University of Technology, AMU, the national labour market organization and 20 companies share the use of the knowledge centre and form a vibrant, modern and constantly changing learning environment for more than 7000 people. The availability of well-equipped educational premises, costly, but shared educational and technical equipment and a rare combination of personal skills makes this both an exciting and cost-beneficial place to learn and work. It is shortly to be supplemented with an Enterprise Park to attract more education–industry co-operation, more high-level research and more resource-sharing.

Finally a resource-sharing example, quoted in the European Round Table of Industrialists 1997 book, *A Stimulus to Job Creation*, involves collaboration between large and small companies and local government employment offices in the Netherlands. Here, small and medium-sized companies have difficulties in training their own people. They rarely have the resources to seek or train recruits. So, in order to address this problem, the Philips company makes room in its Dutch divisions to give a year's work experience to 800 long term unemployed people, falling mostly into four categories:

- those with no, or the wrong, qualifications;
- women re-entering the labour market;
- foreign nationals who need training or re-training;
- disabled people.

The students are chosen in co-operation with the local labour office, and between them they match the training to the current and future demands of local companies. So far over 7500 long-term unemployed people have been trained and about 80 per cent of the trainees find paid jobs after their training. In addition, SMEs acquire new staff who are immediately productive. One interesting aspect of the course is that it is essentially a learning-by-doing experience concentrating on satisfying the future, as well as the present, marketplace. The company maintains that the programme does not cost very much to run. The number of work-experience places is set at 2 per cent of the regular Philips payroll staff in the Netherlands.

In the same booklet, the example of Iberdrola, Spain's largest electrical power company, provides more evidence of an innovative approach. Regional development is fundamental to the company's corporate strategy. It has established a small office in Bilbao to energize links between Iberdrola and regional governments in which the company helps in several ways. These include training individuals, promoting innovation and new technologies, providing consultancy services and diagnostic studies, mentoring SMEs and promoting the region. Since this is a collaboration activity which does not compete with academic or indigenous industrial institutions, these are all done on a matched funding basis – the company pays half and the regional authority the other half. It is not altruism. The company maintains that every wealth-creating activity it performs for a region also creates wealth and influence for the company. But within a seven year period in the 1990s it developed 12 regional technology institutes, 11 computer and electronic centres, 24 technology days for universities and SMEs (creating further links between these), 30 SME Management courses, and 3 diagnostic studies.

These are just a few examples of the way in which resources from one sector of the community can be used to provide resources for others, not just in the same community but in neighbouring cities, towns and neighbourhoods. They are but the tip of the iceberg. Learning cities can profit from developing such links in every way – wealth-creation projects, learning development using up-to-date techniques, productive partnership programmes, equipment donation, mentoring – the list is long. It is perhaps worth mentioning that, according to Logan, only 26 countries have a GDP larger than General Motors' annual revenues, and that the company is responsible for the livelihood of about 9 million people around the world. Its educational commitment is huge and highly innovative. And it is shareable with the many cities in which it has a presence, as is that of the many other multinational companies in the corporate environment.

To recapitulate the points made in the first paragraphs of this chapter, the physical, conceptual and human resources in every great city are waiting to be tapped. To initiate the lifelong learning process, great efforts need to be made to unlock the potential of its people, and make better use of buildings, equipment, expertise and open spaces, to mention but a few. It could be the subject of a creative brainstorming session in every city.

Chapter 13

Networks in the learning city – communicating with the world

A Learning city nourishes tolerance and outward-looking mindsets through innovative projects to link citizens of all races, ages and creeds locally, nationally and internationally.

Modern communications technology, and particularly the Internet, offers the possibility and the implicit excitement of linking people of all ages to each other as never before. They respect no local, regional and national boundary, nor do they prevent open communication between different races, creeds or age. The son of a Glasgow carpenter can interact freely and openly with the daughter of an Indian rice-grower, exploring and contrasting ways of life, the constraints of weather patterns, food and drink, belief systems and all the richness and diversity of their respective lifestyles. A retired French baker can converse with a young Vietnamese garage owner and each can step outside of the mindsets dictated by lack of time, finance and understanding into another world of international fascination. A Russian entrepreneur from Perm can contact an American industrialist from Cleveland, Ohio, and each can understand the marketing constraints and opportunities in their respective communities. All of them might be fulfilling one of the precepts of the distinguished Brazilian educationist, Paulo Freire, that real liberation is possible only through popular participation.

Genuine learning cities are by nature outward-looking. Learning itself is outward-looking. It opens up the mind. Those cities with cybercafes or Internet facilities in libraries, as in the Manchester Community Information Network (see Chapter 14) or other public places know that their clientele covers all ages, all groups and all dispositions. None of them report a lack of commitment or interest, rather the opposite. Such facilities enable new people, moving from one community to another, to recognize in each the ambience of learning and use it as a means of integration. A learning city, like a learning organization, never stops learning from others. Once it does so it is no longer a learning city. It draws in the experiences, knowledge and insights of other places and other people for the development of its people and the growth of its trade. Figure 13.1, at the end of this chapter, shows one of the goals of the European Lifelong Learning Initiative, shared by the European Commission, to create a vast network of Learning Cities throughout Europe, learning from each other and linking their citizens and organizations in a complex web of interconnection and interaction. The relative cheapness of international electronic mail and interest forum networks makes this a real possibility. This is backed up through the ELLIcities forum of the Learning Highway project to provide case studies of good Learning City practice, forums through which city planners and educators, among others, can discuss topics of common interest, and even Internet-delivered courses and seminars on Lifelong Learning.

Industry and business have communicated in this way for several years, but now the facility is expanded to schoolchildren, professional interest groups, city councillors and third age groups. Yet again, Edinburgh provides an example of the latter. The evocatively named 'Cyber Grannies' project is a collaborative venture between the Community Education Service and Craigmillar Community Information Services (CCIS). In the Jack Kane Community Centre a group of third age pensioners supplement their lunch club activities by 'surfing the net'. Community leaders established the scheme to dispel the 'fear and mystery' often expressed by the older generation about modern technology. Every Monday morning the group took part in 'sessions' at the CCIS office. During one such session the name 'Cyber Grannies' was coined. The 'Cyber Grannies' are now e-mail account holders, and they spend even more time developing their skills at the centre itself. They are involved in cross-generational work with the 'Keyboard Kids', another CCIS project and have visited Internet cafes on three occasions. They are now planning the next stage of their project and exploring ideas surrounding genealogy, reminiscence, or producing a worldwide recipe book. Their interest now extends to contributing to the Internet. More recently, Craigmillar has extended its range of network-based projects to include 'Digital Dads', 'Modem Mums' and 'Techno-tots'. One could perhaps wager that the latter make the most progress the most quickly. Next 'Fibre-optic families'? There is no doubt that Craigmillar is creating the future in a very visible and exciting way, and that the participants in these projects are leading the way into a century in which communication is a prerogative, and a learning pathway, for everyone. Nor is it alone. Similar community-based projects are spreading rapidly into other cities and towns around the planet.

The PLUTO project provided several other examples in the late 1980s. This was established to provide links between teachers in training in several different countries of Europe and extended into the schools through teaching practice. Among the common databases established were dietary habits in different countries, acid rain measurements for comparison between the UK, Belgium and

Norway, and language learning links between pre-service teachers and, in one case, supervised language learning links between schoolchildren in Manchester and Copenhagen. The power and the novelty of the network not only encouraged active and fruitful English language learning for the Danish children, marked by the English pupils, but also provided the motivation in some of the English children to learn Danish. This is unusual in English schools.

It is in schools that the effective use of networks will have the most benefit. Inter-school networks across Europe are proliferating from the European Schools network, to the national networks of Denmark, Finland (freenet) and Norway, to which all schools are linked. Goteborg in Sweden has put every child onto a special version of the Internet and Southampton secondary schools are also well endowed with computers and network access. Its Executive Director of Education somewhat wryly points out that already he knows of two secondary schoolchildren who have made more than £50,000 each from the Internet this year.

One forward-looking European programme 'Cyberspace Learning for Kids' aims to develop an intercultural network across Europe for children aged 5–16. This ten country project was described at the Theme Conference of the European Year of Lifelong Learning organized by ELLInet Finland on behalf of ELLI. Its remit is large: 'The network provides an environment within which children can learn together and play together, teachers can develop and deliver learning activities, databases of information and teaching and learning resources are accessed and parents can be involved in the process of education and child development.' It was particularly aimed at disabled and disadvantaged children. Results demonstrate that it is possible to give children the facility to see the world through the eyes and minds of other children and adults whose viewpoint may be very different from their own.

A similar network operates on a much grander scale in Canada. Schoolnet, a network of the provincial providers of electronic networks for education, is available to every school. Further, although it is neither free nor public, its board is packed with educationists who make sure it remains affordable. It negotiates preferential telephone rates for schools and is linked to organizations which can provide less expensive refurbished computers. A number of computer databases are made available, including local and national history, and the full books of remembrance of Canadians who fought in wars, and wetlands and sustainable development. Educational games and simulations likewise. The benefits and uses are described in its descriptive pamphlet produced by Industry Canada.

Students, it claims, can stimulate their imagination, develop the confidence to explore challenging new subjects, gain a broader knowledge of the outside world and develop marketable skills in information technology.

Teachers can access a global reservoir of information complementing their expertise and including experts and databases around the world. They can discuss the best educational practices and resources nationally and internationally, and create their own deliverable learning materials. One might add that they can also

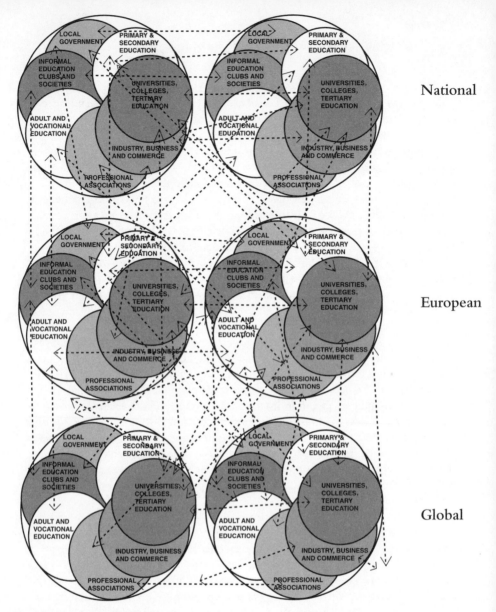

National

European

Global

Linking for what?

1. Business to business for wealth creation.
2. School to school to teacher training for collaborative learning, accessing and creating databases, language learning, research into learning, teacher updating, etc.
3. University to university to industry for joint research, joint curriculum development, student exchange, continuing education, professional development, etc.
4. Third age to third age for social communication, etc in the later years.
5. Hospital to hospital for medical comparison, exchange of ideas and practice, etc.
6. Local government to local government to adult education to museums for collaborative learning projects twinning activities, language learning, leadership development, etc.
7. Professional associations to members in all communities, etc.
8. Vocational education to adult for open and distance education development and training, etc.
9. Individual to individual, community to community, organization to organization for everything under the sun. Schools/industry links, inter-community mentoring, volunteer services, etc.
10. Developed to developing world to improve global performance.

Figure 13.1 Linking learning communities in a learning world

develop courses which challenge students to learn individually, in teams with their classmates, internationally with others from other countries and with a wide variety of experts, including their own teachers and parents, as required of a lifelong learning world. The role of the teacher as an empowerer of knowledge and an enabler of learning activity, inserting him/herself into the communication, has already been discussed as a new and urgent skill in Chapter 2.

Through Schoolnet and other networks parents can participate in their children's education, make homework into a family adventure and encourage children to higher achievement levels. They can communicate with teachers and access information on developments in educational practice, grants, universities etc.

Administrators and those who sit on the governing bodies of schools cam communicate better with each other between meetings, forge stronger links with the community and make economies in bulk purchases for the school. All in all, this is an impressive range of activities for all which can transform the school into a learning, communicating, challenging and exciting environment. It will also transform the role of the teacher beyond recognition.

Such links are exciting and innovative, and they open up real possibilities for understanding and co-operation, but the secret of success lies with enthusiastic and sensitive teachers and community leaders, who understand the power of the technology to motivate and stimulate. The advantage of such schemes is that, once set along the right road, very little further training is needed. Ownership of the learning passes quickly onto the participants.

Finally to the power of the technology to link learning cities with each other as shown in Figure 13.1. So that cyber grannies can communicate with cyber grandads in other cities, schools and colleges in collaborative learning programmes with schools and colleges, health carers with health carers across social services departments and last, but certainly not least, the role of networks in developing wealth-creating trade links between companies of all sizes increases. How this can be done is explained in greater detail in Chapter 16.

Chapter 14

Information in the learning city – broadcasting the learning news

---

A learning city increases participation in learning by devising innovative strategies to provide information where people gather, and proactive publicity campaigns to promote learning.

To take advantage of learning, citizens of a learning city need to know about learning. Further, they need it from accessible places, presented in an attractive way that stimulates them to want to learn. A learning city will make information available at the workplace, at community centres, in shopping malls, through the media and everywhere people congregate.

The University of Sunderland in the UK has long been a pioneer of lifelong learning activities in this area. Perhaps its most well-known project is the learning centre established near the Gateshead Metro Centre, one of the largest under-cover shopping centres in Europe. Here a drop-in learning centre, fully equipped with computers and training staff, is available to shoppers as and when they feel they want to use it. Over time, and as people drop their defensiveness to learning, it is becoming much more popular and offering a range of courses according to demand. At Learning World, as it is called, people can combine their weekly shopping with courses ranging from MBA through Open University facilities to National Vocational Qualifications (NVQs). Access to the Internet allows people to obtain information about other courses in the region of Tyne and Wear.

But Sunderland University is also pioneering the way in other initiatives, now being taken up by the vast University for Industry Programme of the British Government. It operates a free telephone helpline, which the British Government now does on a national basis; it uses commercial marketing techniques to sell 'learning'; it offers its courses in 35 learning centres outside of the university in football stadia, schools and libraries as well as shopping centres; its one stop shop approach gives people access to hundreds of courses, materials and free taster lessons. This is an excellent example of a proactive approach, taking learning and information about learning directly to the people.

In the Hertfordshire region of the UK, the local TEC (Training and Enterprise Council) has adopted a focused approach to increasing the general educational level of the population. As a part of this, information and guidance is a key strategy. The TEC identified seven groups likely to have different sets of learning needs within the learning framework. These are (in alphabetical order) Employed People, Employers, the non-Employed, the self-Employed, Third Agers, the Unemployed and Young Adults (16 to 21).

Within each of these categories the differences in gender, ethnic origin, ability and motivation are recognized as is the fact that many groups may have different reasons to embrace learning. Third age groups for example would not see career advancement as a major reason for learning but they could have a very beneficial influence on the learning of others.

A strategy has been set in place to ensure accessible provision for each of the groups to information, advice and guidance and to learning itself. The strategy involves the co-operation of all institutions in the county either as 'Learning Information Points', 'Learning Advice Centres' or 'Learning Centres', while some may combine two functions (eg 'Information and Learning Centre') and others encompass all three. The county has been divided into 29 smaller localities both for information-giving and delivery of education, though of course citizens of any one locality can attend courses in any other. In this way the demand for particular publications attracting people to learning can be determined and all groups are kept informed through the network of information centres.

Of course the new technologies can also provide more sophisticated help with the process of information dissemination. The Manchester Community Information Network is an example.

It combines the opportunity to make ordinary citizens more familiar with the use of computers with an information service for citizens. In an article published in the *Electronic Library,* Alec Gallimore, Central Library Manager of Manchester Public Libraries, describes how this works. The public library has joined with the Citizens Advice Bureau, a national firm of management consultants, local voluntary groups and city council departments to establish the Information Network. It provides information on demand to members of the community through public terminals in the form of World Wide Web pages with access to local databases. There is also a project to develop public information touch screen kiosks. As in Edinburgh, the partners have established themselves as a limited company called MCIN with a board of directors containing representatives from each of these organizations.

Each partner brings its own Web pages, local database resources, premises and experience to MCIN. These are mounted on the Manchester host computer by

Poptel, a local Internet service provider. The library service has provided two venues for the terminals in north and south Manchester and two further terminals are being placed in other libraries as part of a new development originally called TARDIS, which will offer an improved kiosk version of the MCIN information.

The system provides access to Web pages from the main partners and databases. One of the most popular sources is Jobs Update, giving details of City Council job vacancies. The Citizens Advice Bureau operates its own community advice pages, while MIND maintains a database of mental health services. There is also an A–Z of Council services.

The partnership started out by looking for solutions to the problem of community information provision and realized the potential of Web browser software and Internet techniques to do something different. Poptel was responsible for mounting the Web pages and database on their server. KPMG provided expertise in the early phase in designing the user interface, which was based upon Netscape. This was modified to prevent general Internet surfing and to confine users to the MCIN information.

Apart from the time of individuals involved and the running costs on site, there have been no major financial burdens on either the City Council or on voluntary groups. Funding for the project worker came from SRB or European funding via the Economic Initiatives Group of the Chief Executives department of the City Council. The equipment used was donated by KPMG.

Many private organizations are now looking to get in on the act, usually technology-based companies, which want to find a market for their systems. MCIN partners have now realized that their locally-based information is quite valuable for such ventures. Whatever technology comes along there will be a demand for useful content. MCIN may see itself more as a content provider in future rather than trying to cope with an ever-expanding electronic community information infrastructure.

In many ways MCIN, as a public–private partnership, is leading the way in the delivery of community information, although other councils are catching up fast. It has put in a bid for National Lottery money for future growth and it has become a registered charity. TARDIS, a European-funded project involving the cities of Manchester and Barcelona. SEMA is providing the software and the kiosks and Virgin is acting as sponsor. Magic Touch terminals are being placed in six venues in Manchester. These represent a technological advance and more information is being added. There will also be some advertising to help pay for the running costs. The kiosks will have information held on local drives rather than the Internet, and this will be updated regularly using ISDN lines.

But sometimes there is a need to be even more proactive and to take the possibility of learning more directly to the potential learners. The European Year of Lifelong Learning encouraged other projects to bring learning and learning information to the people. NIACE, which co-ordinated that effort, reports a number of innovative examples. In the Yorkshire area of the UK, Airedale and Wharfedale

College carried out an outreach project to people who remain sceptical about learning. With the help of Tetley's Breweries members of the college developed a questionnaire on learning and visited six inner-city pubs in Leeds. They discovered that 40 per cent of the people sampled had taken no courses in the last five years and 21 per cent had had no further education since leaving school. However they went further and asked whether they would be interested in taking courses if they could be brought to the pub. 56 per cent thought this an excellent idea. Thus courses were delivered by members of the college staff on local history, ordering drinks abroad, calligraphy for Christmas cards and fitness for stress management.

In a similar vein, Rycotewood College in Hertfordshire targeted women who might consider returning to learning at their hairdressers. With the agreement of the owners they left leaflets detailing learning opportunities in the locality and trained stylists to talk about it in their conversations with the women.

The process of information-giving is well recognized to be a key element in a company strategy to get people into the learning habit. So it is with the Learning City, though it is a much more complex and varied task demanding creative and innovative initiatives. Interesting the uninterested, including the excluded and motivating the unmotivated is an uphill task. The example of these two initiatives can be extended to restaurants, sports stadia, shops and department stores, medical centres and hospitals.

But in many cases, information on a take-it-or-leave-it basis is not enough. Both the format and the content of the message will need to be attractively presented. The approach to the potential learner has to proclaim the advantages and the enjoyment to be had from learning. It will need to use the same media techniques used to market everyday products – television jingles, eye-catching advertisements, promotional events and special deals.

Appendix 2 describes a Learning Festival in Japan. This is the sort of event which all cities aspiring to become Learning Cities should consider. There, Lifelong Learning was presented as a pleasurable activity, something everyone does, a celebration of being human and able to learn.

The results of learning can be proclaimed. Motivation is much greater if for example children's art is to be displayed in a company foyer, as happened in the IBM scheme, or the English composition is to be highlighted in the local press, or language work is shared with parents and the community around, or project work is presented on radio or television. Lessons on particular subjects can draw in the experts, professional and amateur, as arbiters and helpers – the local ornithological or historical or geographical society.

The media can offer a sympathetic and understanding ear to the world of learning, emphasizing new methodologies positively, explaining the why, the what and the how and describing success stories.

Such positive publicity for learning has become commonplace in Japan. In a comparative survey of Lifelong Learning, it is reported that 3115 out of the 3200 City Boards of Education use magazines for Public Relations purposes. 2865 of them frequently distributed pamphlets about learning matters, 2435 offered learning counselling via a hotline. Many of them inserted articles about learning in newspapers and had local radio programmes. Posters are to be seen frequently in Japanese towns, while 58.4 per cent of local authorities put computer systems in libraries for the use of their citizens. Some libraries even had lifelong learning centres, rooms where adults could obtain advice on learning and where and how it could be carried out.

LEARNING CAN BE FUN

ONLY YOU CAN MAKE IT SO

BUT WE CAN HELP TOO

Telephone xxxxxxx

Figure 14.1 Learning can be fun

What message does all of this give to aspiring learning cities? First, that information given on a take-it-or-leave-it basis will only attract existing learners to learn more. What has to be transmitted is the excitement, the advantages and the pleasure of learning – taking away the terror which some people have of exposing themselves to further humiliation in the learning environment. Second, that innovative strategies to take information about learning directly to the people will often reawaken a latent learning desire. Third, modern marketing techniques using every medium at the city's disposal will succeed where other approaches have not, and therefore the city should deploy its marketing expertise in the service of learning. Fourth, the information should be available 24 hours a day, 7 days a week. A city learning hotline would not be such a bad idea.

Chapter 15

Needs and requirements in the learning city – discovering the demand

---

A learning city nurtures a culture of learning by proactively auditing the learning requirements of all its citizens and providing the opportunities to satisfy them.

How can a community satisfy the learning needs of people if it has not taken steps to discover what these are? It is probable that more than half of the learning desires of citizens lie latent and unarticulated because few people have been asked or, better, stimulated to express their learning needs.

Certainly there is an increased focus on finding out what these needs are. But this is linked to the supporting issue of quality control. In Britain three organizations have carried out surveys for the government on the state of learning. All of them contribute valuable data. The MORI survey on *Attitudes to Learning* carried out for the UK Campaign for Learning increases our understanding of how far Britain has progressed toward a learning society. It rightly distinguishes between taught and non-taught learning, recognizing that not all learning is classroom- or computer-based. The conclusion reports a wide interest in learning, a collective appreciation that learning is valuable, but a low commitment among half the British population to actually doing something about it, for a wide variety of reasons.

Cities are now beginning to commission their own learning requirements surveys, for example Glasgow. Many of them are aware that producing meaningful data from them is notoriously difficult. As the organizations carrying them out will readily agree, the answers are based on the existing knowledge of the surveyed. For example, people who have only ever experienced one style of learning, usually classroom-based, are not readily in a position to make judgements about alternatives they have never experienced, such as self-learning through CD-ROMs on the computer. People with no knowledge of the Internet cannot be expected to reply sensibly to questions about learning on the Internet. Despite the best efforts of surveyors to simplify language and make it intelligible and unambiguous, those not immersed in the ambience and the vocabulary of education may find it hard to relate to the full meaning of the question. Further, it is almost impossible to eliminate subjectivity from the questions.

This is not to undervalue the surveys. They provide a time-slice of opinion about learning and learners from a cross-section of the people, which is valuable in its own context, that is, as an expression of opinion. They point too to where educators need to work in order to improve public understanding of their field. Repeated over time, they chart the changing attitudes of the population of the city. From the results of most surveys, it can be said generally that a lot of learning is still to be done.

But recognizing the problem of obtaining unbiased data, the proliferation of surveys also offers new opportunities. At a time when the definition, the approach and the whole image of learning and learners are changing, is there a sense in which the surveys themselves can be used to change perceptions of citizens? Can they be used as learning instruments such that the questions would stimulate informed thought rather than non-informed reaction? Purists would of course say no. Proselytizing is no substitute for empirical study, and statisticians have spent years trying to eliminate the independent variables from data-gathering. They measure what is, not what we would like it to be. And that is a very seductive argument, and highly relevant in many cases. But in this day and age when many parts of the media present opinion as fact, and data as knowledge, there is a case for an alternative approach.

The Audit of Learning Requirements, described in Chapter 2, and carried out by the European Lifelong Learning Initiative was not the most scientific of surveys, though a major proportion of it was the collection of hard, non-biased fact. But, in certain aspects, it did try to educate responders before they gave a reply, sometimes by presenting a controversial sentence to provoke thought and reflection, sometimes by providing an explanation of the question's meaning and sometimes by extending a concept beyond its raw boundaries. The following is an example from the audit, concerning employment and employability.

Example 15.1: *These are statements which have been made in the press as a result of research carried out. Please let us know your opinion about the degree of truth of the statements on a scale from 1–5.*

	1= Strongly Agree	2= Agree	3= Don't know	4= Disagree	5= Strongly Disagree
Many skilled and semi-skilled jobs (more than 50%) will disappear in the future as a result of new technology.					
There will be an increasing demand for higher level skills in the workforce.					
Many industries are beginning to work in an entirely different way; they keep a smaller core staff and buy in the expertise they need.					
If so, people in the future will need to have a much wider range of skills.					
Companies are becoming more international, more mergers with foreign companies are likely and language skills will be highly valued.					
The amount of work available is decreasing and there will never be a return to full employment.					

Having asked the participants to reflect a little on this, they were then asked follow-up questions, such as Example 15.2:

'Who is responsible for dealing with problems of this kind? If any or all of the things above happened, do you think your job would be affected? Would this create a need in you for further training? If yes, how?'

And then asked to think outside of themselves. Example 15.3:

'If you have children, what would you advise them to do?'

Similarly, since the audit was carried out in small and medium-sized enterprises, another question asked about the relationship between the interviewee and company, giving an explanation to clarify the meaning comprises Example 15.4:

'Some large companies are becoming 'Learning Organizations' as well as commercial organizations. This means that they encourage their staff to take courses which develop their own potential in a wide variety of subject areas and to take charge of their own learning. This, it is argued, increases the commitment of the company to its people and the commitment of its people to the company and thus keeps the company up to date, lively and competitive in the market place. To what extent do you believe that your own company is moving in that direction?'

This again is designed both to educate, motivate and encourage thought. And the purpose of the questionnaire is described at the end:

'Lastly, we said at the beginning that this is about the development of human potential – your, and we hope your children's, potential – and you may have understood from the words we have used what we are about. This is the first step in what will be a long road. We thank you for helping us to take it and hope that the results will be of benefit to us all. Now, as a last opportunity, we have some lines for you to record anything you think we have missed, or got wrong, or misunderstood, and to mention your own opinions and ideas on the subject of learning. Thank you.'

Such surveys are of course difficult at street level. A personal interview handled by an impartial but knowledgeable person is preferable, and so it was with the ELLI Learning Audit, although several people responded without this help. The information obtained, though still subjective, tends to be more informed, better considered and more easily converted into useful knowledge and action. From the interviewees' point of view, they are more likely to feel valued because they have been stimulated to think, they are more likely to feel motivated to react positively as a result and they might feel they have learnt something. In a hyper-democratic world, where instant opinions are being sought daily, the capacity to reflect as well as to react can be important. And so it turned out. As reported earlier, the audit uncovered a huge reservoir of unfulfilled learning needs, which may not have been expressed in more formal surveys.

However, the proliferation of Learning Surveys raises other issues. The main one is what both the interviewee and interviewer understand by learning and being a learner. In the MORI and other polls, most responders considered learning to be important. But then so is motherhood, and a sense of morality and decent behaviour, and citizenship and a whole host of other 'good things'. When answering, what image do the responders have of learning? How do they know if they are 'a learner'? At its most basic, everyone learns every day, and the belief that this is so is a feature brought out in the MORI survey, as well as in the UK National Institution for Adult and Continuing Education and the Ministry's National Adult Learning Surveys. Every time we switch on the television set we learn something. Every time we pay a visit to a town, we learn something new. In that sense everyone is 'a learner'.

This osmotic view of learning acquisition is reinforced by the definition used by the UK Department for Education and Employment in its National Adult Learning Study and extensively used in the surveys:

> Learning can involve either formal, taught learning or informal, non-taught learning. Taught learning for example, includes training sessions at work, driving lessons, evening classes and teaching yourself using distance learning materials. Non-taught learning, for example, includes studying and developing your skills on your own without being enrolled on a course, learning on the job at work, and keeping up to date with your own interests by reading books, etc.

For good or bad, the second part of the definition certainly creates a high number of learners. My mother would interpret watching a documentary, or a quiz show, on television as de facto learning by this definition, since it keeps her up to date with her own interests. Every time I play tennis I meet a new situation or opponent and learn how to deal with it. We are learners and we are proud of it. Or are we? It is surprising to find that the results of most surveys show such a high lack of commitment to actually carrying out learning in the sense of developing potential, in spite of such a liberal interpretation.

And yet, there must be something more to it than that. And of course there is, and learning cities can themselves learn something from this. Quite apart from the need to stay updated to remain employable in a changing employment environment, which requires a personal commitment to a more structured learning environment, there are other factors to be taken into account – the quality of the learning, the uses to which it is put, creativity, learning levels, active vs passive learning, fact acquisition and retention vs understanding, and the intellectual and behavioural improvements which learning allows individuals to achieve. A nation of television watchers, whatever type of programme they are watching, or tennis players or dog-walkers, would not necessarily constitute a 'Learning Society'. We would not be learners simply by changing our behaviour to avoid a bus as we cross the road. There is some other ingredient.

In one sense, learners might be defined as 'people who, for whatever reason, are continuously motivated to acquire new skills, perceptions, competencies, knowledge, values or behaviours'. It is a challenging concept, in which the learner is both the adversary and the beneficiary. The word continuously is particularly contentious. It might be a description an academic, steeped in the world of learning, would use. And yet, there are many academics who would not meet these criteria, just as there many poorly educated individuals who would. But this stretches well beyond current definitions and would decimate the number of learners in the poll figures.

Learning cities, in their efforts to understand learning requirements, should be honest in their interpretation of the results. They should beware of adopting easy definitions in order to give a rosy picture of the state of learning in the city. This is not a perfect world.

So, as an exercise in understanding what sort of vision the learning city might expect from its citizens in, say, the year 2020, and as a personal challenge for those who wish to aspire to greater things, perhaps there is a need to define the characteristics which would distinguish the real learners from those who simply play at learning – let us call them 'super-learners'. Figure 15.1 suggests some of these more qualitative virtues, the desirable attributes each learner needs to espouse in order to demonstrate effective learning. As an *aide-memoire* (and an exercise in word-play), they are presented as a mnemonic.

It is not suggested that all true learners would need to satisfy all these requirements. Not every learner is a super-learner, or aspires to be so. We will all be 5 per cent or 30 per cent or 60 per cent or 90 per cent learners. But the table presents a yardstick to which people can aspire and perhaps even be expanded into a personal or reward/recognition-based monitoring system for individuals organized by the community, much in the same way that the Duke of Edinburgh's Award in the UK rewards achievement in a number of personal and community challenges.

None of this is merely an academic argument about definitions. Learning cities can understand much about how to find out the true learning need in their regions, and they can understand how to respond to it. The step increase in the standard of education required to produce a learning city able to cope with 21st-century work patterns; the enhanced understanding of the technological tools which will come into common usage in many households; the environmental imperative to safeguard and sustain an ecologically sound and stable environment in the city; the threat to democracy caused by a lack of interest and informed thought on issues affecting the livelihood of millions; these will not be addressed without the stimulus of a new learning environment accessible to, and comprehensible by, all people.

L	Listen	They take heed of those who can extend their knowledge and skills and of their own inner voice which says develop your potential
E	Evolve	They climb the learning ladder which leads from ignorance to knowledge and eventually to understanding and wisdom
A	Adapt	They modify their thinking, their behaviour and their mindset to cope easily with the changing world in which they live
R	Reciprocate	They recognize their own creative power to change their world through learning and participation in the community in which they live
N	Network	They look outwards to the world and gather strength by sharing their learning and its results with others in the wider international community
E	Enjoy	They enliven their own learning and that of others through their enthusiasm and their determination to make learning fun
R	Reflect	They learn from the past, make sense of the present and contemplate the future through learning
S	Support	They stimulate others and act as empathetic mentors and guides in their voyage of self-discovery through learning

Figure 15.1 Superlearners – qualitative learning

They, and other challenges of the next century, can only be met if a culture of Life-long Learning permeates throughout society, organizations and people. Listening and adapting, reflecting and evolving, contributing and supporting, creating, enjoying and networking are all vital and active constituents of the learning process. They define it and they make it happen. They are the what, the why, the when, the where, the how and the how to. What cities should be planning for is the time when, at some time in the future, present-day super-learners become ordinary learners. Then we can define anew the super-learner of the future, perhaps in terms of contribution to the learning of others and to the city itself as a living, breathing organism.

Chapter 16

Growth and the creation of wealth and employment – stimulating the economy

A learning city generates wealth and employment through innovative use of existing resources and through creative projects with other learning communities.

In the same way that companies are being urged to become 'world-class', learning cities will also increasingly need to accept a similar challenge. They can learn much from industry. Kanter (1995) suggests that the city which can creatively harness the talents of its institutions will be the city that succeeds in generating wealth and employment in a globalized world:

> Future success will come to those companies, large and small, which can meet global standards and tap into global networks.And it will come to those cities and regions which do the best job of linking the businesses that operate within them to the global economy. Forces of globalization are so powerful that communities must connect the global and the local and create a civic culture to attract and retain 'footloose' investment. The challenge is to find ways in which the global economy can work locally by unlocking those resources which distinguish one place from another. Universities are one such [means] . . .

This is a powerful argument for a new sense of purpose based on lifelong learning by the development agencies of cities. Kent, Region of Learning, agrees: 'All regions are part of what is now a vast-developing global economy. To survive and prosper in such an economy the people must aspire to and achieve world-class standards.' While this is more easily said than done, the county of Kent has been pursuing policies to improve the general educational standard of all its citizens for several years now. Chapter 25 describes some of the strategies it has put into place.

Maintaining full employment is currently one of the most sought-after pana-ceas by local communities. In a highly competitive international environment, in which labour-intensive manufacturing industry has migrated away from the developed to the developing world, the production of high added-value goods and services becomes increasingly important. This is turn demands a new focus on lifetime high-order skills and competencies in highly adaptable and flexible citi-zens, with continuous upgrading and change to keep them both employed and employable. The provision of an education service which can create such knowl-edge, values and attitudes is one way to stimulate wealth-creation, though other initiatives will also be needed to encourage the entrepreneurial spirit in a caring enterprise society. Some of these arise from the partnerships built up between industry and schools, from such bases as the Young Enterprise Scheme. Others will arise from the contacts and ideas developed through the inter-company net-works fostered by the twinning of learning cities illustrated in Figure 13.1. Yet more will be created within the context of international programmes like the European Development and Social Funds.

Often growth-generating innovation can be left to the private sector. ICI's work in creating a technology park at Belassis Hall in the United Kingdom is a case in point. The three major industries of the Teesside region were steel, ship-building and chemicals. Nothing is left of the first two and the third has reduced employ-ment numbers by two-thirds. ICI, as the major Chemicals Industry employer of the region for many years felt that it had a social responsibility to create new employment. It therefore donated land worth £2.5 million at Belassis Park to build a technology park which would not only attract the branch offices of large compa-nies, but also new innovative SMEs. More than that, with the help of a partner organization, it seconded senior managers to supervise the establishment of more than 125 work space units in a period of eight years and provided basic services such as marketing advice, computer training, technical information facilities and help with research and product development. As time progresses and the SMEs become more viable and profitable, the cost to the company diminishes. But the value to the community in terms of wealth and employment generation is price-less, and has entailed very little financial outlay on its part.

Perhaps Teesside is fortunate to have such a generous and socially responsible employer, but other fine examples of how international education and training community partnerships can lead to the growth of trade are provided in the Euro-pean Social Fund booklet, *Meeting the Challenge of Change at Work*. Take the project between the UK, Sweden, Austria and Italy pioneering the use of computer links to develop support networks for SME Training and courses by CD-ROM. It is aimed at upskilling people who are switching jobs or taking on new responsibilities at work. Stage one involves setting up the computer links between learning centres and SMEs to provide information and training on business issues. Stage two devel-ops new multimedia materials for the businesses to use – titles such as personal business assessments, strategic business planning using the Internet, and starting up your own business were all produced in the first year of the programme. Advisors and mentors are at the other end of the helpline for all participants. While the jointly developed methodology is the same in each country, the Swedish partner concentrates more on computer training for doctors in the health service and the Italian consortium is developing a CD-ROM on health and safety at work. In Austria materials are developed looking at the legal framework for tele-working.

Such collaborative ventures not only help to increase the amount of available learning material but also establish a new insight into the needs of businesses in other countries and a potential expansion of international trade. In Denmark, a scheme for job rotation was developed in Silkeborg. Its goals were to improve the skills of those already in work and to help the unemployed find work by sending existing employees on to training courses and replacing them for the duration of the course by unemployed people who have themselves undergone preparatory training. It is a rolling programme run by a co-ordinator who acts on behalf of many companies. It is of interest here since the scheme and the method have now been exported to 11 other countries of the European Union and provided 5000 training places. The company benefits in two ways – its own employees become better trained on their courses, while a new reserve bank of trained labour is created for the future. In addition both the companies and the people become much more flexible in the operating environment and SMEs become much more like modern Industrial Learning Organizations.

And let us not ignore the contribution a large company can make to the development of growth. One of the growth generating initiatives a learning city can stimulate is the creation of synergy between large and small industries in a locality. Business happens in specific localities. Jobs are created, not just anywhere, but in a specific place, a city neighbourhood, a town or a river valley. There is a continuous give-and-take between companies and the communities where they operate. When a company thrives, the benefits spill over to neighbouring businesses and the community at large.

The presence of a large company in the community will almost certainly stimulate local SME growth and job creation. The return to the company from its local investment is an improved supply in local skilled labour, better relations with local and regional governments, and easier integration into the community. All these things will raise local living standards and improve the overall image of business and industry. So the impact of a large company will stimulate the local community to come to grips with present realities and prepare for the future. In return the company may benefit from a better supply of quality labour; better relations with the machinery of government, and more co-operation from local people in general. Business can contribute to local leisure and cultural activities, raising the quality of life in a way that will help to attract other businesses.

However, success is not guaranteed. It is vital that large companies work in close co-operation with local authorities and vice versa and that local managers assure themselves of backing from their head offices. The complex of local relationships will not work for the large company unless its local managers are totally committed to making it work, with full backing from company headquarters. And it will not work for the community unless its own political and official leaders are fully committed to co-operating with business. The European Round Table of Industrialists suggests that eight lessons can be learnt by both sides to create a win-win situation for each.

- Large companies give their greatest stimulus to local job creation when they use their creative and professional energies to drive community partnerships. There are multiplier effects when regional activities are co-financed by large companies and public authorities.
- Large companies should work with public authorities; they cannot be expected to and should not try to do their job for them.
- Joint financing of local development activities by large companies and public bodies can provide a valuable multiplier effect.
- Managers from large and small companies can work with local educators to assess the demand and supply of current labour markets and make tentative predictions for the future. Local facilities can then be used with imagination to satisfy companies' needs, equip young people for real jobs and help the unemployed back into work.
- Both active and retired managers from large companies can pass on their management and marketing know-how through courses at universities, schools and other local centres.
- It takes people with a spirit of enterprise to make small companies succeed, and schools should see what they can do to develop such traits among children of all ages. This particularly matters in localities where large-scale industries used to provide the jobs and the spirit of small business entrepreneurship needs to be rekindled.
- When participating in regional and local development programmes, large companies achieve more when they work with local authorities than by trying to act in their place.
- Technology parks and SME incubator sites contribute to local development, stimulate the growth of SMEs, and can do much to strengthen the local image of a large company with greater cost-effectiveness than a short-lived publicity campaign. They provide safety, flexibility and valuable contacts, which money alone cannot buy. They not only provide local jobs but also attract other SMEs into the community. SME incubator sites and technology parks need not be expensive or luxurious, but they do need to be properly supported in the early years. Incubator sites are designed to provide start-up micro- and small-sized companies with flexible premises and add-on services to suit their size, budget and growth rate. Established SMEs are expected to move out of incubator sites when they are ready to expand, but the experience of ERT companies is that

only 30 per cent of them will do so. Perhaps 20 per cent of those that stay put will collapse, while the rest will survive and possibly expand.

In all of these, the concept of learning from each other within an entry Learning Community is important and implicit.

Links with communities in other parts of the world can also be useful to Learning Cities exploring growth and regeneration. The concept of pan-European 'Bootstrap Business Networks' is a scheme to share experience among SMEs in the throes of restructuring. Originating in Sweden, but now extended to Germany, Greece, Portugal, Austria, Italy and the UK, it defines and develops new processes and fresh ideas, provides counselling and training and computer-based networks for SMEs facing changes not only in their production processes, but also in their management systems and how they provide services. It helps them to develop new strategic business plans and identify and train for future skills. The programme started out as an information and training network – now it exchanges workers and managers between organizations to better understand markets and processes.

The establishment of electronic working links between learning cities helps to generate social and financial benefits. They will breathe new life into the old 'twinning' arrangements which cities already have, and at the same widen the number of potential 'twins'. Figure 13.1 shows the possibilities when all sectors and agencies of the community can be involved in fruitful interaction with each other and with those in other learning cities.

Chapter 17

Change management in the learning city – preparing people for the future

A learning city cultivates programmes which allow citizens to cope positively and without fear in a world of rapid change.

Many people are unable to come to terms with the idea of living with rapid change and uncertainty. Unfortunately or otherwise, stopping the world to get off is not an option in most communities. They are subject to decisions and actions taken elsewhere. In industrial areas, fishing ports, rural paradises, whole communities have lost the source of their livelihood, either because the major industry has become obsolescent, or through overproduction or overexploitation of resources. It is a process that the effects of globalization will accelerate as we progress in the 21st century. After a period of despair, some communities have recovered through the development of new, modern industries, while others continue to struggle or are just entering decline. A true learning city would be able to anticipate change and empower its citizens to be sufficiently adaptable, flexible and versatile to quickly recover confidence and employment. This of course is much more easily written than carried out in practice. However, there are some precedents from which cities can learn.

Territorial employment pacts

In order to address this problem, particularly in the context of job creation, the European Commission introduced the idea of local territorial employment pacts within its Leader programme. These combine all sectors of a community into a concentrated attack on understanding the sources and the effects of unemployment and on the creation of new opportunities for employment, based on the development of new skills. Their stated aims are:

- to identify both the difficulties and the prospects in the employment field facing each territorial player;
- to mobilize all available resources in favour of an integrated strategy for the creation of new employment opportunities;
- to improve the integration and co-ordination of measures for creating and sustaining jobs.

Overall the effect is to turn change into opportunity. Many of the excellent examples described in the booklet, *Territorial Employment Pacts*, emphasize the importance of partnership, innovation and a 'bottom up' approach, that is, the involvement of the citizens themselves in the process of regeneration.

Pacts vary considerably in scope and form. For instance, some represent aspects of tripartite institutional arrangements common in several European countries, whilst others can be *ad hoc* solutions. Some partnerships pursue comprehensive strategies and some focus on particular sectors or types of action. Some have started as, and remain to date, informal partnerships whilst others have been formally endorsed, as in the case of recently signed agreements, *patti territorioli,* in Italy.

The provinces of Caltanissetta, Rovigo and Lamezia Terme are characterized by weak co-ordination of industrial and agricultural activities and a consequent decline in both. The former, on the island of Sicily, has also suffered from the closure of its main employer, a petrochemical plant, and is an area of high unemployment and low skill. The territorial pacts aim to rectify this through the promotion of new SMEs, job creation and training and co-ordination of activities. This is done through a variety of strategies:

- co-ordinating spatial planning policies;
- setting up networks of services for new and old companies in the area;
- promoting SME co-operation;
- facilitating access to funding for technological innovation and training;
- establishing easily accessible channels for obtaining continuous training;
- dealing with the endemic undercapitalization of companies;
- supporting local market in its effort to become more competitive and international;
- introducing new industrial initiatives in the fields of agro-industry and tourism;
- combating parochialism and a lack of communication at local level;
- developing markets for SMEs at home and abroad through co-operation projects.

In all three regions, training and quality are the foundation of all activities, since it is recognized that none of the above will continue to exist without a trained and highly motivated workforce.

Glasgow's intermediate market scheme – Glasgow works

From rural reskilling to urban regeneration, 'Glasgow Works' is an innovative example of how unemployment benefit can be used to create jobs for long-term unemployed people in activities which the city and its people need.

'Glasgow Works' is an initiative forming part of the Glasgow regeneration strategy involving all the key public agencies in the city of Glasgow. It is an intermediate labour market approach to reintegrating the long-term unemployed into the labour market through a package of work, training and personal support.

The project finances its training and project costs partly by using benefits normally paid to unemployed people participating in the national Training for Work (TfW) programme. This funding is made up of the statutory unemployment benefit allowance together with an additional training allowance. This 'benefits transfer' resource can then be used to match European Structural Funding, the other principal source of finance for projects.

'Glasgow Works' has developed a pathways approach to reintegrating long-term unemployed people. Thus all entrants to the programme receive personalized assessment and guidance before starting the programme, and receive training in personal development, heavily 'learning to learn'-oriented, to help them learn how to maximize its benefits. Training emphasizes the development of the core skills which are most attractive to employers – team-working, problem-solving, flexibility, communications skills and the use of information technology. Assessment and guidance is provided throughout the project through the support of a counsellor or mentor.

A key element is the full commitment of all the key agencies in the area. It is a partnership led by the Glasgow Development Agency and involving the local authorities, Scottish Enterprise, the Employment Service and the Scottish Trades Union Congress. Within this are smaller location-specific partnerships, including a wide range of organizations operating locally. These are training providers, local regeneration agencies, private companies and voluntary organizations. The Glasgow Development Agency provides a team of four development agents assisting with the development of project ideas, guidance and operating rules, funding for the projects and monitoring and evaluation. Such a three-pronged approach involving an overarching partnership, a core team and local partnerships ensures the continuation of political and financial backing, administrative support, and a co-ordinated approach reflecting the needs and opportunities of the local community.

'Glasgow Works' focuses on projects which not only provide valuable work experience to unemployed people participating in the scheme but also contributes to the quality of life and to the economy of Glasgow. Jobs created do not displace existing employment. Among the many projects are:

- 'Theatre Works' – plays developed for schools on issues such as drug abuse, crime etc. These have led to the setting up of a professional theatre company;
- Electrical Goods Remanufacture – the refurbishment of refrigerators and washing machines for sale;
- City Centre Representatives – people trained and employed as guides and wardens for the city centre.

As a project this is a good example of creative development. But, on a larger scale, perhaps one of the best examples of changing perceptions comes from the Vienne Region of France. It is quoted in the notes for the high-level seminar on competitive strength and social cohesion conference hosted by OECD in January 1998. Vienne is, and has been throughout history, a predominantly rural area, suffering in the late 20th century from depopulation. In 1986, the regional government made a political decision to invest in new technologies in order to bring the region into the future. At its centre was the designing and building of Futuroscope, a technological theme park which could be, and indeed has been, visited by millions of people, and which also provides training, research business, education as well as leisure activities. It was based on the premise that the knowledge society related to lifelong learning, at all levels.

As the project advanced, the research capability of Poitiers University was considerably enhanced through new commissions, the schools were equipped with new computers and a new model of continuous cradle-to-grave education was monitored by government offices. The results are impressive. 6700 new highly qualified jobs created, new industry research laboratories, more educational institutions and a host of new businesses. The lifelong learning model continues to attract new investment.

The need for change management happens most frequently in industry, where it is an economic imperative. Learning cities can learn much from the way in which large companies treat the subject. Guinness is an excellent example. John Findlater believes that 'the key lesson is to move when you are strong'. Accordingly, Guinness employees are urged to develop change management and leadership skills, that is to both understand and communicate the need for change and to develop the skills to make it happen. Learning and involvement are the built-in processes by which this transformation in attitude, values and knowledge can be made. Guinness provides workshops and courses for all its employees on learning how to learn, knowing why, growing confidence, dealing effectively with people, team and organizational learning and a wide range of other subjects.

To support these it encourages personal goal-setting, provides well-equipped learning centres, develops learner networks, mentoring programmes and encourages involvement with the local community where Guinness facilities reside. Examples of the latter include helping local schools with reward schemes for attendance and project work, running workshops developed for in-company purposes with 15 year-olds, sponsoring university students, employment guidance interviews for school students, work experience and others. Guinness workers and pensioners contribute to a project providing start-up finance for entrepreneurs who have difficulty borrowing from other sources. Every Guinness worker is also a learner and is encouraged to question the way things are done. A city that learns will aspire to this as a vision of the way it can not only use its own resources to change perceptions in its citizens, but tap into the resources of those forward-looking companies and other organizations to help it become more effective and cost-beneficial.

These are all excellent examples of the combination of job creation, community contribution, personal skills development and preparation for a more flexible future, which many cities and towns can copy in the context of the Learning City or Region. The new needs for new information services, better learning through technology and networks, learning audits, leadership strategies, greater use of community resources, environmental care and family learning described as essential for learning cities in these pages can extend the fund of creative ideas into new areas, providing employment and a return on investment.

Chapter 18

Investing in the learning city – making everything count

A learning city influences the future by linking learning strategies to cross-departmental financial and other strategies.

Lifelong learning is not the territory of the education department alone – it is a social, a political, an economic, a health and sometimes even a spiritual phenomenon. It lasts throughout life and affects every aspect of it. Learning cities recognize this and take steps to educate and involve all departments of the city administration, as well as the voluntary sector, in creative projects to foster learning. This is why it is often not a good idea to give the responsibility for policy design and implementation to the Education Department. The task belongs to a supra-departmental body, or to a company specially charged with implementing lifelong learning policies, as in Edinburgh – a combination of the elected, the appointed and the participators. It also presupposes that the members of this body are fully cognisant of the characteristics and implications of lifelong learning and that they have the power to make and implement far-reaching decisions.

In Japan, this process starts at governmental level. As we saw in Chapter 3, every ministry is required to produce, and have implemented, an annually updated set of lifelong learning programmes for the whole population. Thus there are more than 160 plans for the third age, and more than 200 for youth produced by Ministries of Education, Employment, Industry and Social Services, plans in fact for every age group. What can happen at a national level can also happen at local level. Of course there are cultural differences between nations, but these are often used as excuses for inertia.

We can learn much from those countries in the forefront of the action. But more than that, a learning city cannot be created without the consent of its people. As discussed in Chapter 14, a city strategy should aim to involve as many people as possible, both in the development of projects and programmes and in the direction the city will take to implement them. At the very beginning, a series of seminars needs to be developed for key people, who in their turn deliver the same seminar to other key people in a cascade process that reaches out eventually to the whole city. The centre for the learning city at Sheffield Hallam University is currently developing such workshops. The guidelines should be not only practical and realistic but also imaginative and inspirational. Hearts need to be turned as well as minds. A learning city is, like a child, a candle to be lit as much as a vessel to be filled. Knowledgeable consultants will be needed to start the process moving, to involve and animate the partners – councillors, counsellors, teachers and lecturers, administrators, the media people, the leaders of voluntary groups, the businessmen and the opinion-formers. Progress will need to be measured, monitored and reported back over a period of years.

It is important to realize that a true learning city will not be created this year or next. This is a 20 to 50 year strategy, starting now, to make a learning city into a dynamic community which recognizes and satisfies the learning and developmental needs of all its citizens, which gives them the opportunity to contribute to the creation of a learning city and grows with them in their understanding of themselves and others. The creation of wealth, the development of human potential and the minimization of exclusion follow naturally from this process.

One story from Scotland illustrates how initiatives started in one sector expand to another and eventually become cross-departmental. It concerns a co-operation between the national education inspectorate, local education authorities and schools aspiring to become 'learning schools'. According to Jardine (1997):

> The learning school is defined as one where staff as well as pupils learn, where teachers review their own and the school's work against its aims and then take steps to bring about improvement. Through this process of review or self-evaluation, linked to the school's development plan, staff development activities will be identified at school, team and individual levels. The school development plan is a key document in this, and the development planning process of aims, audit, planning, implementation and evaluation is one which is identical to that in most successful business organizations.
>
> If people are an organization's most important resource, the organization has to make a commitment to the training and development of all its staff. Accordingly, the Scottish schools' inspectorate have installed the Investors in People (IiP) standard, a challenging set of personnel development requirements usually associated with business and industry, into some Scottish schools. IiP accreditation is not usually granted until as many as 33 performance indicators have been satisfied, including those in the area of staff development plans, management performance indicators, communication of vision and targets and career development. A training package for schools offering advice, questionnaires, checklists and frameworks was delivered to those schools which wished to take up the challenge, while further support was available from the inspectorate.

Jardine reports that in the first two years of the project, up to June 1997, 9 secondary schools and 5 primary schools were successfully accredited, while more than 100 schools have made a commitment to meet the standard in the future. One Local Education Authority is now taking all its schools through the accreditation procedures. The concept is becoming so popular and pervasive that local authorities and schools are beginning to adopt this as a national standard and using it as a quality indicator in their communication to parents and the community.

But one interesting development is that local councils are feeding off this and extending it to all their activities and organizations. Jardine reports that the one council which started to do this in 1997 is now joined by others. Both of these are interesting developments for learning cities. First, they set a high quality standard for staff development in schools and council offices. Secondly, that standard extends to the quality of the information they provide and the communication methods they use. Thirdly, it inserts a degree of creativity into the process since people who are now continuous improvers will need to demonstrate it. And fourthly, it highlights in practical terms the essential interconnectedness and interdependency of local authority organizations. The application of quality in one depends upon the application of quality standards in the others. A lack of commitment to quality in any part of the system can affect the whole system.

It also gives food for thought to aspiring learning cities about how this principle can be applied right across the city institutions, including local government offices. Some cities may wish to devise their own quality standards rather than use an externally moderated programme, but, whatever they do, they should be applied and monitored in every part of the city's activities.

The development of the 'full service school' concept in the USA is another response to the over-compartmentalization of social, health, employment and education services which, according to MacBeath (1998), 'often seem more adept at serving the needs of the professions rather than those of their clients'. 'The idea,' he says, 'is to bring together under one roof the range of agencies whose job it is to serve families and communities, making it easier for professionals to meet, share their knowledge, and respond flexibly and swiftly to issues as they arise.' This appears to be an idea of which learning cities can take cognizance. In a city, the needs of families, or indeed individual citizens, do not occur in the neat and tidy parcels which local government has set up to deal with them. Everyone has personal, psychological, health, learning, housing, and a range of other needs. In particular, those trapped in the bottom layers of society suffer greatly from the fragmented system of benefits, education and other support services available. The notion of full service, client-centred cradle-to-grave focus, which concentrates on empowerment as much as on care, is said in the USA to cut truancy and raise achievement by streamlining services to young people. As the focus of education is changing from teaching to learning, and on the problems of the learner in order to satisfy the needs of the customer, so the focus of the service departments of our cities will change from reactive caring to proactive enabling of individuals in order to help them to help themselves. This will entail not just better cross-departmental communication, but a total rethink of the way services are administered in a more holistic way.

Chapter 19

Technology for the learning city – creating the future

A learning city transforms the city into a modern centre of learning by the effective use of the new learning technologies.

Many governments base their strategy of more effective learning in the future on a strategy of more effective use of education technology, including open and distance learning and delivery through networks. The flagship project of the UK Government strategy for Lifelong Learning, the University for Industry, is heavily technology-oriented. The Green Paper, *The Learning Age*, says 'As the UfI will demonstrate, one of the best ways to overcome some of the barriers to learning will be to use the new broadcasting and other technologies. We expect their role in learning to increase significantly.' Another project for schools, the 'National Grid for Learning', will help teachers and students to obtain access to a wide range of learning materials on-line. It will include a 'virtual teachers centre' to use the Internet for teacher support and training.

Cities already recognize the need to invest in computers into schools. The number of computer classrooms has increased vastly over the past five years, though it is still not, and probably never will be, enough. In the middle 1980s, the IBM Europe Computers in Schools plan put as many as 50 computers into one 400 pupil school in Sweden and called it the 'Viskjo Project'. At the time this was a breakthrough in the use of computers by all parts of the school for administration, for teaching in all subjects and for learning programming languages in the Mathematics department. The results of the project showed a moderately successful use of technology in some science-based subjects, a large increase in the use of the computer as a word-processing tool and the real breakthrough in the use of the computer as a tool for administration. The reported drawbacks were lack of

167

teacher familiarity – in some cases a real fear – lack of time to prepare for computer-based lessons, lack of good educational software and not enough computers to satisfy the demand! While some of these have improved over the past 12 years, one suspects that many of them are recognizable today despite the massive influx of new machines into schools.

While computers may be important for open learning, they are not the only items of technology in education. The successful use of sophisticated broad-band networks for the delivery of education are a common-place in multinational industry, and, particularly in the United States, many universities have such facilities to satisfy a range of customers from industry to public broadcasting networks. Such high technology is not normally considered useful in schools, either because it is expensive or because it is unsuitable for the type of education delivered there. Westfield, Indiana, is an exception and perhaps indicative of the way in which public education systems at all levels of the community will change over the first part of the next century. The following is distilled from a report written by Jim Steele, Ball State University.

Westfield High School is a small school in a small town in rural southern Indiana – a school that only a generation ago would have been restricted by its isolation. But today, thanks to the school's investment in technology, its social studies teachers are able to enrich their instruction on international trade by bringing into their classrooms live coverage of French farmers demonstrating in Strasbourg, or by discussing the subject live with a university teacher in California who is an authority on sanctions and embargoes. New technologies have opened up the world to students in the school. Thanks to the largesse of GTE, a local employer, several other technology companies and nearby Ball State University, every classroom and office in the three-school, 919-student school district is equipped with a TV monitor and wired into a fibre-optic network.

Teachers can use a simple channel changer in their classrooms to display everything from newspaper articles and educational graphics to films and, in the case of Westfield, live programming via satellite. Much of the material is stored in a single technology distribution centre serving the entire school system. Teachers in their classrooms electronically check out of the library-like centre the material they want to use, and it is 'delivered' to their rooms with the push of a button. The technology also allows Westfield teachers to create their own multimedia materials.

To students nurtured on Nintendo, multimedia materials make learning more fun. To teachers eager to improve the quality of instruction in the nation's classrooms, such technology offers opportunities for less teacher lecturing and more hands-on, interdisciplinary learning of the sort advocated in lifelong learning. Students become active rather than passive learners in many high-tech classrooms.

Technology also can help address the problem of teacher quality that plagues so many schools. Westfield Washington District's satellite hook-up will permit its middle school to offer courses in Japanese, Latin, French and Spanish for the first time in 1998. The courses will be taught by certified teachers hired by TIIN Network, a provider of distance-learning programming.

Steele believes that, if introduced on a large scale such cutting-edge technology has the potential to cut the finances of public education significantly, a notion which would send shivers of apprehension throughout the teaching profession. The USA Congress's Office of Technology Assessment reported a general consensus that the appropriate assignment of new technologies within effectively organized schools could make a big difference in academic performance. But the cost of getting the newest technology into classrooms is likely to be high. The computers in many schools are outdated and used primarily for drilling students in basic skills. Buying hardware and software, wiring schools with fibre optics and training typewriter-generation teachers to use the new equipment are all expensive. Yet in the long run, technology can produce savings. The total cost of the new foreign language courses in Westfield Washington will be about $2000, a fraction of what it would cost to hire teachers locally. While no amount of techno-wizardry is going to do away with the need for high-quality books, teachers and schools, educators are beginning to see technology's potential to transform and improve teaching and learning.

Learning cities may wish to learn from this. And so may the schools themselves. For some teachers this is the ultimate horror story, a mechanized world in which machines take over the education of our children. The reality of course is different. Technology is there to be used when appropriate, not abused for a majority of the time. But perhaps the major drawback is that it presents an idealized picture from a relatively rich part of the world. The situation on the ground in most communities is more prosaic. Funding difficulties for technology remain one of the major concerns. And even where the technology has been installed, it has not created the educational revolution forecasted. Classroom practice remains much the same, embedded in out-of-date constructs and teaching, rather than progressing to learning-based techniques. The newly introduced technologies, which would lead to individualized learning, more intense and faster learning through new cognitive tools, and emphasis on small-group and individual inquiry over lecture and rote exercises, have not yet delivered their promise. Despite some wonderful materials and good classroom or school models, the technologies have been far more commonly appropriated to the ways things are traditionally done.

The truth is that technology cannot be seen in isolation from the rest of the school system. Timetables must become more flexible, the curriculum more open and accessible, the assessments systems more adaptable – a difficult task in those countries where the curriculum is national, the targets are rigid and the threat of exposure by league table is strong. There is no model technical development programme reproducible in every school. Teachers need to be involved at every stage of development if they are to accept the new methods – again an almost impossible task, given their already overcrowded task list and their natural defensiveness to new methodologies.

But new technologies will gradually make their way into the schools, and it is as well to be aware of how to introduce it wisely. The booklet *Bringing Business into Schools* offers some advice for those schools introducing new technology:

- Make up a five year plan to assure the continuity of the process;
- Reserve a specified amount of money in the school budget for the use of the Internet at school;
- Involve the total school community, including parents. A broad support is essential to the project;
- Discuss with the teachers the role that the Internet could play and the social structure of its use;
- Don't forget that teachers and heads need help in taking their own 'small steps of invention';
- Define the possible 'partners' (local authorities, industries, publishers, telephone companies,etc) who could support the process;
- Make a sponsor plan;
- Try to find partner schools to co-operate in the project.

These are all sensible and sound guidelines to which might be added:

- Identify the software which is suitable for use in different parts of the school;
- Focus on specific projects which involve each of the partners – teachers–pupils, home–school, school–industry etc and search out the added value which provides learning to both sides;
- Keep your computers up to date enough for them to do the job you want them to do. Seek strategies for replacing them – industry sponsorships, guidelines for purchase to parents, fee-paid computer literacy courses for the community, tap European, national and local funding sources etc;
- Run regular courses for all teachers in the school each dealing with a different aspect of computer usage;
- Join in projects and networks with other schools nationally and internationally, and again involve all the teachers.

One of the more exciting new programmes in the UK is the creation of Education Action Zones. These are mostly in regions of the country where social, political and cultural problems dictate a more flexible and relaxed attitude to education. In the first 30 zones, announced in July 1998, Local Education Authorities have a greater freedom to deliver the education which befits the local situation. If successful, it may herald a more general break away from the tyranny of an unsuitable and unworkable nationally imposed system. More finance is available for such items as new computers and it is here that the technology will have the opportunity to prove its effectiveness, where the experimentation with ownership of learning, personal learning plans, mentoring and the stuff of 21st century educational methods will stand or fall. If it can work in these places, how much more can it work in the more affluent parts of the world?

But schools are not the only organizations concerned with the effective use of technology. The digital revolution offers a much greater opportunity to Learning Cities. Not far into the next century, cities will have their ingenuity and their genuineness as a true Learning City challenged by the use they make of the new broadband channels made possible by the digitalization of television and cable networks. And the network is widening. Many cities have already set out along that route. All the Further Education Colleges in Glasgow for example are now linked by a 2Mb broadband network equivalent to 10 TV channels. It includes the capacity for e-mail and videoconferencing links with faster ISDN access for remote learners. The Glasgow Telecolleges Network now has the capability to deliver interactive courses, information, support networks and seminars remotely to teachers, students, SMEs and community groups in many parts of the city. It will link in to the fast-developing Scottish National Grid for Learning and the University for Industry to widen the trawl of available material, and expand into those parts of the city not yet reached through cable networks and into the entertainment channels. It allows for participation in collaborative research and development of all kinds. By anticipating the growth in demand for Lifelong Learning over the next decade, it is well-placed to satisfy it.

Glasgow is not the only example. The wired and cabled city is now a fact on every continent. Already, many cities in the USA, (Edmonton, Pittsburgh, San Francisco and others), are offering learning channels to their citizens, broadcasting self-learning courses from universities, colleges and private education providers to those who want to receive them. But that is just the tip of the iceberg. The proliferation of available space will lead to the possibility of neighbourhood channels offering information to the citizens of a single housing estate or a small city ward. Schools will be able to broadcast to people in their catchment area, perhaps transmitting the school play, providing essential information to parents, even involving children who are unable to attend, giving them the opportunity to receive lessons – not at present a popular idea among the young. Schools will be able to involve parents, advertise the school fête, explain their philosophy.

The possibilities are endless. Special interest groups – environmentalists, ornithologists, sports clubs, religious organizations, might have their own, or a shared, channel to involve people in the care of their own environment or the development of a new hobby. The opportunities for feedback are also in place, making this a two-way communications experience. Watchdog bodies may be needed to avoid abuse, but the technology is there to be used. Add this to the further development of Internet facilities, potentially available to every home and the sheer power of technology to change and expand people's perceptions, activities, lifestyles, and access to learning into the new millennium is obvious. It adds flexibility, versatility and a new mental minefield of potential.

It will certainly help the cultural industries to develop more rapidly and provide employment for a great number of people. In a way, the city of Sheffield in the UK has been preparing for this through a territorial employment pact first started in the 1980s. Sheffield, England's fourth largest city, has for decades survived on steel-making and cutlery production. The decline of these industries has resulted in a loss of some 50 000 jobs since the 1970s. The need to develop a more diverse economic base became a necessity if the city was to survive and prosper. The City Council therefore started to work alongside the private sector to focus on the development of activities in the cultural sector – mainly video, sound-recording, film and broadcasting – to create employment and regenerate the city.

One area of the city centre was designated a Cultural Industries Quarter (CIQ). Here the private sector was supported in a number of ways, including training and business support for potential entrepreneurs, the provision of managed workshops at favourable rates, the provision of facilities, particularly redundant buildings such as factories, at favourable rates and support in redeveloping such buildings. For its part, the private sector provided significant financial support to the CIQ initiative and small businesses have been supported to grow and prosper. The establishment of a cluster of cultural industries has provided those businesses with added value from sharing resources and exploiting new opportunities though networking with related businesses and organizations.

The CIQ has emerged as a lively vibrant location for business, education and culture and is home to 132 media and science-related businesses. Significant music and arts venues have emerged, inducing the 'works Station and Media Centre' opened in 1993 and a new cultural business and training complex housing 35 companies in a managed workspace environment providing conferencing, child care, reception and exhibition space. The Scotia works, a former cutlery factory, was restored and developed into an arts and media training centre. The Yorkshire Arts Space, with twenty studios for printing, sculpture, furniture, jewellery, ceramics, instruments, crafts, photography and fine arts, was created. The Northern Media School brings together the courses provided by Sheffield University in film, video and photography, with those provided by the City Council, and the 'Audio Visual Enterprise Centre' provides managed work space for new businesses.

The funding for this ambitious initiative comes from a combination of sources including the UK Urban programme, the European Regional Development Fund, the European Social Fund, the City Council, and the National Lotteries Fund. And it leaves Sheffield in an excellent position to exploit the new possibilities of the technology for learning.

But in all the euphoria about the potential of technology, a word of caution has to be injected. Most networks are still in a situation of technology push rather than learner pull – have technology, will accept content, ideas and expertise on how to use it. While many of the network managers are well aware that the use of new technologies imposes new challenges and new learning imperatives, the take-up will be determined by the customer. Not only are many end-users unfamiliar with, and therefore wary of, its use, the providers themselves may not have realized just how different the pedagogical approach has to be. For sure, technology can help the development of Lifelong Learning, but in the new paradigm, the education is no longer a provider-client relationship. When the focus is on the needs of the learner, learning becomes at worst an equal partnership between them, and at best a means of passing on ownership of content and method to the customer. It is this pedagogical turn-around which needs to be urgently addressed.

Chapter 20

Involving people in the learning city – harnessing the talent

_____

A learning city inspires citizens to contribute to city life and culture by building a database of their skills, knowledge and talents and encouraging them to make them available to others.

A learning city is also a contributing community. It is a two-way celebration process in which citizens both develop and donate skills, talents and knowledge for the wider benefit of others in the community. This, properly managed, is one of the largest resources available to every organization and every individual in the learning city. And it is largely untapped. Several examples have already been discussed. Mentoring and partnerships, both valuable ideas with a great deal of unused mileage still in them, are a basis for further explorations into community contribution, and their use is growing. The sense of community is strong and growing in many parts of the world, notably in the United States, where vast resources have been devoted at grass roots level to help solve deep-rooted problems.

But it is not only the USA and not only in times of relative stability. According to the Japanese National Institute for Educational Research in *Lifelong Learning in Selected Countries*, the Kobe earthquake caused in Japan, a country hitherto not noted for its volunteer activities, the mobilization of thousands of volunteers to improve facilities, many of them for the first time. 78 per cent of these reported that they would want to continue to work in an appropriate capacity back in their own home areas.

A 1998 report from the UK Advisory Group on citizenship headed by Sir Bernard Crick emphasizes this trend. This group has added three new basics to the already long list shown by Longworth and Davies in *Lifelong Learning*. These are social and moral responsibility, community involvement and political literacy and, in its opinion, they are 'what every child should have more than a glimmer about' on leaving primary school. It goes further. It recommends that children should learn such things by doing – by taking part in the political processes, by experiencing democracy in the classroom and by learning how to use their knowledge. 'Rights are balanced by responsibilities,' it says. Children should be taught to become 'active citizens', and to play a full and energetic part in local democracy.

To some this can be seen as a blueprint for anarchy. It is certainly subversive in many ways. Political literacy involves much more than receiving and comparing party literature at election times, which most people do not do anyway – it means understanding the values and premises under which each party operates and their effect on trade and commerce, the quality of life, the effect on the non-self. Community Involvement means more than helping out in voluntary activities – it implies doing something about perceived injustices and making a positive difference to the life of the city and the people who live there. In the late 1990s we have moved a long way from the notion that only the individual counts into the belief that an individual has a responsibility to contribute to and improve the society in which he or she lives. That belief also underlies the concept of the Learning City.

Many examples of community involvement abound. The European Round Table of Industrialists book on partnerships describes the work of the Dutch foundation Kleinnood, established as long ago as 1979 to channel advice from retired executives of Shell and Unilever to SMEs in Holland. Their consultancy to SMEs is offered for free while travel expenses can be claimed back. In 1997 it had an annual clientele of around 2500 and employed over 200 consultants. This gives rise to the notion that Learning Cities might wish to pass the establishment of a register of volunteer workers, whether they be retired businessmen, willing housewives, eager youngsters, or any other member of the community to a private company or foundation. The return on such an investment could be high.

In another national project organized by the British charity 'Community Service Volunteers', budding contributors were invited to join the 'Yellow Pages Make a Difference Day'. The Yellow Pages refers to the sponsor of the event, being a subsidiary company of British Telecom. As the title indicates this was a day event to encourage participation in community improvement projects, and followed a successful British television programme describing such work. It provided an opportunity for those who may not want to make a long-term commitment to contribute for a defined period of time. Participants were invited to look around the local community to see what needs to be done. They were encouraged to make this a fun event with a defined outcome – the building of a community shelter or the painting of an old person's house. They were encouraged to join or gather together a group and divide out the tasks of making the outcome happen – one person would be responsible for publicity, another for fund-raising and obtaining sponsors, another for recruiting experts, etc.

Each year on 'Make a difference day' the Community Service Volunteers organization provides the publicity leaflets, recruits celebrities to help locally (a good way of motivating people), gives hints on how to volunteer and make things happen, creates a database of projects, approaches national sponsors, encourages national and local media support and in general markets the idea to both organizations and people. It is presented as a fun day out, meeting new people, learning new skills, and accomplishing something which would not otherwise be done.

Make a Difference project examples include a group from Reading, in which 30 employee volunteers packed up boxes of baby clothes for Bosnia. They achieved 1500 boxes in six hours on the premise that the 'next person to look in that box would be a Bosnian mum'. In another project a group of 5 to 8 year-olds set out to recruit people to reclaim an inner-city estate park. The playground had been vandalized. 200 young volunteers turned up with their mothers and fathers and completed the job. Such was the commitment and the sense of achievement that the group continued, one of their next tasks being to design and man a float in the following year's procession.

Several groups identified old people as the recipient of their volunteering. More than 200 old people had their houses re-decorated free of charge, using free end-of-line paint and wallpaper donated by local shops and hundreds of willing hands.

A 1950's science fiction book by Eric Frank Russell related the adventures of the crew of a spaceship from earth sent out to re-establish contact with groups which had left the planet some centuries earlier to colonize the galaxy – a sort of Startrek without the Klingons. On one of these remote planets, the intrepid explorers landed to find a society to which the concept of money was alien. In effect the only currency was 'obs' – the obligation to do a good turn to another member of the society, and an elaborate system of values had been worked out to measure the worth of an ob. Taking your neighbour to hospital might be worth 2 obs for example or helping to build a house for the community might be worth more. Food, medicine and all the trappings of community life were purchased through this system.

Modern community life is imitating science fiction art in a story originating in *The Independent* of June 1998. 'Taking your elderly neighbour to a hospital appointment might soon be an investment rather than just a good turn,' it said. 'A scheme to "pay" volunteers who take part in charitable work is to be launched next spring. Instead of cash, they will be paid in time. If they spend an hour taking a grandmother to hospital, they will be entitled to an hour of another volunteer's time. The "service credit" programme originated in America and is a key element in a presidential effort to rebuild fragmented communities in inner cities. There are more than 200 schemes in the US and one in Japan.'

The system is spreading. Edgar Calm, the inventor of service credit, gave a talk to 20 Local Government Chief Executive Officers in Britain to explain how the system works. It is said to be an important plank in the Government's plans to rescue some of the worst areas in Britain. When the social exclusion unit starts work next month, one of its major tasks will be to motivate people to 'turn around' problem estates and localities, starting with a 'Fair Shares' project in the Forest of Dean, Gloucestershire. It will work in conjunction with the Barnwood Trust, a voluntary charity.

In the USA, participants earn one 'time dollar' for each hour spent helping someone else. A simple computer programme records every dollar earned and spent and volunteers receive regular statements. The Clinton administration has ruled that time dollars are tax-free. This is important for volunteers who use them to 'pay' for health care. Several companies have agreed that time dollars can be exchanged for goods. Credit accounts can also be used as a form of old-age insurance. People do voluntary work now to qualify for help when they become infirm. Time dollars can also be traded for such services as meals-on-wheels, house cleaning, nursing care, neighbourhood security patrols and computer training work. In Chicago, teenagers who agree to 'mentor' younger pupils can 'cash in' their dollars on computer software.

Young people in Washington DC are paid in time dollars for participating in youth courts. Young delinquents are tried by their peers and, if convicted, face community service punishments. The offenders are then paid in time dollars for their community service. In Brooklyn, time dollars fuel an alternative economy for the aged. They can be spent on telephone bills, bereavement counselling and in reducing health insurance costs.

While ideas such as these may not be universally possible, or even desirable in some places, the concept of an alternative 'community currency' is well worth exploring in learning terms. Already learning card credit systems exist in several parts of the UK and Europe. It would not be too difficult to create a 'learning credits account' in the 'learning bank', earned through a variety of voluntary activities.

Thailand provides an example of community activity in villages. The village learning centre is the Thai's main source of knowledge and is run by villagers themselves with help from national and local government. Indeed they are often the only local source of knowledge for the villagers and fit into the particular Thai structure and philosophy of Lifelong Learning. Some of the centres are attached to schools, some to Buddhist temples and others are situated in the village square. They give rise to a variety of self-help activities, using mentoring and active learning techniques in the quest for their own learning society. The story is told of a garage owner, fluent in eight languages, which he had learned mainly from the radio with some help from the knowledge sources available at these centres.

The Leader II programme of the European Community has supported a similar self-help project in Finnish villages. The Village Action Movement is a well-known example of the Learning Community at work. In response to the increasing isolation from decision-making centres, the movement started by establishing voluntary committees to energize village life. At the beginning, training is provided for village leaders to help them understand how the village can be vitalized into a more active living community. When they return to their own community, the ideas are discussed with the villagers themselves and plans to implement them are put in place with their consent. In this way villagers start small tele-cottaging businesses, and create novel new services.

For example, the village of Muurikkala in south-east Finland has established a village service centre, runs its own school and provides tourist services to its municipality. Alkuvoima is a women's village group contacting young farmers in Europe to determine their daily life. Since unemployment in Finland is as high as 20 per cent many village groups are examining job creation opportunities, and how to expand local economies. Many villages have now taken charge of their own physical, economic and cultural development. The emphasis is on mobilization and motivation through greater self-esteem, the building of confidence and the discovery of creativity. Theatre and other cultural activities abound and projects to repair piers, build ice hockey rinks, parking lots etc are carried out as a matter of course. Schools, community centres, individuals join in. The whole is supported by a strong system of regional co-ordinators who can offer advice and assistance whenever needed.

Perhaps the Philippines set an example to us all in fostering community involvement from an early age. The State Constitution says, 'The State shall encourage non-formal, informal and indigenous learning systems as well as self-learning, independent and out-of-school study programmes, particularly those that respond to community needs, and provide adult citizens, the disabled and out-of-school youth with learning in civics, vocational efficiency and other skills.' Learning cities can build upon national statements of intent by providing the means by which people of all ages can make their own contribution to the community in which they live, and by challenging them to do so through innovative projects to satisfy pressing needs.

Chapter 21

Environment in the learning city – improving the future quality of life

---

A learning city energizes programmes, which enable all citizens to take positive action to care for the environment.

'Lifelong learning is also linked to sustainable development. Unless all peoples recognize the threat to the planet, and are educated in alternative ways in which its resources may be husbanded, the outlook for the world by the Year 2050, for example, looks increasingly bleak. Thus lifelong learning is linked to the idea of continuous education for all as a means of creating a society able to respond intelligently to the world predicament.' So said John Dewar Wilson in a fascinating article on Australian developments. Supra-national governmental organizations are well aware that environmental matters are not just important, they are a potential threat to continued survival on the planet. They also know that action has to be taken in local communities not just to educate both children and adults about environmental issues, but also to promote projects in which the citizens of a learning city, for example, can preserve and improve their own environment.

We may learn from Thailand, where the concept of 'Khitpen' involves people in the preservation of harmony with their own environment. It is a part of the Thai culture and a key principle in the development of a learning society in that country. But the need for effective management of local environments extends beyond a single community. The depletion of resources and the destruction of ecosystems is a threat to survival, not just of human beings but of all other species on the planet. Despite a continuous assault on individual consciousnesses by environmentalists, complacency is still rife. As has been observed ad nauseam, 'Think globally – act locally' is a well-known environmental watchword with wide implications for local communities. The care and maintenance of our only planetary habitat starts in kindergarten in local communities and continues throughout the education chain into late life. There is a crucial need to educate continually all people in environmental matters as a basis for the survival of species on earth. In this the learning city can be inventive and innovative about how environmental information is kept constantly in the forefront of popular consciousness, and how it can mobilize its citizens to take care of the local environment.

Since the publication of the Brundtland report on sustainable development, environmental matters have caught the imagination of schoolchildren all over the world. They, as inheritors of the planet, more than any group want to do something about it. UNESCO has fed that desire through the designation of one day each year known as 'Earth Day'. All the schools in its 'Associated Schools Project' participate, and the creativity displayed can give ideas to many a Learning City. In Bangladesh, for example, students of the Viqarunnisa Noon School and College of Dhaka decided to start Earth Day activities by cleaning up their immediate surroundings, their classrooms and school grounds.

In order to involve as many students as possible, they organized three different contests. A poster contest on environmental pollution allowed individuals and groups to increase awareness in the school and the neighbourhood by designing posters to illustrate its effects on people. A speech contest involved pupils in preparing and making a speech on four different topics: the greenhouse effect, air pollution, water pollution and health hazards caused by chemical wastes. An article contest, the winning entry to be published in the local newspaper, was also organized on 'How to keep the planet free of pollution and how to maintain the ecological balance of this earth which is our abode'. The winners were rewarded at a prize-giving ceremony in the presence of members of the community as well as the Bangladesh National Commission for UNESCO. This was accompanied by an exhibition of posters and drawings displayed in the hall.

In Chad, where there is an acute problem of deforestation, teachers, students and parents from schools in two villages, Gaoui and Koundoul, embarked on an intensive tree-planting campaign. Both villages are located in the vicinity of the capital city, Ndjamena, a semi-desert region where there is also a 30 per cent rate of illiteracy. The population lives primarily from agriculture which is dependent on rainfall. Because of deforestation, the immediate environment is threatened by the advancing desert. Hence, the young people worked together to improve their immediate communities by planting 1320 trees. The project also enabled the students from the two villages to understand each other better. Such was the success of this event it is now an annual project and a long-term environmental education programme is being developed.

In an ASP High School in Parral, Chile, an 'Ecological Brigade' was established which mobilized volunteer students to take an active part in defending their environment against pollution and neglect. These are some of the initiatives used:

- The preparation and maintaining of a mural journal on one of the walls of the school in which information was provided on local, national and world environmental topics.
- The launching of a publicity campaign during which articles were written for publication in the local press. The local radio station was also contacted to help disseminate information on the ecological concerns of the school. Posters with such captions as 'Have a good vacation but . . . be careful not to start forest fires' and 'Have a good vacation but please do not litter' were displayed in public places.
- The use of stickers bearing environmental messages on notebooks, car windscreens, etc.
- In co-operation with local officials from the municipality and engineers from wood-processing factories, a special ceremony was held on Earth Day which involved the planting of 150 native trees.
- The 'First Student Ecological Encounter' was organized involving students from several other schools in the city which led to proposals for a permanent form of action in defence of the environment.
- The city of Parral was declared an 'ecological community' and the school believes that its work contributed to receiving this distinction.

In Greece, the students of the Third High School of Naoussa conducted a project entitled 'Streets – Squares – Suburbs', which aimed to provide them with more knowledge and a better understanding of the history, traditions, architecture and environmental issues of their city. All 125 streets in the city were recorded and students collected information and completed a questionnaire concerning each street – its historical characteristics, problems and solutions. The pupils took photographs and slides of many streets in order to better document their research and undertook action to beautify the streets through cleaning parks and collecting and recycling products made from paper and aluminium.

The students tried to sensitize the members in their community about their project by publishing articles in the local newspaper and by giving interviews on the radio and television.

At the end of the year, an exhibition illustrating the students' work and efforts was displayed at the Town Hall. The students also gave a performance on an environmental issue at the municipal theatre which was attended by many students from the city and their parents.

An attractive illustrated calendar on the theme 'Vermio – Our Mountain'was prepared by the students and sold for the benefit of the project. A book highlighting the project is under preparation. It explains the environmental problems facing the community and possible solutions. Upon its completion, it will be presented to the Mayor.

The marketplace at Dubreka, in New Guinea, is a natural meeting-point for the local community, but was not as clean as it ought to be. So the students of the

Secondary Teachers' Training College of Dubreka decided to make what they considered the most useful contribution towards improving the hygiene of this very crowded area: ie to build some latrines and washing facilities. By combining their forces they built two toilets and a washroom that can also be used for ritual ablutions. Apart from saving a lot of time for users of the market, these buildings are part of a campaign to improve sanitation and make the urban population of Dubreka aware of the importance of a clean and hygienic environment.

Among the activities carried out by the Trefort Teacher-Training School in Budapest was the conduct of a conference on pollution and their cultural heritage. In Hungary, 9575 buildings are protected as historical monuments and 10 per cent of them are in an endangered state. Due to water and air pollution, caused mainly by the use of leaded fuel, the buildings are crumbling and falling into pieces.

In an effort to sensitize young people to their threatened cultural heritage and to seek ways and means for improvement, the school invited some 160 students from 14 European countries to discuss the issue at stake. A number of field visits to such places as the Szentendre Folk Museum, the Esztergorn Museum of Christian Art, Buda Castle, the Parliament, the Dutch and Italian Embassies, provided the students with an opportunity to see for themselves the restoration work required.

The students also took part in a simulation exercise. They were divided into groups, each one representing a delegation of a country (17 countries in all). Information on environmental pollution in Hungary was provided by the Hungarian National Commission for UNESCO and student delegations tried to find out information about the respective countries in order to identify the common problems shared by all countries.

Such stories provide many ideas for Learning Cities on how educational organizations can involve themselves in the environmental community. However, there are also possibilities to engage a wider cross-section of the community in the care of their own environment. An example of this might be a series of 'watch' schemes which preserve and monitor the local environment. Organized along the lines of a neighbourhood watch programme, a UK programme in which groups of people keep guard in the neighbourhood against burglars and crime, the idea could extend to tree-watch, weather-watch, bird-watch, river-watch, coast-watch, insect-watch, and any other project which involved people learning about, and monitoring, aspects of the environment.

Technology, such as acid rain kits, air and water pollution testing equipment, small hand-held computers could also be used to record, analyse and describe changes. National and international links would bring in new learning and opportunities for useful and fascinating collaborative work. They could also provide the basis for a constantly updated local environmental database not only giving information to local officials but usable by schoolchildren and other members of the public as well.

Chapter 22

Strategies for the learning city – celebrating and rewarding learning

A learning city stimulates the community and whole families to learn by running festivals, fairs and other fun events which promote the habit of learning.

The need for communities to celebrate learning and the achievement of learners is an important part of the work of the learning city. Much research into learning shows that reward systems are a significant part of the participation process. Chapman and Aspin (1997) point out that: 'A prime prerequisite for lifelong learning for all is that schools and other institutions for education offer environments in which students experience a sense of self-worth, a sense of excitement and challenge in learning, and a sense of success and lasting achievement in making their learning gains.' Even recreational activities produce competencies in learners that need to be recognized by the community in a way that is consistent with the local culture.

Longworth and Davies (1996) reported that, in Japan, many people have their own learning and achievement record, a sort of annually updatable curriculum vitae which includes details of significant events in the life of the holder during the year. It is celebrated in the learner's own family and among the community at large, usually on birthdays. The acceptability of that process in other cultures may be questionable, but the principle of learning celebration is one for attention in the Learning City.

Recommendation 11 of the European Commission High level committee on the Information Society is entitled 'Celebrating the local community':

> A vital step towards reinvigorating the spatial community is to promote cultural production and consumption at local level. This is important as part of helping to reassert a sense of place and pride, to develop people's natural creativity (especially

in remote or peripheral areas) and as an educational process. The natural place for cultural expression is in the public sphere, and policies for the Information Society should be expressly committed to developing public arenas and the shared celebration of culture.

This recognition of celebration in the learning city is typical of the way in which government organizations are paying increasing attention to the value of reward and learning as fun.

However, one of the greatest celebrations of learning at any level would be for learning to be recognized as a great achievement in itself. Longworth and Davies (1996) suggest:

> There could be annual competitions in the community for the school, the company, the teacher, the local government department of the year. The judging could be done by those who have been excluded from the system – the unemployed, the homeless, the under-educated and this would provide a way of extending learning and motivation to the currently unmotivated. Local well-publicised 'learning days', coinciding with the start of a new school, adult education and vocational training terms, and incorporating parades, concerts and plays, are another way of injecting fun.

Families too are important. Special programmes to enhance the role of the family in the community should be initiated. Longworth and Davies in *Lifelong Learning* suggested that 'families which learn together are more likely to stay together'. Schemes might include joint family qualifications, family learning days, inter-family links through e-mail to others in the locality, the country or internationally, the family learning album and the development of special family courses.

An example comes from Colombia, where pupils of Grade XI of the INEM Santiago Perez school centred on the integration of school and community. This included school activities for the fathers of families with the participation of specialists and artisans in the community and teaching staff from the school. The activity has two aims:

1. To improve family relations so that fathers fulfil better their role as fathers of families.
2. To improve the living standards of the population by providing courses for fathers to improve their skills, thus leading to a higher income and a better standard of living.

The UK think tank DEMOS has also been concentrating on family learning. It identifies five types of learning:

- Informal learning in the family.
- Family members learning together.

- Learning about roles and relationships and responsibilities in relation to stages of family life.
- Learning how to understand, take responsibility and make decisions in relation to wider society.
- Learning how to deal with agencies that serve families such as schools and social services.

It recommends that Government should take much greater note of the opportunities which family learning offers for social stability.

Following suit, the UK Campaign for Learning ran its Family Learning Day in the September of 1998 and will make this an annual event. In its publicity leaflet it describes the purpose of the day:

> Family Learning Day is an opportunity for families and their friends to get together and have fun learning something new. The learning may be new to the whole family or may be a chance for one family member to share skills or knowledge with the rest of the family.

It points out that the family was, traditionally, a significant source of learning, which passed to the school with the introduction of compulsory education. Nevertheless, even today, children spend less than 15 per cent of their waking hours in school, and this is where the opportunity for learning in the family arises. The Campaign believes that lifelong learning will be essential for survival in the 21st century. In the past an adult may have expected to learn the majority of skills and knowledge required to earn a living in the early years of life. In the future that early learning will only be the foundation stone for a lifetime of learning. A family life that embraces learning can help to confirm the habit of continual learning from early life. Adults can no longer assume that they are familiar with everything being taught in school. By learning with their children, they not only support the children's learning but also discover new things themselves.

Ideas which arose from the day were:

- for libraries
    - invite authors to discuss writing about family relationships;
    - run a competition for children to write family stories;
    - provide family history tracing packs and the impetus to produce a family history scrap book.
- for mueums and galleries
    - promote family visits through local schools;
    - organize a paint a family portrait competition.
- zoos, aquariums, etc
    - work with local newspaper to produce a feature on animals in the community.

- residential homes
  - interview the residents to provide a picture of family life 30 years ago;
  - organize a teach-in for older people given by youngsters;
  - preserve memories of family life through audio and videotapes.
- universities
  - organize a family fun day;
  - give a discount on fees for more than one family member.
- youth clubs
  - make displays on members' family history;
  - use the Internet to teach older people;
  - organize a family learning day.
- schools
  - organize an after-school family activity;
  - run a weekend family learning activity;
  - organize a family competition;
  - launch a family literacy project.

Indeed, in Britain, several initiatives have taken place on this theme through a competition organized by the National Institute for Adult and Continuing Education. Courses for parents from 'Helping your child at school' to 'Making Christmas Gifts in the Family' abound. In Calderdale, classes in 'Learning for children and adults together' gathered 500 parents and their children. Moreover, it encouraged many of those parents, many of whom had dropped out of regular education, to continue with other classes offered by the authority.

Kent TEC has established a Children's University' (see Chapter 25) and travelling roadshows on learning. These are just the thin end of a very fat wedge of creativity being encouraged to bring families closer together in community events. In fact, the Campaign for Learning identified 29 organizations interested in family learning in England and Wales alone. These include the nicely named University of the First Age, which runs learning experiences for parents, older students and members of the community to support young people aged 11to16 as they learn.

Learning cities are the natural catalysts for the celebration of learning. Ideas from the learning festival in Sapporo (see Appendix 2) to the use of schools and other institutions as community centres for family learning abound. This is a topic for yet another creative development session in each city.

Chapter 23

Summarizing the learning city – putting it together

Part 2 has tried to provide an overview of the essential characteristics of the learning city and examples of what is happening in some of them. Those readers with a passion for word games will have noticed that the chapters have followed an acronymic progression. Figure 23.1 below summarizes the points that have been made.

The list is of course incomplete, partly because the list of projects and activities taking place throughout the world is enormously long and partly because new concepts and new perceptions of what a learning city is and what it can do for its citizens will evolve over time. It is a self-generating experience. Like a learning organization, the moment a learning city stops learning about itself, stops trying to be innovative and looks inwards into itself is the moment it ceases to be a learning city. Moreover each learning city will inject its own cultural identity into the development process.

Cities are now making great strides to develop their infrastructures, their organizations and their people to cope with the increase in demand for learning already taking place. That effort will increase exponentially in the future, some of it required by government, but mostly because it is the most obvious and most effective way to implement lifelong learning into the 21st century, the learning century.

By the millennium, no city can afford not to be a city of learning. It is the new imperative for cities. But it needs to be more than just a label. In the city we are now seeing the fusion of the individual as a sentient human being with personal needs, dreams and talents, and the individual as a member of a community within which those needs, dreams and talents and requirements are not only fulfilled, but also donated to others. It is a rich and exciting time.

A learning city is one with plans and strategies to encourage wealth-creation personal growth and social cohesion through the development of the human potential of all its citizens and working partnerships between all its organizations.

L	Leadership	Links its strategy to the development of leadership and learning counselling courses and skills in and for the whole community
E	Employment and Employability	Effects plans to define and develop skills and competencies which make all its citizens employable
A	Aspirations	Activates the creative potential of its citizens through a Strategy for encouraging the use of personal learning plans, mentors and guides in citizens of all ages
R	Resources	Releases the full potential of community resources, including human resources, by enabling mutually beneficial partnerships between public and private sectors
N	Networks	Nourishes tolerance and outward-looking mindsets through projects to link citizens of all races, ages and creeds locally, nationally and internationally
I	Information	Increases participation in learning by devising innovative strategies to provide information where people gather, and proactive publicity campaigns to promote learning
N	Needs and Requirements	Nurtures a culture of learning by proactively auditing the learning requirements of all its citizens and providing the opportunities to satisfy them
G	Growth	Generates wealth and employment through innovative use of existing resources and through creative projects with other learning communities
C	Change Management	Cultivates programmes which allow citizens to cope positively and without fear in a world of rapid change
I	Investment	Influences the future by linking learning strategies to cross-departmental financial and other strategies
T	Technology	Transforms the city into a modern centre of learning by the effective use of the new learning technologies
I	Involvement	Inspires citizens to contribute to city life and culture by building a database of their skills, knowledge and talents and encouraging them to make them available to others
E	Environment	Energizes programmes which enable all citizens to take positive action to care for the environment
S	Strategies for the Family	Stimulates the community and whole families to learn by running festivals, fairs and other fun events which promote the habit of learning.

Figure 23.1 Learning cities – facing the future

Chapter 24

Valediction – starting the process

What this book has tried to outline is nothing less than the total transformation of cities, towns and regions into places ready to meet the challenge of the 'learning century'. It is an investment in the development of the environment, the workplace, leisure opportunities, the family. But most of all it is an investment into the sort of learning which reaches into the hearts and minds of people. For many, the process is already happening. An increasing number of people are already making the personal investment into their own future. But this also has the effect of marginalizing those who, for whatever reason, do not have the vision, the motivation, the resources, or the means to protect themselves from the process of rapid and inevitable change. And this creates instability both in the individual and in society as a whole. There is a need for new rites of passage based on learning, and encompassing both the acquisition and the contribution of talents, skills, values, understanding and expertise from and into the community.

This predicates a rapid cascade system of education for those people who will be the movers and shakers of the new learning city, spreading knowledge and awareness of the benefits it can bring to its citizens. At the end of the ELLI/Southampton conference, I was asked by several delegates to say what the initial steps should be to kick-start the process into a sustainable strategy. Thus, the following are seven initial recommendations made to these as a first action plan. They are in the process of being implemented in some cities now. For cities now setting out on the journey, key projects should aim at three targets:

- creating consensus and a sense of common purpose among the leadership groups in the city;
- collecting data on learning requirements which the city can use;
- preparing and informing citizens through publicity and promotion campaigns.

The following therefore proposes actions to do this:

1. Organize a one-day launch conference for key people – 'xxxx – a learning city for a learning century'. This might be for 50 to 500 city leaders and would include creative development and discussion sessions inviting ideas and comment on the different aspects of a learning city. Topics might include:

   - how to give and receive information to citizens;
   - how to deal with problems of exclusion;
   - how to motivate citizens to care for their own environment;
   - how to discover Learning Needs and Requirements;
   - how to mobilize people in the Community;
   - how networks can be increased and used positively;
   - how can existing resources be more equitably shared?
   - how can leadership skills be developed and used?
   - what are the skills and attributes needed to promote employability?
   - how can the learning city promote new investment and growth?
   - what are the new uses of digital technology in the learning city?
   - what strategies can we put in place to promote the family?
   - what type of partnerships will benefit the city and how can they be of benefit to all partners?

And, of course, other topics with specific relevance to the particular city. Speakers should be knowledgeable, inspirational and from inside and outside the city, and include well-known celebrities who can describe how learning has contributed to their success. Each small group session should be prepared with a list of questions, led by an expert who inspires the creative expression of ideas and opinions. Feedback is important.

2. Organize and run 12 one-day Lifelong Learning workshops for different audiences and groups within the city. These might be, in no particular order:

   - The Learning City Committee;
   - Business, Industry and Commerce, Chambers, TECs, etc;
   - Higher Education;
   - Local Government staff;
   - Local Government Councillors;
   - Schools – teachers and heads;
   - Adult Education Groups, etc;
   - Community Leaders – NGOs, informal education groups;
   - Schools and Industry;
   - Local Government and Higher Education;
   - Mixed Audience.

The workshops, for 15 to 20 people each, should be delivered by knowledgeable experts and promote a cascade model, in which the participants are expected to deliver similar workshops for 15 to 20 other people. Materials should be developed by the expert with copyright release to enable them to do this. At least three-quarters of the time, participants in the workshops should be actively involved in case studies, creative discussion sessions, brainstorms, etc the outcomes being the ideas and actions which that group from that sector can contribute to the development of the city as a learning city. Topics from the list in 1 above may be useful.

3. Start a Learning Requirements Audit (Needs Study and Contribution Survey). This may be based on a tailored questionnaire agreed by all parties and led by higher education researchers in the city universities. The actual collection of data could be carried out by a variety of people, including the unemployed, who would themselves learn much from the exercise. The questionnaire might be carried out in industry and in the community and could include the potential contribution of the interviewee to the city or to others in the city. In this, citizens would be requested to think about what their own contribution could be to the development of the learning city in terms of their talents, skills and knowledge and encouraged to make these available, either as mentors for others or as advisers to organizations developing courses. Initially it may be a pilot project involving, say, 210 people from different sections of the community eg:

   - 30 unemployed
   - 30 graduates in work
   - 30 skilled people in work
   - 30 semi-skilled workers
   - 30 unskilled workers
   - 30 young people under 18
   - 30 Third Age

Categories may change but it should be a cross-section. Based on the results of this study, the decision may be taken to extend the exercise to involve many more people and lead to a database of the learning needs of all citizens, made available to the learning providers at all levels. Grants may be made to the latter to help them carry out their own learning audits from which they can develop new courses based on awareness of need.

4. A pilot action project to develop and administer three of the key tools and techniques of Lifelong Learning – Personal Learning Plans, mentoring programmes and e-mail/Internet links. Personal Learning Plans should be designed, developed and tested from existing prototypes that can be used to encourage learning and personal development. They may be individual to the city. The

guides and mentors encouraged by the questionnaire in 1 above. Mentoring programmes might be developed for schools or generally within the community. E-mail or Internet links could target groups generally regarded as excluded, such as third agers, the unemployed or the handicapped and should include local and international links. They can be carried out as part of a local, national or European programme such as Socrates, Leonardo or ILA.

5. Prepare a Millennium Learning Conference to bring together all parts of city life and launch the 21st century.

6. Prepare for 21st century educational methods and partnerships by developing and delivering a course on Learning Counsellors (see Chapter 2). This should be done in conjunction with Teacher Training Colleges, Higher Education and Industry and incorporate the best of existing practice and knowledge with the new tools which are also useful to the learning city, eg:

   – moving the focus from teaching to learning;
   – empowering learners through new learning techniques;
   – identifying and profiting from individual learning styles;
   – failure-free learning;
   – the role of the personal tutors;
   – administering personal learning plans (as above);
   – personal mentoring;
   – using networks effectively;
   – developing open learning materials;
   – using distance learning and self-learning programmes;
   – using educational databases;
   – keeping records of achievement, smart cards, passports, etc.

Many of the skills listed here are available from a variety of sources within the city, What is proposed therefore is to develop a cut down course which would give an overview and some practical hands-on practice to a core of people who would then be the new generation of teacher/counsellors.

7. Develop a Publicity/Information/Promotion Campaign to market the Learning City concept to its citizens. This should be sensitively and professionally carried out. Communication is always the most important, and the most difficult, aspect of changing perceptions and creating new concepts like learning cities. Most people are not educationists and are unfamiliar with either the jargon or the new education methodologies. Most are not even familiar with the term 'Lifelong Learning' and remain unconvinced of the need. The activities under this heading would include jargon-free, attractively presented booklets, pamphlets and other reading materials, a poster campaign (including smaller posters for

shops, offices, schools and other organizations), media promotion through TV and radio, press coverage, and the development of a Learning Festival to take place with the millennium conference (see Appendix 2). Booklets/pamphlets might include such titles as:

– Learning and the citizen – making the most of our potential (cf the booklet for all families issued with the Sapporo Learning Festival – see Appendix 2)
– xxxxxx – City of Lifelong Learning
– Learning is fun
– How to learn
– What you can do to make xxxx a City of Lifelong Learning

They should be entertaining, interesting and engage the reader as an equal without talking down. Different booklets may have to be written for different age groups or target audiences.

8. Design your own city 'learning charter' outlining the philosophy and vision of the city *vis-à-vis* its Lifelong Learning policy. The ELLI cities model shown in Figure A1.1 (Appendix 1) may be sufficient, but cities may choose to modify this.

9. Join an organization which can help the city and its people to make contact with people and organizations in other aspiring learning cities to participate in learning forums and expand their knowledge and vision. The ELLI cities network, described in Appendix 3 is one such.

Many of these activities might be carried out by local universities such as Sheffield Hallam Centre for the Learning City.

Following the idea mentioned earlier of 'we shall know when we have learning city when . .', cities may also wish to set overall targets based on progress and destination. An example of this might be:

– when 75 per cent of the City's organizations are practising learning organizations (according to the suggested definition in Appendix 4); and
– when 75 per cent of the city's people are actively involved in learning; and
– when 75 per cent of the city's people are contributing to the further development of the city as a learning city; and
– when 75 per cent of the city's people have personal learning plans; and
– when 75 per cent of the city's people act as mentors for other people's learning.

And so on. The percentages and the targets may differ, the journey to becoming a learning city may have interim objectives, and many cities will wish to be more specific for each sector of the community. But such statements help to articulate the vision expressed in the city charter and create a more positive mindset.

Learning cities will follow their own star, inserting their own culture and their own inspiration into the strategy they adopt. They should not be diverted from their long-term vision by the vicissitudes of political, social and economic life. Such short-term crises inevitably occur in every city, but more effective learning is common to all politics outside of dictatorships, and its benefits extend across all aspects of city life. For most this is a long journey stretching well into the 21st century. Lifelong learning is both the incentive and the goal, and its tools and techniques are the methodology by which cities become learning cities. It is a worthy cause.

Chapter 25

Case study: Kent – region of learning

The region of Kent has, since 1996, embarked on a multi-organization strategy for raising the learning levels of its population and for improving knowledge of the need for lifetime learning across its geographical area. The following account by Steve Matthews and Nicholas Fox, to whom I am indebted, charts its progress and the places where it needs to improve its performance. Many of the initiatives described here echo issues raised in earlier chapters, particularly the suggestion that lifelong learning is a holistic mission requiring combined and co-ordinated commitment by every sector of the community. Kent is in no doubt that this process will not be complete until well into the next century.

Introduction

This case study describes in some detail how Kent has responded to the challenge of becoming a learning region. We explain the successes of the *Kent Learning* strategy, but also share what we have learned from our less successful ventures. We also aim to shed light on the daily challenges faced by the many people, from a variety of public, private and voluntary sector organizations, who have worked to deliver the objectives of the 'cradle to grave' regional learning strategy.

Firstly, we provide background information on Kent and give an overview of the *Kent Learning* strategy. Next, we explore *Individual Commitment to Learning*, the research basis of interventions by Kent Training & Enterprise Council (Kent TEC) and provide five case studies of lifelong learning initiatives developed in Kent. Finally, we review our progress against Norman Longworth's *Learning Cities* checklist and conclude with some reflections on our experience to date and aspirations for the future.

Kent – garden of enterprise and learning

Kent is located in the south-eastern corner of England, between London and the Nord Pas de Calais, France. 1.5 million people live in the region, which is also home to some 43 000 businesses and has an active workforce of around 700 000 people. In 1996, after extensive research and consultation, major local institutions launched the *Kent Learning* strategy and *Kent Prospects*, the complementary economic development strategy. The basic thrust of these key strategic initiatives was to link the economic success and social cohesion of the region to ambitious plans for more and better learning across all ages and in all contexts.

While the *Kent Prospects* strategy identified twelve priority sectors for action by a regional strategic partnership working to specific performance indicators, *Kent Learning* sought to engage the *entire population* of Kent by targeting all individuals and all employers. Taken together, these two interdependent initiatives, which secured the active support and engagement of all key public, private and voluntary organizations, set out a vision of success, labelled *Invest in Kent*:

> By the year 2006, we see Kent – the 'Garden of England' – having become a garden
> of enterprise and learning, where innovation and excellence thrive alongside the
> county's rich legacy of countryside and heritage.

The achievement of this vision would be reached by the implementation of a learning strategy which sought to raise the volume, quality and accessibility of learning across a continuum of ages and life circumstances. Specific sections of the strategy and dedicated subsets of the regional strategic partnership would work to specific targets in six contexts:

- Parents and families;
- Pre-school;
- Primary and secondary education;
- Post-16 education and training;
- The working years;
- Third age.

Nine key priorities, ranging from universal access to pre-school education to special provision for people with disabilities, are to be addressed by the partners and specific targets set to measure the success of the initiative. The targets are ambitious and seek to redress the relative underperformance of the Kent population when compared with other parts of the south-east of England. Divided between *Foundation Targets* for young people and *Lifetime Targets* for the adult population, the Kent Education and Training Targets (KETTs) even included measures for employers by proposing that 70 per cent of large firms and 30 per cent of small firms should achieve the *Investor In People* standard by the year 2000.

Research by Kent TEC conducted in 1997 gives an indication of the likely success of these targets. There has been progress towards the achievement of Lifetime Target 1, which aims for 70 per cent of the workforce to have a National Vocational Qualification (NVQ) or equivalent at Level 3 by the year 2006. From 1993 to 1997, Level 3 qualification had grown from 34.8 per cent to 38.9 per cent, while Level 4 qualification (Lifetime Target 2) rose from 20.7 per cent to 21.9 per cent. Although promising, these results are disappointing, when compared with the rest of the south-east of England, where growth in both target qualifications outstripped that in Kent (by a further 1 per cent and 0.4 per cent respectively).

The results for employer support of learning are equally positive. As the local agency responsible for assisting firms in achieving the *Investor in People* (IiP) standard, Kent TEC has excelled when compared with similar organizations in the UK. From 57th place in national league tables for IiP recognitions in employers with over 50 employees in 1996–1997, Kent TEC rose to first place in 1997–1998, while a Kent employer, Swaleside Prison won the national *Key Champion Award*.

In general terms, the picture in Kent is one of progress towards the achievement of the *Kent Learning* targets, but at a rate which is insufficient to meet the sponsors initial ambition. So, while the proportion of the workforce with qualifications is rising, Kent managers remain relatively underqualified when compared with their colleagues in the rest of the south-east.

More worryingly, the labour market is polarizing, as the number of people in Kent with no recognized qualifications remains high (19.9 per cent of the workforce, compared with only 16.4 per cent for the south-east as a whole) and the earning gap widens between the learning 'haves' and 'have nots', evidenced by the wage disparity between those with higher level qualifications and those with lower level or no qualifications. Thus, annual earnings for people with no recognized qualifications is £11, 573, while those for people with Level 4 qualifications is £22, 898, almost double the average (£16, 581). On the positive side, earnings figures in Kent demonstrate that 'learning pays', disproportionately better than in the rest of the south-east in fact, perhaps due to the relative scarcity of qualified staff.

In 1998, the partners to *Kent Learning* and *Kent Prospects* commissioned the consultants Ernst & Young to assess the impact of the strategies to date. The resultant *Competitiveness Report* identified significant progress towards the objectives for parental and pre-school learning, while progress in post-16 achievement, Further Education and Higher Education was more modest. The important contribution of the *Kent Forum for Lifetime Learning* (KFLL) was recognized, but re-structuring recommended. In particular, it was recommended that the links between the KFLL and its economic counterpart, the *Kent Economic Forum*, be strengthened. Greater commitment to the partnership and better co-ordination of sponsor strategies was also proposed, as was the idea that the partnership should be 'deepened' to increase the role of local district authorities. These issues are being addressed through a recent initiative led by Kent TEC to produce a Workforce Development plan in co-operation with key strategic partners.

Individual commitment – a research model for learning development

As a tool in the design and implementation of Kent TEC interventions and product development, the Individual Commitment to Learning (ICL) model has provided a framework for understanding learner behaviour and motivation. It has supported Kent TEC's policy of seeking to support individuals in their efforts to maintain their employability, benefit their communities and contribute to the competitiveness of the regional economy. The research model is statistically based, updating is ongoing and the approach has formed the basis of significant investments in the learning infrastructure by Kent TEC.

Initial research in 1994 clustered Kent learners into six groups, described briefly in Figure 25.1:

Learner Group	Outline characteristics
1 Learning enthusiasts	Typically female (18 – 24), more likely to stay in full-time education, have few barriers to learning, work in 'other services' (eg: public administration, clerical or professional occupations).
2 Committed to vocational learning, but unsure of wider possibilities	Typically male (35+), limited range of work experience, will learn for work purposes, often managers, administrators or professionals, less likely to study at home.
3 Learning is good if help provided	Typically public sector workers (25 – 34) but many unemployed, with a wide range of work experience, motivated to learn but not in traditional learning environments, main barriers cost, lack of family support, lack of time.
4 Learning for its own sake	Older, well qualified workers in managerial and professional occupations, few barriers to learning, keen to improve but sceptical of the benefits of learning.

5 Poor experience of wider opportunities	Narrow range of work experience, do not value their experience of education, mainly unemployed or working part-time and caring for children, typically female (25 – 34), have the most barriers to learning, such as family pressures, lack of finance, low estimation of the benefits of learning due to bad past experiences.
6 Switched off	Typically work part-time as plant / machine operatives and craftsmen, often aged 15 – 17, and have few opportunities for training and promotion at work.

Figure 25.1 Learner classifications in Kent

Further research in 1996 revisited the groups and assessed the effectiveness of targeted learning initiatives. There was little statistically relevant change in the relative size of the groups in the workforce, but new trends appeared to be emerging. Not least, that men's participation in learning decreased, while that of women increased. More encouraging findings emerged in terms of attitudes, auguring well for future changes in behaviour. Significantly higher proportions of the 1996 sample expressed the view that learning is something that people do throughout their lives and is a source of personal satisfaction. More people also reported having learned new skills at work and there was greater recognition of the work satisfaction to be gained if training is available. This significantly more positive attitude towards learning has yet to result in an equally significant increase in numbers actually in learning.

Case studies from Kent – success through partnership

Five brief case studies (set out below) give an indication of the breadth and impact of learning development work under way in Kent. They also demonstrate the value of the strategic approach taken by the *Kent Learning* partners and the contribution of strong local partnerships to success.

Kent Children's University aims to raise the aspirations of 7 to 9-year-olds by offering non-curricular Saturday morning classes in schools and universities on Saturday mornings. The number of participating schools has risen from four to forty, and special events have involved parents and relatives in exciting learning activities. Driven by the local Education Authority, the initiative has drawn wide support from employers, other agencies and talented individuals.

The Real Game, a careers game discovered during a senior-level study tour by the *Kent Forum for Lifetime Learning* to the Second Global Conference on Lifetime

Learning in Ottawa, is now running with 21 schools and 2445 14-year-olds, and has recently been adopted by the UK Department for Education and Employment for wider trials across the country. While a tribute to the commitment of Kent Careers Services to improving careers education for young people, it also demonstrates how international partnership networking can benefit local communities.

The Kent Guidance Consortium, a voluntary grouping of 19 providers of adult careers and educational information, advice and guidance, supported by Kent TEC, has developed and implemented a set of Quality Assurance standards which aim to guarantee a client focus to guidance delivery in Kent. Devised by senior practitioners from organizations as diverse as universities, colleges, voluntary organizations and specialists working in the private sector and with ex-offenders, the Consortium is now seen as a model of best practice by national guidance bodies and Government. In particular, an assessment and accreditation process based on peer assessment, but with external rigour has cemented cross-organizational co-operation and identified a common agenda for future joint improvement of practice and service.

The new network of Community Learning Utilities has enabled 14 user communities built around voluntary sector networks, neighbourhood ties, common interest and common need. With sponsorship by Kent TEC, the growing network has provided access to learning to several thousand non-learners in a non-traditional, community-based setting.

Kent has pioneered the development of Individual Learning Accounts, by devising account systems and learner support infrastructure. Delivered by Kent TEC in partnership with a wide variety of employer, voluntary, public and labour organizations, over 300 people will benefit from funding for learning paid into a special bank account and matched by a small individual contribution. Once the pilot trials have been completed the accounts will be made available to up to 30 000 individuals across the region.

The learning cities checklist – how Kent measures up

The 14-point checklist for effective learning communities developed by Norman Longworth provides an interest benchmark for assessing the success of the *Kent Learning* partnership. Figure 25.2 is self-assessment by the authors of the Kent case.

Learning Cities Category	Assessment of Kent
Leadership	Key leaders of opinion from business and education have endorsed the *Kent Learning* strategy. An effective network of guidance provision exists, but provision is not universally available to all adults due to insufficient funding, which can only be guaranteed to those seeking employment, studying or intending to enrol on a course. No initiative to expand the supply of leadership and counselling at present.
Employment & Employability	The *Kent Forum for Lifetime Learning* has set up a special group to define work readiness for all ages and educational levels. Collaborative research is expected to take place in 1999, to be followed by a Kent-wide initiative with employers.
Aspirations	The *Kent Learning* strategy includes the express objective that everyone in Kent should have a Personal Learning Plan (PLP). Kent TEC funded PLPs for 2500 people in 1997 – 1998, and will encourage all 30 000 Individual Learning Acount holders to do the same.
Resources	In addition to the *Kent Forum for Lifetime Learning*, most lifelong learning initiatives in Kent are delivered by and through partnerships. Work is in hand to 'deepen' and widen partnerships at local level and across organizational boundaries.
Networks	The very basis of the *Kent Learning* strategy is that Kent is special because of its location close to the heart of Europe and the workforce's need to compete in a global economy. Equal opportunities are a key element of each partner's agenda, and many projects aim to overcome barriers to learning and employment faced by disadvantaged groups.

Information	Significant resources have been deployed into mobile learning facilites, local learning centres and new locales for learning, such as shopping centres. With other partners in the South East, Kent TEC has launched a web-based online information resource of learning opportunites. A mass media marketing initiative led by Kent TEC in 1996 failed to generate enrolments on a scale required to justify further investment. However, in 1999, direct telemarketing of learning opportunities will take place in support of a variety of employer and individual learning initiatives.
Needs & Requirements	The Further Education colleges of Kent have led a special partnership which aims to widen participation in learning among groups disadvantaged in social, economic and physical terms. Kent TEC is producing a Workforce Development Plan, which will catalogue the learning needs of the workforce and form the basis of partner initiatives and external funding.
Growth	The Kent partnership has added significant input value in attracting external funding for lifelong learning initiatives into the region, but it is not clear yet whether the strategy is generating wealth in output terms.
Change Management	Many partners have measures to assist communities facing economic and social change. While projects are typically focused at very local level, mature partnerships with a county-wide sphere of influence tend to provide weight and support to local groups.
Investment	All direct pooling of agency resources is relatively rare, projects are typically based on a web of mutually supporting financial contributions from a variety of partners.

Technology	ICT lies at the heart of plans to widen access to learning in Kent. A regional Centre of Excellence is being established in Medway, while the *Kent Access* strategy aims to maximize connectivity and coherence of the ICT infrastructure.
Involvement	No database of the skills of the Kent population exists and the creation of such a major piece of infrastructure would probably be prohibitively expensive. Management information and learning market intelligence, though, will be a key feature of the Individual Learning Account system, and serious consideration is being given to joint resourcing of larger samples for the Kent Business and Household Surveys.
Environment	In addition to many local authority, employer and voluntary organization initiatives, European funding is being sought to create a dedicated virtual learning network to support Sustainable Business Partnerships. A desire by many to maintain the traditions of rural Kent, though, is often seen as a barrier to economic development, perhaps resulting in a disproportionately large traditional small firms sector not noted for a progressive attitude to employee development.
Strategies for the Family	The *Kent Learning* partners frequently combine resources for local events to promote and celebrate learning. Given the large geographical spread of the population, a Kent-wide celebratory initiative would probably be beyond the partners' combined discretionary resources.

Figure 25.2 How Kent matches up to Learning City Characteristics

The above discussion of the Kent experience viewed through the lens of the ELLI Checklist points to significant past successes, and, perhaps more importantly, to important plans for the future. A key brake on the more ambitious aspects of the Checklist is the cost of such interventions in a large geographical area like Kent. Lacking the compactness and accessibility of metropolitan areas, Kent may just be too big and too diverse. Despite these limitations, and the logical caution of partner organizations in committing limited discretionary resources to projects beyond their catchment areas and core activities, we feel that the Kent case generally scores well.

Conclusion

This brief review of the achievements and activities of the *Kent Learning* partnership points to three key lessons which can be drawn. First, specific plans – with specific, measurable targets – for learning regions provide a valuable focus for partner activity, even if some targets later emerge to be too ambitious or a change in circumstances leads to a change in emphasis in the activity of some partners. By measuring our performance against targets we set ourselves in 1996, we have learned much about what can and cannot be done. More importantly, we have been encouraged to reflect in detail on what we can do as individual organizations and in partnerships to deliver the *Kent Learning* vision.

Secondly, we are convinced that a strong research base significantly enhances the prospects of success in learning development initiatives. Although we are constantly reviewing the Individual Commitment to Learning learner motivation model, it has provided a valuable conceptual framework for the development of learning products and interventions by Kent TEC. Similarly, annual surveys of individuals and businesses, especially when supplemented with special studies of motivation, identify real trends which partners can seek to address. Perhaps more importantly, the research process itself provides valuable insights which can be incorporated into future activities.

Finally, we have learned to value the power of partnership in bringing regional learning strategies to life. Although through evaluation we have discovered that our partnership arrangements can be improved and that there are still barriers to more effective joint action, we have identified major benefits to be derived from the process. In addition to the coherence of purpose engendered by a shared vision, our experience shows that regional learning partnerships add value by allowing more effective use of partner resources and in attracting new ones. We have also learned that partnership requires new ways of working, based on a recognition of the specific concerns and needs of individual organizations and a willingness to take risks and operate across traditional boundaries. We look forward to working through the Kent Partnership to carry forward the vision of *Kent Learning* in the coming years.

Appendix 1

The ELLIcities charter for learning cities

The idea of a learning cities charter was a central tenet of a European conference on learning cities held in Southampton in June 1998. The difficulty is to put together a form of words with meaningful content to which every city can subscribe – presenting some of the why and how-to as well as the what. A document simply extolling the value of learning in a city would be so anodyne and analgesic as to be worthless – all vision and no action. Cities already value learning as a function of their statutory duty. The ELLI definition of a Learning Community as 'a city, town or region which goes beyond its statutory duty to provide education and training for those who require it, and instead creates a vibrant, participative, culturally aware and economically buoyant human environment through the provision, justification and active promotion of learning opportunities in order to enhance the potential of all its citizens'. This is somewhat long-winded but it is a big concept with big implications covering the three major OECD requirements of personal growth, social stability and wealth creation.

The draft ten-point charter shown in Figure A1.1 contains generic words covering many of the topics discussed at the conference and identifies key issues which learning cities can focus on in their learning journey as a matter of urgency – environment, partnership, technology, exclusion, contribution, celebration and proactive guidance and support.

Cities may choose to adopt the charter as it is written or to make modifications which conform to their own culture and approach. Those cities wishing to implement such a charter are invited to make this known to the ELLIcities organization, a European, and eventually global, network of learning cities being established in several cities and universities and described in Appendix 3.

A Charter for Learning Cities

WE RECOGNIZE THE CRUCIAL IMPORTANCE OF LEARNING AS THE MAJOR DRIVING FORCE FOR THE FUTURE PROSPERITY, STABILITY AND WELL-BEING OF OUR CITIZENS.

We declare that we will invest in lifelong learning within our community by:

1. **DEVELOPING PRODUCTIVE PARTNERSHIPS** BETWEEN ALL SECTORS OF THE CITY FOR OPTIMIZING AND SHARING RESOURCES, AND INCREASING LEARNING OPPORTUNITIES FOR ALL
2. **DISCOVERING THE LEARNING REQUIREMENTS** OF EVERY CITIZEN FOR PERSONAL GROWTH, CAREER DEVELOPMENT AND FAMILY WELL-BEING
3. **ENERGIZING LEARNING PROVIDERS** TO SUPPLY LIFELONG LEARNING GEARED TO THE NEEDS OF EACH LEARNER WHERE, WHEN, HOW AND BY WHOM IT IS REQUIRED
4. **STIMULATING DEMAND FOR LEARNING** THROUGH INNOVATIVE INFORMATION STRATEGIES, PROMOTIONAL EVENTS AND THE EFFECTIVE USE OF THE MEDIA
5. **SUPPORTING THE SUPPLY OF LEARNING** BY PROVIDING MODERN LEARNING GUIDANCE SERVICES AND ENABLING THE EFFECTIVE USE OF NEW LEARNING TECHNOLOGIES
6. **MOTIVATING ALL CITIZENS** TO CONTRIBUTE THEIR OWN TALENTS, SKILLS, KNOWLEDGE AND ENERGY FOR ENVIRONMENTAL CARE, COMMUNITY ORGANIZATIONS, SCHOOLS AND OTHER PEOPLE
7. **PROMOTING WEALTH CREATION** THROUGH ENTREPRENEUR DEVELOPMENT AND ASSISTANCE FOR PUBLIC AND PRIVATE SECTOR ORGANIZATIONS TO BECOME LEARNING ORGANIZATIONS
8. **ACTIVATING OUTWARD-LOOKING PROGRAMMES** TO ENABLE CITIZENS TO LEARN FROM OTHERS IN THEIR OWN, AND THE GLOBAL, COMMUNITY
9. **COMBATING EXCLUSION** BY CREATIVE PROGRAMMES TO INVOLVE THE EXCLUDED IN LEARNING AND THE LIFE OF THE CITY
10. **RECOGNIZING THE PLEASURE OF LEARNING** THROUGH EVENTS TO **CELEBRATE AND REWARD** LEARNING ACHIEVEMENT IN ORGANIZATIONS, FAMILIES AND INDIVIDUALS

On behalf of the City of ....SEAL

Signed ....

Title ....

Appendix 2

The Sapporo learning festival

As a by-product of opening a conference of Teacher Educators at the Educational University of Hokkaido in Asahikawa, I was privileged to spend a couple of days with Yoshihiro Yamamoto at the Sapporo learning festival. Yoshihiro is one of the lifelong learning luminaries in the National Institute of Educational Research, a division of Monbusho, the Japanese Ministry of Education. He is also doing sterling work in raising awareness of WILL in Japan and South-east Asia.

The festival was a fascinating experience. Its first impact was its size – the impression was of a Pacific Ocean of stands and demonstrations promoting every conceivable facet of Lifelong Learning for all sectors of national and community life and for all ages. It was not simply an exhibition of learning products, though IBM, Toshiba, Intec and the rest were certainly all there in force. Learning visitors could find, in addition, leisure products and pursuits of all kinds from fishing to fiddling, from sailing to skiing, from knitting to networking. It seemed that the whole of life was there. The spiritual side of Lifelong Learning was not neglected either – several religious groups were strongly represented – the sacred and the secular co-habiting under the flag of learning. There was a stand representing the 25 public Lifelong Learning Centres in Japan (there are also many private ones) and a large exhibition area promoting the virtues – economic, personal, familial, communal – of Learning. A telephone hotline was available to any who still harboured doubts.

On the central stage third age choirs sang anything and everything from traditional Japanese folk ballads, through American glee club numbers to classics; magicians and fire-eaters plied their trade and fast-talking presenters involved the passing public in games and quizzes and activities. The ectoplasm of vitality and energy was phenomenal, and smiling faces showed how much it was a fun occasion – a celebration of the learning condition.

I saw visiting classes of schoolchildren, including a set of 5-year-olds, mesmerized by the 'magic of learning' stand, complete with magician. A constant procession of visitors of all ages, all backgrounds and all interests mixed and mingled and meandered, ever, it seemed with a smile. Sapporo is a provincial city with a population of about a million souls, akin perhaps to Bordeaux, Newcastle, Thessaloniki or Dusseldorf, and the organizers expected to receive 600,000 of these during the five days.

In the evening more cultural events connected with the festival were held at the city hall. My host had managed to obtain tickets for the opening musical event and we arrived just five minutes before the start. This was impressive to say the least and it was played to a packed audience. The overture comprised a five minute film depicting the considerable natural beauties of the island of Hokkaido – and then faded out to a darkened stage containing a group of four people – two instrumentalists playing a primitive flute and a two stringed sitar respectively, and two singers – a mother and a child. Together they produced some of the most remarkable and evocative folk sounds I have ever heard. It was an epiglottal tour de force – all throat and lungs – a vocal tone poem describing the mystical sadness of the sea, the majesty of the mountains, the symbiotic maternal link between man and his environment, the joys and the sorrows of community and conflict in the natural world. These were sounds not heard outside of this area of Japan – a celebration of a thousand years of Ainu aboriginal culture, reminiscent of a Hebridean folk song, an Irish step dance, an Auvergnian mountain call, a Catalan lament or a Portuguese fado. To say the least it was an event which one experienced as much as heard, felt as much as saw.

The evening continued with three speeches from the Minister of Education, the head of the Hokkaido prefecture and the Sapporo city boss, all of them extolling the virtues of learning and the opportunities in the locality and all of them, mercifully for both stranger and citizen alike, not more than five minutes long. After that, further music from the city's close harmony group which rivalled the King's Singers in purity of sound, though not in breadth of output, and the City of Sapporo Symphony Orchestra.

For a provincial orchestra the quality was surprisingly high – it confined itself on this occasion to selections of light music, though one had the impression that it would have been equally at home with Bach, Beethoven, Brahms, Berg and Birtwhistle (well, OK, perhaps not Birtwhistle). In between whiles the local television personality interviewed the performers and extracted from them how learning had contributed to their success.

Every citizen received two attractively coloured pamphlets – one produced by the city and another by the island prefecture. These were 16 pages each, describing the rationale behind the joys of lifelong learning and explaining where, why, how and when the citizens of Sapporo could take advantage of them. They were surprisingly sophisticated and, in some ways, quite visionary. They dealt in simple terms with every facet of Lifelong Learning – networks, open and distance learning, the interaction between sectors of the community, integrated learning, qualifications etc and on an age-by-age basis from pre-school to third age. Their purpose was to broaden the horizons of the populace and even to encourage a strong international outlook.

There was a festival mascot – a Disneyesque character called the manabee (Honey bee). This was omnipresent whether as a huge blowup balloon, a print on festival products, a picture on shop windows and public notices, as badges to wear, or on T-shirts. It was the symbol of the festival – a sort of learning Mr Blobby. Manabee could hold a honey pot or a computer screen or walking stick or indeed could be adapted to help to market each product individually. Who said the Japanese are not creative? The overriding impression of the whole festival was exactly that – creativity and the enjoyment of learning.

How can I summarize this experience? Yes, of course it was a product of the Japanese culture and of course we are aware that there are cultural differences. It was a Japanese festival for Japanese people. It was one of a series planned on an annual basis for different parts of Japan – rather like the European cities of culture. Yes, of course we have to take into account cultural differences between nations. But there was an atmosphere about this event which transcended these. It was not brash or authoritarian – its aim was to stimulate, sensitize and coax rather than to exhort – to celebrate the joys of learning and the personal benefits to be gained therefrom. Perhaps 50 000 people, perhaps more, perhaps less, came into the learning fold for the first time.

We in Europe have much to learn about the marketing of learning, its representation as a way of life. This festival was an example of what happens in Japan – there are other beacons of lifelong learning activity there – such as the establishment of 25 lifelong learning research departments in Japanese universities, and the Lifelong Learning Centres springing up in each prefecture.

The 1996 European Year of Lifelong Learning helped both to educate and stimulate creative ways in which the peoples of Europe can become learners for life. In the same way that there is an annual European City of Culture, perhaps there should be an annual City of Learning, from which the rest can learn. Perhaps a competition to find the European learning city, perhaps the use of modern technologies to link people and organizations into learning networks between cities, perhaps the carrying out of a learning audit of the learning needs of whole populations and the establishment of a city-by-city database of these. ELLI has an interest and some initial experience in these. The possibilities are endless, and perhaps more to the point in a world of structural unemployment, the creation and satisfaction of learning opportunities is in itself a huge job creation scheme involving designers and planners, counsellors and councillors, researchers and promoters, and teachers and learners. Sounds good – let's do it.

Appendix 3

ELLI and ELLIcities

The ELLIcities network

Readers will know that almost every European government is producing strategies and policies to promote lifelong learning, This is because lifelong learning is known to be at the heart of the future and one of the most powerful influences on its development in education, society and national economies. But readers are also close enough to the action to know that most of the real development will take place at local and regional level, where organizations are situated and where people live. This explains the recent massive growth of 'learning cities, towns and regions' throughout Europe and the world at large.

ELLIcities is a major forum for the development of European cities, towns and regions as vibrant, innovative and exciting places whose citizens accept learning as a part of life. The ELLI definition of a Learning City is shown in Figure 8.1. Read it again. It is a challenging definition, covering all aspects of city life. It also has huge implications – for the administrators, public servants and teachers who will have to implement the new lifelong learning strategies, and for the citizens themselves who are on the receiving end of new structures and ideas. The range of activities and ideas for our lifelong learning future is both limitless and confusing.

Learning cities have been a focus for ELLI activities and research for several years. There are ELLIcity forums linked to other pioneering initiatives on lifelong learning in Europe and in the wider world. We are creating new forums so that city specialists can talk to each other, discuss problems and research solutions in good practice. We have plans to construct an electronic learning city, with schools, universities, City Halls, debating chambers, marketplaces, etc to create interaction between the social partners, encourage citizenship and fuel debate between communities. But for those unable to communicate in this way ELLIcities will also be a people network with frequent workshops and seminars to assist in building the learning city of the future.

One of the powerhouses of the ELLIcities work is the Sheffield Hallam University 'Centre for the Learning City'. Its mission is to assist cities to become learning cities through research activities, workshops, seminars and studies in all aspects of the learning city. It is also establishing a European network of such centres, initially based in Finland, Spain, Scotland, The Netherlands and the Czech Republic.

We know that the 21st century will be different and that the development of a culture of learning for life is the way to prepare for it. We know too that local communities will be the wellspring of action. We invite readers to join us in creating that future. It could be the best investment you will make this century. And of course there are the links to all parts of the European system through the ELLI organization.

Who is ELLI and what is it for?

Who is ELLI? It is the European Lifelong Learning Initiative – an organization offering knowledge, debate, support and action across the board at European level. This includes research and advice into the lifelong learning needs of schools, universities, companies, professional associations and cities. This breadth of vision and activity of its membership is the ELLI's strength and is available to the ELLIcities network.

ELLI was established in 1992 to initiate the dissemination of information, the co-ordination of projects and studies, the mobilization of actions, people and organizations to bring Europe into the Lifelong Learning Age. Its groups cover all sectors of society and all European countries:

Business, Industry and Commerce (ELLindustry) – where lifelong learning can be a survival strategy. ELLI provides examples of good practice from around the world and empowers its industry and commerce members through collaborative partnerships for developing lifelong learning strategies, which can be implemented to create learning organizations.

Higher Education (ELLIversities) – Higher Education is in a position to provide the intellectual and practical leadership for the development of Lifelong Learning programmes locally, nationally and internationally. ELLI mobilizes universities to take this leadership position through co-operative projects and programmes and workshops, seminars and conferences.

Schools and Teacher Training Establishments (ELLIschools and ELLIteachers) – lifelong learning begins in childhood, and schools are crucial organizations for shaping those attitudes and values which prepare future adults for a world in which flexibility and adaptability are essential ELLI exists to help and encourage teachers, teacher trainers, parents and others on how to create habits of learning which will last throughout life.

European and National Governments (ELLIgovernment)–they play a leading role in providing vision and setting standards. ELLI members have helped to put together government strategies for lifelong learning. ELLI acts as a link between European governmental organizations on good practice from which good strategies and policies emerge.

Vocational Education Organizations (ELLIvoc), which influence the creation and maintenance of employment for the future. ELLI believes that lifelong learning skills and practices are crucial for effective vocational education and training. It offers its members ideas, actions and solutions through which they can maintain employability as well as employment.

Adult Education Organizations (ELLIadult)–Second-chance colleges, leisure and sports education, Continuing Education, organizations in all areas with responsibilities to their constituencies, Museums, Libraries, Women's Groups, Local Societies. The list of people and organizations in and outside of the formal education system which become involved in the lifelong learning process is endless. They are crucial at all levels of human potential development and ELLI acts as a clearing house for information and activities in these areas.

Professional Associations and Non-Governmental Organizations (ELLIngos) – ELLI offers information and participation opportunities to NGOs and Professional Associations, whose members must keep themselves up to date and who need to know how the concepts of lifelong learning can be applied within their own organizations and for their members.

Towns, Cities, Regions, Communities (ELLIcities) – The ELLIcities group, described above, exists to provide a forum for all municipalities or regions wishing to become learning communities.

Above all, ELLI believes that, only through the integration of many of these sectors, will a Lifelong Learning Society become reality.

Legally, ELLI is a non-profit-making International Educational Organization registered in Brussels with a Board of Directors from Belgian and other European countries taken from its Administrative Council, This comprises distinguished people from industry, Professional Associations and Universities throughout East and West Europe and co-ordinates the guidelines for ELLI activities.

ELLI addresses a reservoir of European needs and demands, including:

- the creation of Learning Communities in every city, town and region;
- the development of Learning Organizations in every company, school, university and government department;

- advice to Governments on lifelong learning strategies for all and how to implement them;
- the development of a society in which the habit of learning throughout life is a part of everyone's personal growth and culture;
- the use of learning techniques and tools of the 21st century – technology, personal learning plans, audits, mentors, purposeful learning partnerships. etc.;
- the development of new skills and values to enable individuals to cope with a rapidly changing workplace and world;
- defining, measuring and monitoring progress to the acquisition of lifelong learning skills, values and habits in schools, universities, government departments, companies, communities, individuals.

Each one is a mammoth task. Each one, and more, presents challenges to those organizations with an awareness of the needs of the 21st century.

If ever we thought that lifelong learning could be implemented easily the (initial) task list should make us stop and think again. Everywhere and for years to come, there is much to be done. It demands insight, wisdom, energy and commitment – and leadership through a professional organization. Interested people and organizations are invited to contact ELLI.

The ELLI organization comprises a President, a Director-General, a Secretary-General, a Director of Strategy and a Director of Operations. But it is the members who are the executive arm of ELLI. They help to organize the learning development groups, conferences, workshops and seminars, participate in European educational programmes and working groups, and develop reports on various aspects of lifelong learning. These activities are increasing through the establishment of the ELLInets – networks of people and organizations which act as centres of lifelong learning expertise in their own countries. ELLInets are active in the UK, Finland, Italy, Germany, Sweden, Benelux, Poland, Russia and the Czech Republic, and others in Spain, France, Portugal, Greece, Ireland and seven other countries are in the process of being created.

Among the conferences which ELLI has organized is the highly successful European Commission's theme conference for the European Year of Lifelong Learning in Helsinki through ELLInet Finland, and the equally seminal Global Conference on Lifelong Learning in Rome, at which the World Initiative on Lifelong Learning (WILL) was created. Several others are planned, including a large pre-millennium conference 'Preparing for the Learning Century', also in Helsinki in Autumn 1999, and a millennium conference in Glasgow in the autumn of 2000.

Other projects carried out by ELLI in the past include the development of a work package to find the learning needs of people working in organizations (Learning Audits), a book on lifelong learning in Schools and Teacher Training Institutions and a brainstorming seminar for the European Commission TEMPUS Programme, which produced an ELLI-written report for greater University–Industry collaboration in Central Europe and changed the focus of the programme in most countries. Members of the ELLI team have given seminars on lifelong learning to government, universities and industry in Poland and the Czech Republic.

ELLI involves itself in and leads funded action research projects. Two of these, both supported by the European Commission through their Socrates and Leonardo Programmes, will serve as examples. The 'Learning Highway' project invites new and old members into an electronic learning space into which lifelong learning courses and case studies can be inserted and accessed. The 'Eurotoolls' project creates, among other things, a Personal Learning Plan template which people and organizations can adapt for their own purposes. These are accessible to old and new members at the following sites on the First-Class conferencing system on the World Wide Web – and http:/cmi.noesis.se.eurotoolls.

ELLI's vision is of a Professional Association relevant and necessary to all organizations, communities, governments and individuals in Europe, and serving its members and Europe with the ideas, information and action which will enable them both to learn from each other, and contribute to the development of lifelong learning of others, both nationally and at European level. It has a global arm in WILL (World Initiative on Lifelong Learning) which is just now beginning to establish 'WILLnets' in various regions of the world.

Please contact: European Lifelong Learning Initiative (ELLI),
Napier University, 219 Colinton Road, Edinburgh EH14 1DJ
Tel: +44 131 455 4607; Fax: +44 131 455 4570
and/or visit the ELLI web-site at http://www.ellinet.org
and/or e-mail: Norman_Longworth@csi.com

For ELLIcities please contact:
Sheffield Hallam University, Centre for the Learning City,
Learning and Teaching Institute, Pond Street, Sheffield S1 1WB, UK
Tel: +44 114 225 4729; Fax: +44 114 225 4755
E-mail: Norman_Longworth@csi.com

Appendix 4

A Learning Organization

---

10 Indicators of a Learning Organization

1. A learning organization can be a company, a professional association, a university, a school, a city, a nation or any group of people, large or small, with a need and a desire to improve performance through learning.

2. A learning organization invests in its own future through the Education and Training of all its people.

3. A learning organization creates opportunities for, and encourages, all its people in all its functions to fulfil their human potential:
   - as employees, members, professionals or students of the organization
   - as ambassadors of the organization to its customers, clients, audiences and suppliers
   - as citizens of the wider society in which the organization exists
   - as human beings with the need to realize their own capabilities.

4. A learning organization shares its vision of tomorrow with its people and stimulates them to challenge it, to change it and to contribute to it.

5. A learning organization integrates work and learning and inspires all its people to seek quality, excellence and continuous improvement in both.

6. A learning organization mobilizes all its human talent by putting the emphasis on 'learning' and planning its education and training activities accordingly.

7. A learning organization empowers ALL its people to broaden their horizons in harmony with their own preferred learning styles.

8. A learning organization applies up-to-date open and distance delivery technologies appropriately to create broader and more varied learning opportunities.

9. A learning organization responds proactively to the wider needs of the environment and the society in which it operates, and encourages its people to do likewise.

10. A learning organization learns and relearns constantly in order to remain innovative, inventive, invigorating and in business.

References

Alexander, T J (1997) *Lifelong Learning, the OECD perspective*, in *Lline*, no 3, pp166-7, Helsinki

Ball, C and Stewart, D (1995) *An Action Agenda for Lifelong Learning for the 21st Century*, Report from the 1st Global Conference on Lifelong Learning, N Longworth (ed), World Initiative on Lifelong Learning, Brussels

Bayliss, V (1998) *Redefining Schooling: A Challenge to a Closed Society*, RSA Journal, vol CXLVI, no 5468, London

Belanger, P (1997) The astonishing return of lifelong learning, in *Comparative Studies on Lifelong Learning*, pp vii-xii, NIER, Tokyo

Botkin, J et al (1979) *No Limits to Learning, report of the Club of Rome*, New York

Bradshaw, C A (ed) (1995) *Bringing Learning to Life: The Learning revolution, the Economy and the Individual*, The Falmer Press, London

Canadian Labour Force Development Board (1997) *Prior Learning Assessment and Recognition*, PLAR97 leaflet, Ottawa

Candy, P, Crebert, R G, and O'Leary, J (1994) *Developing Lifelong Learners through Undergraduate Education,*. National Board of Employment, Education and Training Commissioned Report Number 28, Australian Government Publishing Service, Canberra

Chapman, J D and Aspin, D N (1997) *The School, the Community and Lifelong Learning*, Cassell, London

Cochinaux, P and De Woot, P (1995) *Moving Towards a Learning Society*, A Forum Report by European Round Table of Industrialists (ERT) with Conference of European Rectors (CRE), Brussels

Coffield, F (1997) *The UK Learning Society Research Programme*, in COMMENT, October 1997 p11, ELLI, Brussels

Comenius (Jan Amos Komensky) *Pampaedia*, A M O Dobbie, ed Buckland, 1987

REFERENCES

Commission of the European Communities (1991) *Skills Shortages in Europe,* Industrial Research and Development Advisory Committee of the Commission of the European Communities (IRDAC), Brussels

Commission of the European Communities (1996*) Accomplishing Europe through Education and Training,* Study Group on Education and Training, EC Publications Office, Luxembourg

Commission of the European Communities (1997) *Building the European Information Society for us all, Final Policy report of the high-level expert group*, EC Publications Office, Luxembourg

Commission of the European Communities (1997) *Meeting the Challenge of Change at Work,* Employment and Social Affairs Directorate, EC Publications Office, Luxembourg

Commission of the European Communities (1998*) Second Chance Schools, Combating exclusion through Education and Training,* EC publications Office, Luxembourg

Commission of the European Communities (1998) *Territorial Employment Pacts, Examples of Good Practice,* EC Publications Office, Luxembourg

Commission of the European Communities (1998*) The European Social Fund - an overview of the programming period 1994-1999,* EC Publications Office, Luxemburg

Community Service Volunteers (1997) *Yellow Pages Make a Difference Day*, publicity material available from CSV, 237 Pentonville Road, London N1 9JN

Confederation of British Industry, Human Resources Directorate (1998) *Targets for our Future,* CBI, London

Conference of European Rectors (1997) *Restructuring the University, Universities and the Challenge of New Technologies* , CRE Doc no 1 1997, Geneva

Crick, B (1998) *Education for Citizenship and the Teaching of Democracy in Schools*, Report of the Advisory Group on Citizenship, London

Daily Telegraph (1998), 'Help thy neighbour and cash in later' unattributed article in June 18 edition, London

Davis, S and Botkin, J (1995) *The Monster under the Bed*, Simon and Schuster, New York

Department for Education and Employment (1997) *The National Adult Learning Survey*, DfEE Publications Centre, Sudbury

Department for Education and Employment (1998) *Higher Education for the 21st century, Response to the Dearing Report*, DfEE Publications Centre, Sudbury

Department for Education and Employment (1998) *The University for Industry, A summary*, DfEE Publications Centre, Sudbury

Department for Education and Employment (1998) *Adults Learning, Response to the Kennedy Report*, DfEE Publications Centre, Sudbury

Department for Education and Employment (1998) *The Learning Age, A Renaissance for a New Britain,* (Green Paper on Lifelong Learning) DfEE Publications Centre, Sudbury

Dickinson, D (ed) (1994) *Creating the Future: Perspectives on Educational Change*, Seattle

Downs, S and Perry, P (1987*) Developing Skilled Learners, Helping Adults to Become Better Learners*, Manpower Services Commission (now DfEE), Sheffield

Dyankov, A (1996) *Current Issues and Trends in Technical and Vocational Education*, UNEVOC Studies in Technical And Vocational Education, UNESCO, Paris

REFERENCES

Edinburgh City Council (1997) *Building Strong Communities*, City of Edinburgh Council, Edinburgh

Elsner, P (1996) *Maricopa Community Colleges network,* Maricopa Home Page

Elson, J (1992) Campus of the future, in *Time Magazine*, April 1992 edition

European Round Table of Industrialists (ERT) (1989) *Education and European Competence*, ERT Education Policy Group, Brussels

European Round Table of Industrialists (ERT) (1997*) Investing in Knowledge, the Integration of Technology in European Education*, ERT, Brussels

European Round Table of Industrialists (ERT) (1996) *Investing in Knowledge, Towards the Learning Society*, ERT, Brussels

European Round Table of Industrialists (ERT) (1992) *European Approaches to Lifelong Learning*, ERT Education Policy Group, Brussels

European Round Table of Industrialists (ERT) (1995) *Education for Europeans*, ERT Education Policy Group, Brussels

European Round Table of Industrialists (ERT) (1997*) A Stimulus to Job Creation, Practical Partnerships between Large and Small Companies*, ERT, Brussels

Findlater, J (1998) *Thirst for Learning at Guinness*, unpublished paper issued at ECLO Conference, Turin 1998, Guinness, Dublin

Finland Ministry of Education (1997*) The Joy of Learning, A National Strategy for Lifelong Learning*, Committee Report 14, Helsinki

Franson, L (1998) *A Swedish Perspective on Lifelong Learning*, unpublished paper given to ELLI/Southampton Learning Cities conference, Goteborg

Fryer, R H (1997) *Learning for the 21st Century*, First report of the National Advisory group for Continuing Education and Lifelong Learning' NAGCELL1, PP62/31634/1297/33, London

Gallimore, A (1997) The Manchester Community Information Network, in *The Electronic Library*, Vol 15, no 4, pp 297-298

Gardner, H (1993) *Multiple Intelligences: The Theory in Practice*, Basic Books, New York

Goleman, D (1998) *Working with Emotional Intelligence*, Bloomsbury, New York

Handy, C (1992) *Managing the Dream: The Learning Organisation,* Gemini Consulting Series on Leadership, London

Hartley-Brown, E (1998) Part-time Schooling: Dream or Reality? in *The Independent,* 22 January

Healy, T (1996) *Lifelong Learning for All: International Experience and Comparisons*, unpublished paper read at University of Newcastle international conference on research for lifelong learning policy, OECD, Paris

Hertfordshire TEC (1997) *Learning for Life, Hertfordshire's Learning Framework*, Hertfordshire TEC, 45 Grosvenor Road, St Albans

Hertfordshire TEC (1997) *The Learning Network*, Hertfordshire TEC, St Albans

Hodges, L (1998) Welcome to the new world of Disney Degrees, in *The Independent*, October 8

Hoeksema, R (1998) Adult Education for a Sustainable Society in Europe, in *Lline,* vol 2, pp 98–102, Helsinki

REFERENCES

IACEE (1996)*The Joy of Learning, Implementing Lifelong Learning in the Learning Society*, Report of the theme conference of the European Lifelong Learning Initiative (Otala L Ed), Espoo

IBM Sweden (1987) The Viksjo Project, IBM Sweden, Stockholm

Industry Canada (1997) *Schoolnet, Plugging Kids into the World*, Publicity literature from Industry Canada, Ottawa

International Commission on Education for the 21st Century (1996) *Learning: The Treasure Within*, UNESCO Publishing, Paris

Jardine, S (1997) Investors in People in Scottish Schools, *Jolli Magazine*, no 3, Nov/Dec, Glasgow

Kanter, R M (1995) *World Class Thriving Locally in the Global Economy*, Simon and Schuster, New York

Kennedy, H (1998) *Education For All: an Impossible Dream? RSA Journal*, vol cxlvi, no 5485, pp 76-80

Kent County Council (1996) *Kent Learning: Our Future 1996-2006*, Kent County Council, Canterbury

Korhonen, K (1997)*Educating Engineers of the 21st Century: The Challenges of Higher Engineering Education in Finland*, Helsinki University of Technology, Helsinki

Lessem, R and Palsule, S (1997) *Managing in Four Worlds: From Competition to Co-creation*, Blackwell, London

Logan, D (1998) *Corporate Citizenship on a Global Stage, RSA Journal*, vol CXLVI, no 5468, London

Longworth, N (1980) *The Woodberry Down School/IBM Basinghall Street Twinning Scheme*, IBM United Kingdom Ltd, London

Longworth, N (1994) Lifelong Learning and the Community - Relations with Business and Industry, Towards a Holistic Mission, *New Papers on Higher Education*, no 6, pp 211–12, UNESCO, Paris

Longworth, N (1997) *Close down the school, shut down the Ministry, Is that so outrageous?* unpublished paper delivered to seminar on Lifelong Learning, Bratislava

Longworth, N (1997) *Higher Education responding to a Lifelong Learning World*, Journal of Higher Education in Europe, vol XXII, no 4, pp 517–21, CEPES, Bucharest

Longworth, N and Beernaert, Y (eds) (1995) *Lifelong Learning in Schools*, European Lifelong Learning Initiative, Brussels

Longworth, N and Davies, W K (1996) *Lifelong Learning: New Visions, New Implications, New Roles - for Industry, Government, Education and the Community for the 21st Century*, Kogan Page, London

Longworth, N and De Geest, L (eds) (1995*) Community Action for Lifelong Learning for Developing Human Potential*, Part 2 of Report of First Global Conference on Lifelong Learning, Rome, World Initiative on Lifelong Learning, Brussels

Longworth, N and Gwyn, R (1989) The PLUTO International Networking Project, *European Journal of Education* (N Longworth, ed), 24 (1), pp 79-84, European Centre for Education Policy, Paris

MacBeath, J (1998) Serving Families and Communities, *Jolli magazine*, no 5, March/April, p 7, Glasgow

REFERENCES

Markkula, M and Suurla, R (1998) *Passion to Learn, Benchmarking Good Lifelong Learning Practice*, IACEE Report no 9, Helsinki

McDonald, R et al (1998) *New Perspectives on Assessment*, UNEVOC Studies in Technical and Vocational Education, ED-95/WS-28, UNESCO, Paris

Ministry of Education, Finland (1998) *The Joy of Learning: National Lifelong Learning Strategy*, Summary of the Lifelong Learning Committee, October 1997, Helsinki

Morris, B (1998) *Address to the World Conference on Higher Education*, Maharishi Universities of Management, UNESCO, October 5-9, Paris

Mueller, J (1997) *Interactive Learning: On-line and on-time in Effective Management Development: Linking People, processes and performance*, EFMD Forum 97/2, European Foundation for Management Development, Brussels

Mumbai Statement (1998) see UNESCO

Naisbitt, J and Aburdine, P (1986) *Re-inventing the Corporation*, Futura, London

National Institute of Educational Research and UNESCO Institute of Education (1997) *Comparative Studies on Lifelong Learning Policies*, NIER, Tokyo

Nyhan, B (1991) *Developing People's Ability to Learn, A European perspective on self-learning competency and technological change*, European Interuniversity Press, Brussels

Organisation for Economic Cooperation and Development (1973) *Recurrent Education: A Strategy for Lifelong Learning*, OECD/CERI, Paris

Organisation for Economic Cooperation and Development (1994) *The OECD Jobs Study - Facts, Analysis, Strategies*, OECD, Paris

Organisation for Economic Cooperation and Development (1996) *Education at a Glance, Analysis*, OECD Centre for Research and Innovation, Paris

Organisation for Economic Cooperation and Development (1996) *Lifelong Learning for All - meeting of the Education Committee at Ministerial level*, OECD/CERI, Paris

Padfield, C et al (1997) *SOCRATES Thematic Network in Engineering Education Higher Engineering Education for Europe*, H3E Initial Report of the Working Group on Life-long-learning and Continuing Education, Cambridge

Platform Education Centre (1998) *Time to get your head round it*, leaflet available from Edinburgh Community Education Service, Edinburgh

Price, I and Shaw, R (1998) *Shifting the Patterns*, Management Books 2000, Chalford

Rantama, E and Vaatainen, E (1997) Village Action Movement in Finland: The Power of Human Cooperation, in *Lline*, Vol 4, pp 235-7, Helsinki

Richardson, K (1995) Human Learning Potential, in *Bringing Learning to Life*, ed Bradshaw, Falmer Press, London

Schell, J (1982) *The Fate of the Earth*, Jonathan Cape, London 1982

Schools Council Industry Project (1997) *Bringing Business into Learning*, Centre for Education and Industry, University of Warwick, Warwick

Scottish Office (1998) *Opportunity Scotland, Green Paper on Lifelong Learning*, Stationery Office, Edinburgh

Smethurst, R (1995) *Education - a Public or Private Good*, RSA Journal, vol cxliii, no 5465

Steele, R L (1992) Schools of the 21st Century, in *Time Magazine*, April

REFERENCES

Summa, T (1998) Agenda 21 - A New Challenge for Adult Education, in *Lline,* vol 2, pp 104-5, Helsinki

Toffler, A (1980) *The Third Wave: The Revolution that will change our lives,* Collins, London

Tuckett, A (1997) *Lifelong Learning in England and Wales: An overview and guide to issues arising from the European Year of Lifelong Learning,* NIACE, Leicester

Turkle, Sherry (1984*) The Second Self: Computers and the Human Spirit,* Simon and Schuster, New York

UNESCO (1973) *Objectives for the Future of Education (Fauré report),* UNESCO, Paris

UNESCO Cairo Office (1998) *ICT in Higher Education: Global View and Regional Experience,* Background paper prepared for Arab Regional Conference, UNESCO, Paris

UNESCO Institute for Information Technologies in Education (1998*) University Education in the 21st Century: a Concept Paper,* Paper prepared for UNESCO Conference on Higher Education, October 1998, UNESCO, Paris

UNESCO Institute of Education (1997) *The Hamburg Declaration: The Agenda for the Future,* from Fifth International Conference on Adult Education (Confintea V) UNESCO Institute of Education, Hamburg

UNESCO (1994) *International Understanding at School,* pp 4-8, ASP Bulletin, no 61-62/1991, UNESCO, Paris

UNESCO (1998) *Higher Education in the 21st Century - Vision and Action, Thematic Debate - the requirements of the World of Work,* working document ed/98/conf.202/CLD.17, UNESCO, Paris

UNESCO (1998) *Higher Education in the 21st Century, World Conference on Higher Education, Towards an Agenda 21,* working document ed/98/conf.202/CLD.19, UNESCO, Paris

UNESCO (1998) *Higher Education in the 21st Century, World Conference on Higher Education,* working document ed/98/conf.202/CLD.23, UNESCO, Paris

UNESCO (1998) *Mumbai Statement on Lifelong Learning, Active Citizenship and the Reform of Higher Education,* UNESCO Institute for Education, Hamburg, 1998

Warr, P (1997*)* Learning in the workplace, in *Comment,* October, pp 21-2, University of Sheffield Institute of Work Psychology and ELLI, Brussels

Westfield Washington Schools (1996) *New Dimensions in Education,* booklet available from Westfield Washington Schools, 322 West Main Street, Westfield, Indiana 46074

Yamamoto, Y (1997) *Vocational Education as a Strategy for Lifelong Learning,* Research Bulletin of the National Institute for Educational Research of Japan, no 28, pp 76-9, Tokyo

Young, S and Martin, M (1998) *The Learning Inquiry,* unpublished document available from Glasgow Development Agency, Glasgow

Index

Visit Kogan Page on-line

Comprehensive information on
Kogan Page titles

Features include

- complete catalogue listings,
  including book reviews and
  descriptions

- special monthly promotions

- information on NEW titles and
  BESTSELLING titles

- a secure shopping basket facility
  for on-line ordering

PLUS everything you need to know
about KOGAN PAGE

http://www.kogan-page.co.uk